Failed Images

Arturo Bragaglia, *The Bow–
Anton Giulio Bragaglia*, 1911.

Juul Kraijer, *Untitled*, 2006.

Ernst van Alphen

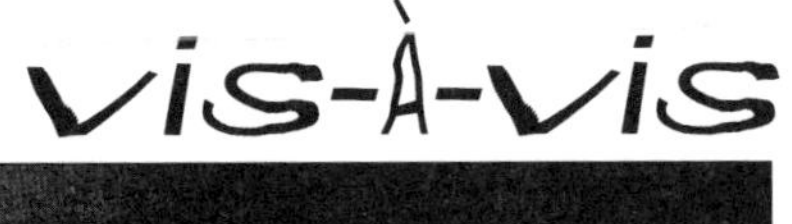

Valiz

Failed Images

Photography and
Its Counter-Practices

Contents

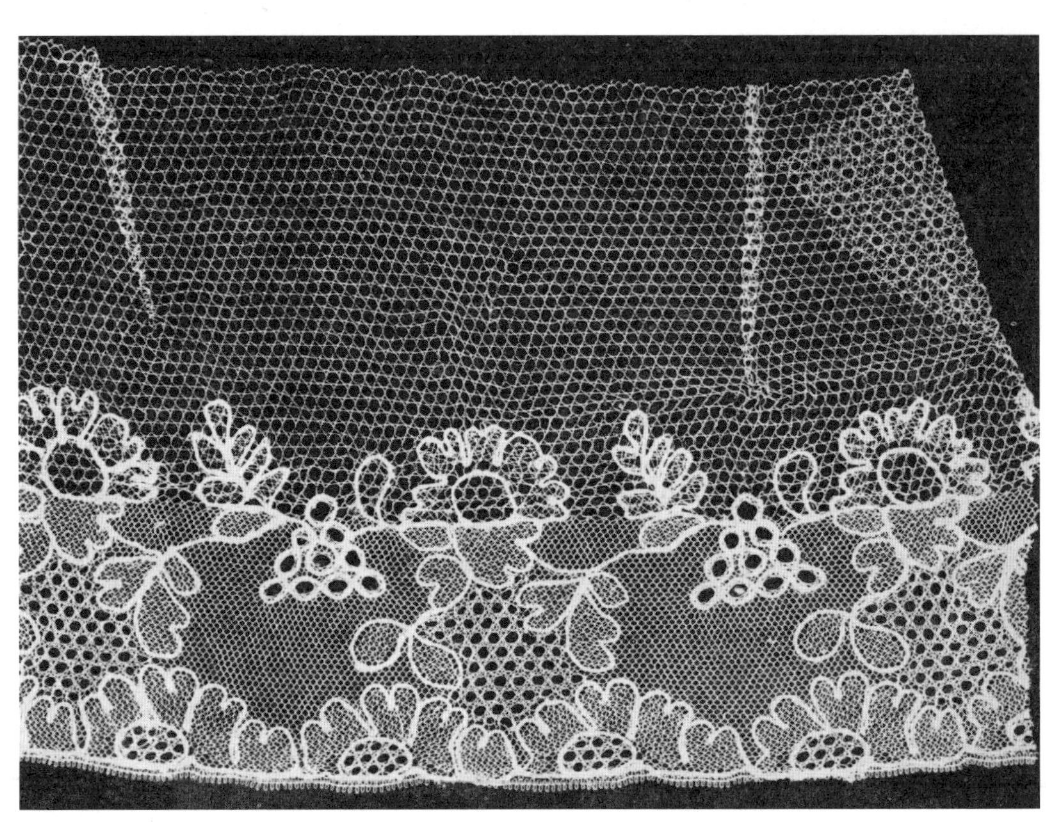

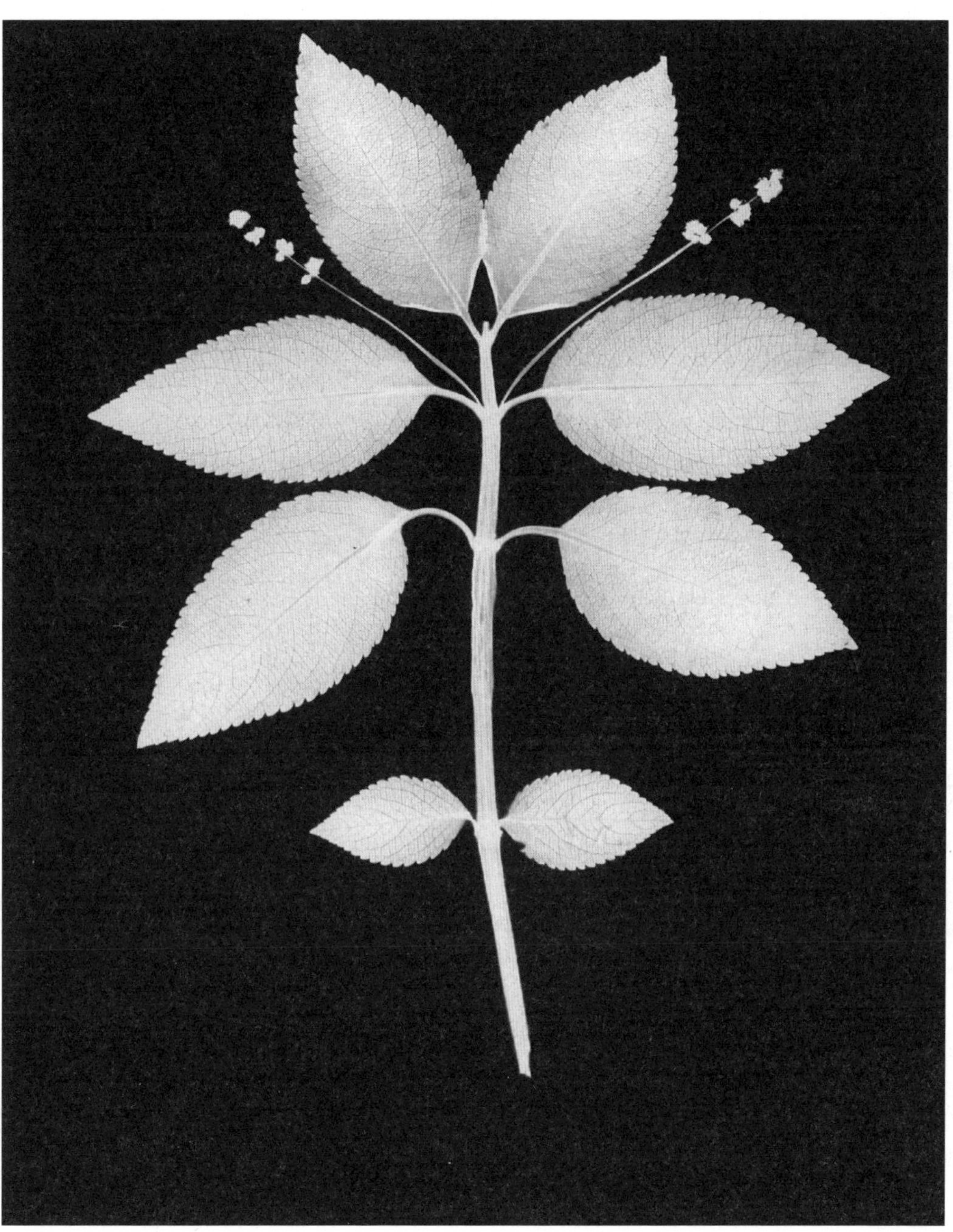

William Henry Fox Talbot,
Photogenic drawing negative,
1839, calotype (salt print),
21.4 × 16.8 cm, coll. Leiden
University Library, inv. nr.
PK-F-65.1034 (gift of J.P. Stam
in 1965).

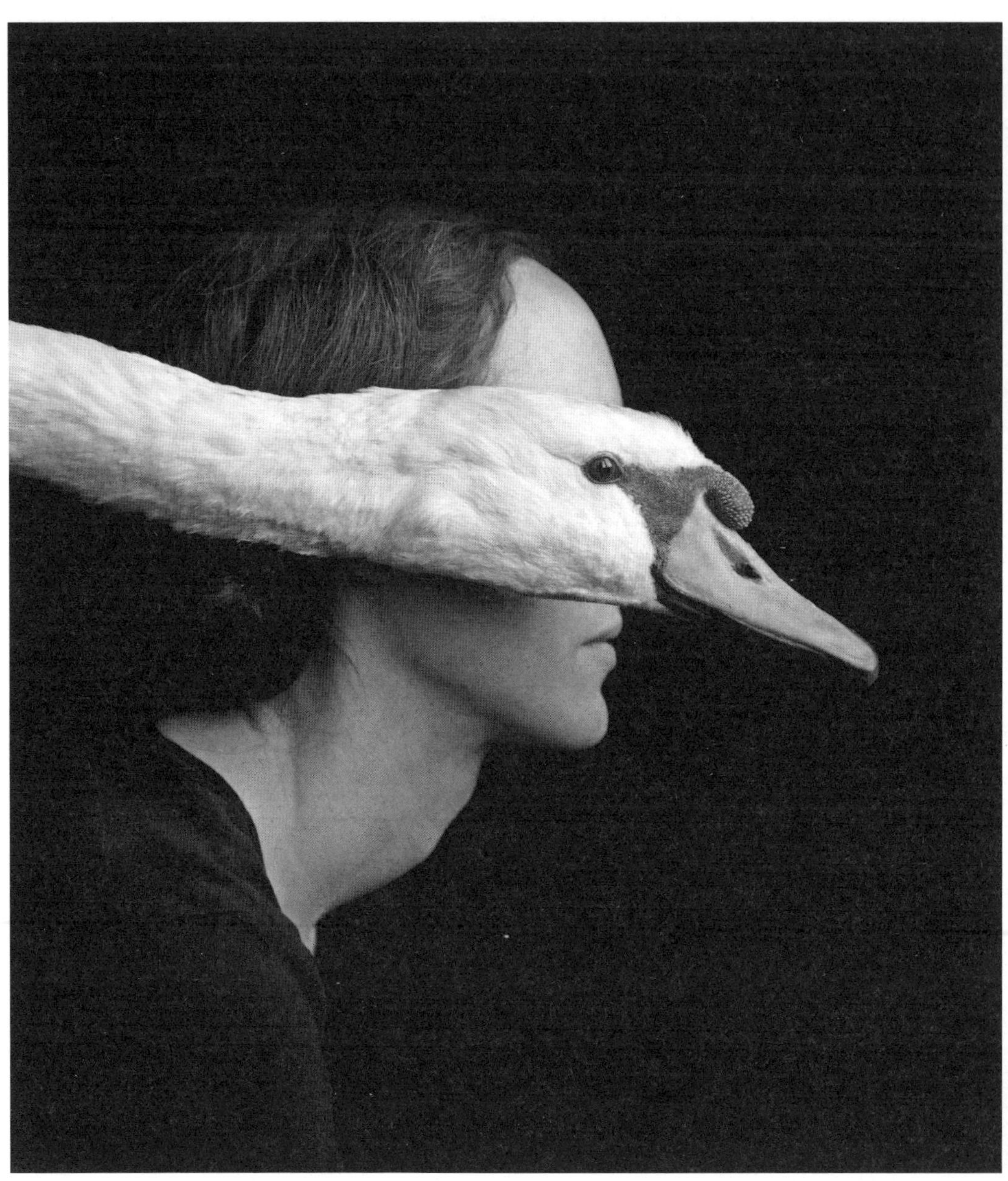

Juul Kraijer, *Untitled*, 2016.

When Does Photography Fail?

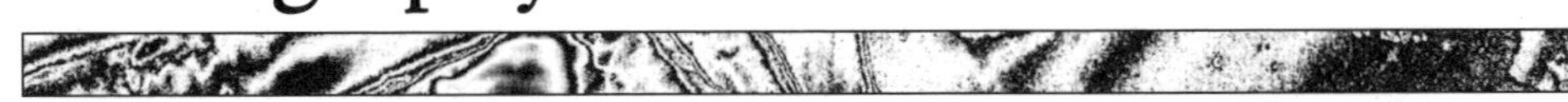

*Photography is not a reflection of the real;
it is the reality of that reflection.*
—Jean-Luc Godard

A 2011 photograph by Dutch artist Juul Kraijer
shows a hand firmly gripping two bronze legs that
stick out underneath bent fingers against a dark
background. The sight of this fist is itself gripping.
Although the image shows what it is, a hand holding
two bronze legs, it also evokes a vision of something
not present in the image, namely that of a giant's
hand crushing a human being. This vision is not
simply visual; by means of a visual sensation other
senses are activated as well. Through synaesthesia,
the integration of different senses, it is especially the
sense of touch that participates here. As viewers, we

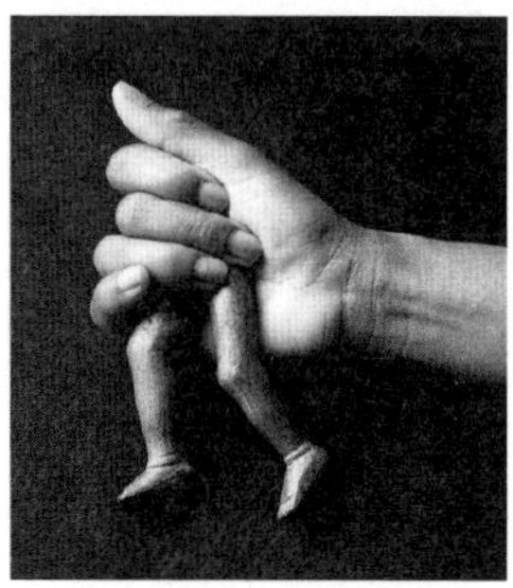

1   Juul Kraijer, *Untitled*, 2011.

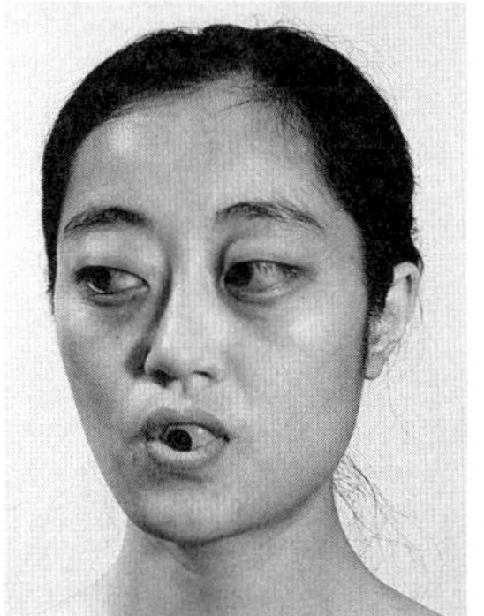

2   Juul Kraijer, *Untitled*, 2006.

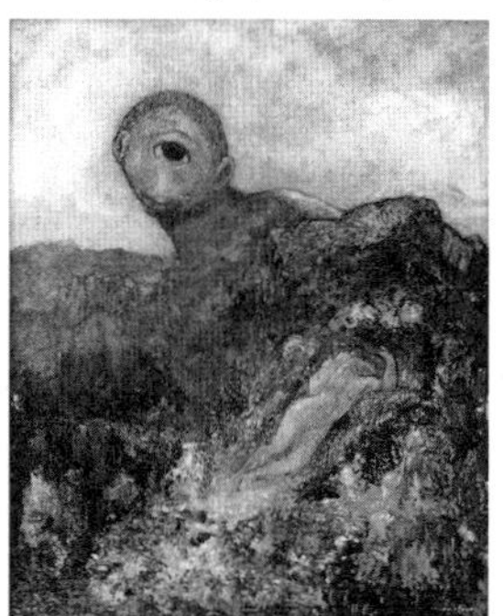

3   Odilon Redon, *The Cyclops*, 1914. This painting is in the collection of the Kröller-Müller Museum in Otterlo, the Netherlands.

feel the hand that crushes the human figure. By evoking this vision, the photograph brackets its indexical contingency with a specific moment and place; in other words, its referentiality.[1]

Another example is from 2006, one of the first photographic works Kraijer made. It shows the head of an Asian woman with something that looks like a glass eyeball in her mouth. Once again, this is a staged posture, this time against a light background, and it is what it is. But the vision this perception evokes is also an example of synaesthesia. The eye in the woman's mouth seems to replace her tongue. It is with her tongue that she sees; it is with her eye that she tastes. Her third eye turns her into a kind of Cyclops. However, she has not one, but three eyes.[2]

The figure is a hybrid of a woman and a Cyclops. She reminds me, for instance, of the one painted by Odilon Redon in 1914.[3] If this photograph points to a referential world at all, it seems to be an intertextual one. These photographs are representative of Kraijer's work. Objects or figures are frontally staged before the camera. These staged situations evoke visions that are both visual and something else. They are not only surreal but even slightly sinister or threatening. They challenge our everyday experience of the perceptual domain.

Each of the photographic images by Kraijer catch the eye in a different way. They do so as images first, as photographs only after this. I begin with the latter. How can her photographic practice be understood in terms of what is considered to be specific to the medium of photography? The specificity of a medium is not only determined by technical and formal features, but also by practices of working with a medium that become prevalent at a certain moment in history, and thus define the possibilities and limits of that medium.[4] Although these practices are dominant for a period of time, they can develop and change. This notion of medium specificity brackets any orthodox, formalist belief in medium specificity.

The German cultural theorist and critic Siegfried Kracauer understood the dominant practices in the medium of photography as 'the photographic approach'. This phrase, 'the photographic approach', which he alternates with 'photographic attitude', integrates the specific properties of a medium with the practices that bring those properties to life. In the case of photography, Kracauer defines the photographic approach as the effort to utilize the inherent abilities of the camera for highlighting the particular nature of photographs.[5] The most important part of this definition is the word that is easily overlooked: 'effort'. That noun refers implicitly to the historical agents responsible for the establishment of a certain practice or 'approach' as prevailing. Historically,

II

4   On the issue of medium specificity, see Rosalind Krauss, 'A Voyage on the North Sea': Art in the Age of the Post-Medium Condition (New York: Thames & Hudson, 1999), especially the introduction. See also Janna Houwen, Film and Video Intermediality: The Question of Medium Specificity in Contemporary Moving Images (London: Bloomsbury, 2017).

5   Siegfried Kracauer, 'The Photographic Approach', in The Past's Threshold: Essays on Photography, ed. Philippe Despoix and Maria Zinfert (Zurich: Diaphanes, 2014), p. 69. Originally published in Magazine of Art March 1951, and also as the first chapter in Kracauer's Theory of Film: The Redemption of Physical Reality (Oxford University Press, 1960).

6   Ibid., p. 69.
7   Ibid., passim.

Kracauer situates the photographic approach in the period during which Realism and Impressionism formed the main paradigm of literature and art. The properties of photographs were at that time 'commonly held to be the hallmarks of art in general'.[6] As soon as painting and literature broke away from realism these properties assumed an exclusive character, defining the nature of photography. This 'dominant approach' could remain dominant throughout the evolution of the photographic medium because the 'realistic' properties of photographs depended upon techniques peculiar to the camera.

The phrase 'photographic approach' immediately makes clear that photography is not only determined by its technical features, but also by an approach to it. In this case, it refers to a specific practice dealing with those technical possibilities and limitations. For Kracauer this approach consists of the effort to utilize the inherent abilities of the camera. This effort is responsible for the particular nature of photographs. Although he described this dominant approach to photography already in 1951 in an essay titled 'The Photographic Approach', it is amazing how his text is still valid in its account for how most people, professionals or not, understand and use the medium of photography.[7]

The first property he assigns to the photographic approach is that photography has an outspoken affinity with un-staged reality.[8] He describes this in the following words: 'Pictures which impress us as intrinsically photographic seem intended to capture nature in the raw, nature un-manipulated and as it exists independently of us.' Photographic portraits are perhaps an exception to this, but, as Kracauer remarks, 'a portraitist who provides an adequate setting or asks his model to lower the head a bit, may well be helping nature to manifest itself forcibly'.[9] It is clear that Kraijer's photographs never present an un-staged reality. On the contrary, the images they present are utterly staged. At first sight, the staged nature of her photos can be seen as surreal. However, surrealist photography usually presents staged situations as if found in reality.[10] Kraijer's photos never pretend to be found. They are always explicit in their staged-ness.

In close relation to the first one, the second property of the photographic approach Kracauer distinguishes is the tendency to stress the fortuitous. 'Random events are the very meat of snapshots.'[11] Photos are plucked in passing and they still quiver with crude existence. This explains why photographic images are seen as the equivalent of the instantaneous. This can even be true for portraits; their likeness to the sitter is caught accidentally. Kraijer's photos, instead, never evoke the fortuitous. Their relation to time is almost the opposite. The

13

8   Ibid., p. 70.

9   Ibid., p. 71.

10   See Rosalind Krauss, 'Photography in the Service of Surrealism', in Rosalind Krauss and Jane Livingston, *L'Amour Fou: Photography and Surrealism* (Washington D.C.: The Corcoran Gallery of Art; New York: Abevillle Publishers, 1985), p. 15–42 and 'The Photographic Conditions of Surrealism', in *The Originality of the Avant-Garde and Other Modernist Myths* (Cambridge, MA: MIT Press, 1985), pp. 151–170.

11   Kracauer, 'The Photographic Approach', p. 71.

12   See Clive Scott, *The Spoken Image: Photography and Language* (London: Reaktion Books, 1999), p. 26.

temporal dimension seems to be suspended. A staged situation is presented in such a way that any awareness of time is cancelled.

Thirdly, photographs look selective, as if cropped. They tend to suggest an infinity beyond the frame. This visual field outside the frame of the photograph is called the blind field, which is 'the extension of space and time beyond the photographic frame'.[12] The selective nature of photography means that they usually present fragments rather than wholes. This is because the frame marks a provisional limit and the presented space continues outside the frame. Kraijer's use of photography never demonstrates this property either. The photo always presents an image with a centre; against a black background an object, a face, a body is presented. The black background against which these objects are shown limits the three-dimensionality of the image. This blackness functions as another, second frame within the frame of the photograph. It definitely cancels the suggestion that the space extends beyond the frame. What exists is only the central focus within the photographic image.

Finally, photographs do not only tend to isolate a spatial fragment from a larger space that extends beyond the frame, they also isolate a temporal moment from a temporal continuity. Like the other properties of the dominant approach to photography, this one also applies to snapshots. When people are photographed, the camera isolates a momentary pose. The function of this pose within the total structure of a personality remains a guess. 'The pose relates to a context which itself is not given.'[13] This explains why photographs can be alienating or depersonalizing. This effect is supposed to be countered by the professional photographer or the artist-photographer. They select or isolate precisely that moment which is emblematic for a personality. This property of the photographic approach cannot be recognized either in Kraijer's images. Her photos seem to suspend time. We never have the feeling that a moment, specific or arbitrary, has been caught. Temporality plays no role in her photographs. This is remarkable, because in most theoretical accounts of photography its specific relation to time is of central importance. According to the phenomenological approach so prevalent today, looking at a photograph usually hits the viewer with the awareness of time past. In the words of Roland Barthes: this-has-been. But long before Barthes wrote this, Kracauer pointed it out in an essay from 1927 with the simple title 'Photography', published in the *Frankfurter Zeitung*.[14] According to him, photography is a function of passing time. When photographs age their likeness to an original evaporates. Aging photographs become like ruins, or deposits of past time. Kracauer's reflections on photo-

13 Kracauer, 'The Photographic Approach', p. 73.

14 *Frankfurter Zeitung*, 28 October 1927.

graphy, on the properties of the dominant approach that I have just listed, seem to go in the opposite direction than that of most thinkers of Barthes' generation. Whereas his essay 'Photography' of 1927 is thoroughly phenomenological, in his 1951 essay he adopts a more formal and structural approach.

Talbot, *The Pencil of Nature*

The four properties Kracauer attributes to the prevalent photographic approach can all be recognized in what is now called a 'snapshot'. It is the practice of snapshot photography that can be held responsible for what many people consider to be the nature of the medium of photography. But as we have seen with Kraijer's images, the medium of photography also enables different practices, and, as a result, different kinds of photographic images. One look at the diversity of photographic images that were made just before realism became the avant-garde movement in literature and art, suffices to realize this. In this section I will explore an example of an early reflection on photography in order to see what kind of photographic images are put forward to demonstrate the 'nature' of the medium.

A good example is William Henry Fox Talbot's *The Pencil of Nature*. This was the first commercially published book illustrated with photographs. Talbot published the book in six parts between June 1844 and April 1846. In the history of photography, this book is often compared to the Gutenberg Bible in printing. In the book, Talbot not only presents some of the first examples of this new medium, he also gives a short sketch of the 'invention of the art'. He wrote this some ten years after his first contribution to the invention of the medium of photography. Besides this historical sketch, he also provides short descriptions of all the plates in the book.

The plates as well as their descriptions cannot be understood in terms of dominant photographic practices because Talbot was writing his accounts at the inception of the medium. This adds significance to his account of photography. For he was looking at photography with his own eyes instead of through a conception of photography that had become standard. First of all, it is rather amazing from our perspective in the twenty-first century that he describes photography as a process and not in terms of the kind of image in which this process results. The ultimate image is constituted by 'ideas which accompany it':

> The picture, divested of the ideas which accompany it, and considered only in its ultimate

15   William Henry Fox Talbot, *The Pencil of Nature*, introd. Colin Harding (Chicago and London: KWS Publishers, 2011), n.p.

nature is but a succession or variety of stronger lights thrown upon one part of the paper, and of deeper shadows on another.[15]

Although the photographic image is the result of a diversity of 'ideas' of which the 'throwing of light on paper' is only the best-known one, the ultimate picture looks transparent because it is divested of all the ideas that built it. Let me now have a closer look at Talbot's accounts of the plates in *The Pencil of Nature*, in order to see if he articulates there the ideas that are no longer explicitly visible in the picture. Or alternatively, they are so visible that they have become transparent and we are no longer aware of them.

The first plate is titled 'Part of Queen's College, Oxford'. His description reveals two elements that constitute the nature of this image. First of all, the image provides a specific perspective on the college. The photograph has been 'taken' from a specific angel: 'The view is taken from the other side of the High Street—looking North.' The end of his description is, however, even more revealing: 'This street, shortly after passing the church, turns to the left, and leads to New College.' What Talbot is implying is that the world framed in and by this image continues outside the frame. Although implicit, this is remarkable, because it distinguishes

the photographic image from the other art media
with which Talbot prefers to compare the new
medium of photography: first of all drawing, but also
painting. The image of a drawing or of a painting
only exists within the frame.

The second plate, 'View of the Boulevards at
Paris' emphasizes again that the image is taken from
a specific position. But it adds something, which has
consequences for the internal composition of the
image:

> The view is taken from a considerable height,
> as appears easily by observing the house on the
> right hand; the eye being necessarily on a level
> with that part of the building on which the
> horizontal lines or courses of stone appear paral-
> lel to the margin of the picture.[16]

Talbot's account of this image demonstrates that the
specific positioning of camera and photographer in
relation to the view orders the view according to the
principles of linear perspective. Although he does
not refer to these principles explicitly, his description
is a demonstration of them. However, in the text that
accompanies Plate xvii, Talbot explicitly refers to
the principles of linear perspective:

> Already sundry *amateurs* have laid down the
> pencil and armed themselves with chemical

16 Ibid.

19

solutions and with *camera obscurae*. Those amateurs especially, and they are not few, who find the rules of *perspective* difficult to learn and to apply—and who moreover have the misfortune to be lazy—prefer to use a method which dispenses with all that trouble.[17]

The camera's inherent application of linear perspective explains the many examples of architectural views among Talbot's plates. Linear perspective works most effectively in representations of architecture. Perhaps it also explains why he did not include any plates with landscapes. With most landscapes it is much more difficult to fully exploit the possibilities of linear perspective. Only when you have a tree, a building or a human figure in the front, via which or whom the viewer enters the image, linear perspective is activated, but not as effectively as in architectural images. The only plate that can be understood more or less as a landscape is Plate x v, but this image also shows a building in the centre: 'Lacock Abbey in Wiltshire.'

From our present perspective, the third plate is amazing both as a chosen illustration of photography's capabilities, and for Talbot's account of it. It is titled 'Articles of China' and shows four shelves each lined with articles of china. In contrast to the two earlier plates which are 'views', this image is divested of 'depth' and is seemingly not organized on the basis of linear perspective.[18]

This almost flat image does not provide a view, but according to Talbot, a visual inventory:

> From the specimen here given it is sufficiently manifest, that the whole cabinet of a Virtuoso and collector of old China might be depicted on paper in little more time than it would take him to make a written inventory describing it in the usual way. The more strange and fantastic the forms of his old teapots, the more advantage in having their pictures given instead of their descriptions. … the Camera depicts them all at once.[19]

Whereas the first two plates can still be understood in terms of the notion of photography which became prevalent not so long after Talbot published his *The Pencil of Nature*, namely as 'snapshots of the world', this picture is an archive. It presents the visual equivalent of an inventory. But it does not use the linear format of the list; it presents all items at once. Whereas Talbot mainly uses the discourse of art in his introduction of photography to the general public, in his account of the third plate he now suddenly uses the legal discourse of evidence:

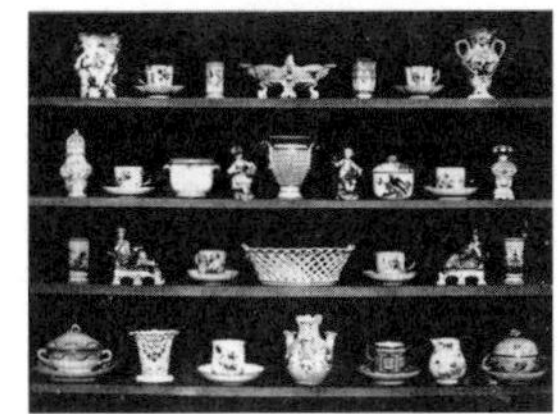

18   William Henry Fox Talbot, *The Pencil of Nature*, 1844, Plate III: 'Articles of China'.

19   Talbot, *The Pencil of Nature*, n.p.

21

20   Ibid.

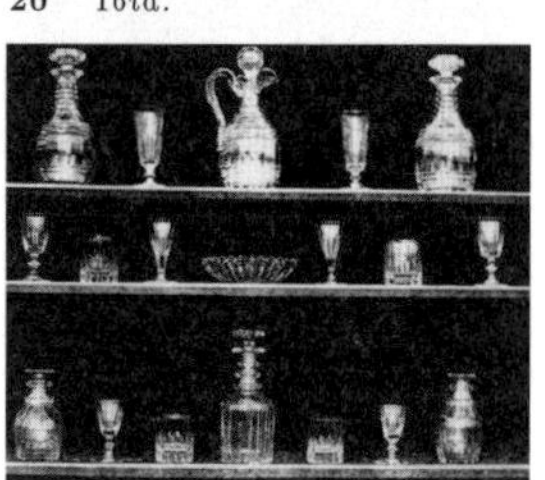

21   William Henry Fox Talbot,
The Pencil of Nature, 1844,
Plate IV: 'Articles of Glass'.

And should a thief afterwards purloin the treasures—if the mute testimony of the picture were to be produced against him in court—it would certainly be evidence of a novel kind; but what the judge and jury might say to it, is a matter which I leave to speculation of those who possess legal acumen.[20]

Plate IV is at first sight very similar to Plate III showing articles of china; it shows articles of glass on three shelves.[21] Talbot explains the difference between the two plates in terms of the exposure time needed for white articles and for dark or transparent articles like glass objects. Glass articles can only be combined with china when it is darkly coloured. Blue china is, however, the exception, because blue affects the sensitive paper as rapidly as white does. The next plate V, 'Bust of Patroclus', is comparable to the one with articles of china because of its whiteness: 'Statues, busts, and other specimens of sculpture, are generally well represented by the Photographic Art; and also very rapidly, in consequence of their whiteness.' Talbot also explains why statues can be better photographed in cloudy weather than in sunshine: because sunshine causes strong shadows. This can be prevented by holding a white cloth on one side of the statue, which blocks the sun's rays. This description is notable from our twenty-first-century perspective, because it does not so much describe the image as a snapshot of the world, but as a material, physical process using rays of light reflected on the object and subsequently on the paper.

Plate xx, titled 'Lace', shows another possible application of photography, namely a negative image. This negative image has been made without a camera and is called 'photogram' instead of photograph. Talbot explains in detail the process that results in a negative image. What we get to see in the image is white lace on a black background, whereas in fact it was black lace on a white background. Talbot legitimizes this kind of image as follows:

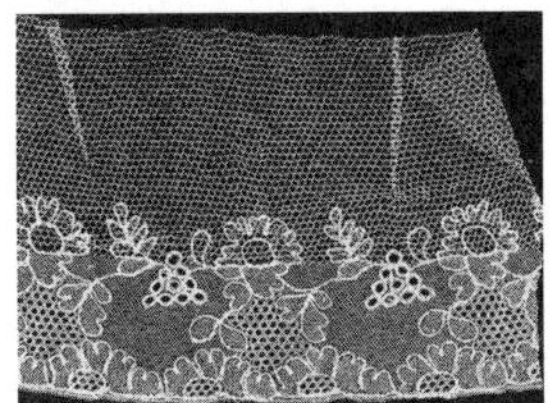

22 William Henry Fox Talbot, *The Pencil of Nature*, 1844, n.p.; Plate XX: 'Lace'.

> In taking views of buildings, statues, portraits, &c. it is necessary to obtain a *positive* image, because the negative images of such objects are hardly intelligible, substituting light for shade, and *vice versa*. But in copying such things as lace or leaves of plants, a negative image is perfectly allowable, black lace being as familiar to the eye as white lace, and the object being only to exhibit the pattern with accuracy.[22]

What Talbot implies when he claims that negative images can be 'perfectly allowable', is that some photographs do not depict the world realistically, but *translate* the world into the contrast between black

23

23 Geoffrey Batchen, *Emanations: The Art of the Cameraless Photograph* (Munich and New York: Prestel), p. 9.

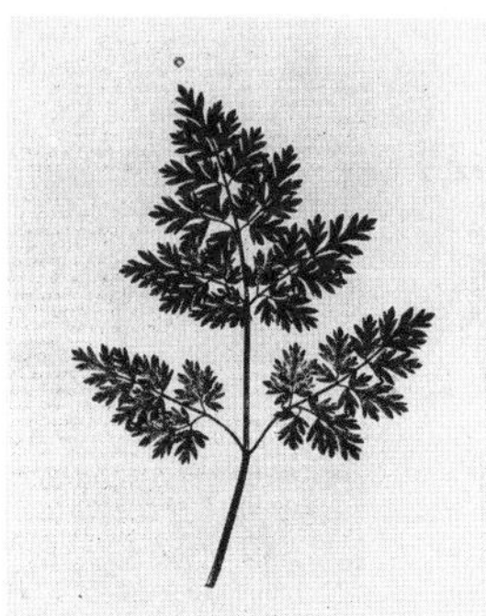

24 William Henry Fox Talbot, *The Pencil of Nature*, 1844, Plate VII: 'Leaf of a Plant'.

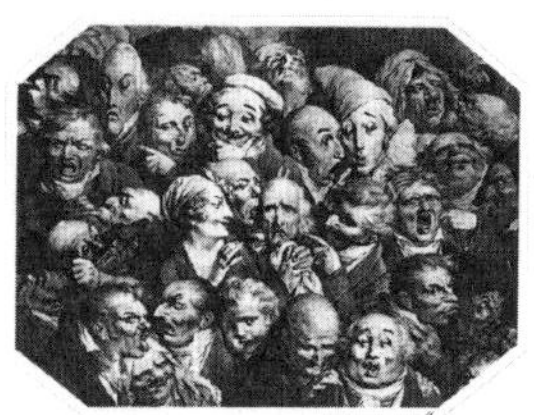

25 William Henry Fox Talbot, *The Pencil of Nature*, 1844, Plate IX: 'Facsimile of an Old Printed Page'.

26 William Henry Fox Talbot, *The Pencil of Nature*, 1844, Plate XI: 'Copy of a Lithographic Print'.

and white. What we see in the image is not the real object, but the photographic translation. That is why it does not matter if black lace is shown as either black or white, as long as it shows a contrast between black and white, because that contrast defines the principle of translation. In the words of Geoffrey Batchen: 'So Talbot recognizes from the outset that photography provides an indexical truth-to-presence, even not necessarily a truth-to-appearance. A photograph, he reminds us, tells us that something was there, but not exactly what it looked like.'[23] In all its elegance, this description of the photographic medium sounds immediately convincing. But it is more subversive than it seems at first, because it challenges the transparency of the medium that is so often assigned to it as its most important feature.

With the plates VII, IX, XI and XXIII Talbot discusses another application of the photographic process. Plate VII, 'Leaf of a Plant', represents an object, a leaf, in its natural size.[24] Plate IX 'Fac-simile of an old Printed Page', shows a printed page of a book from Talbot's library.[25] Today we would call it a Xerox or photocopy. The page is copied in the size of the original by placing it directly on the sensitive plate. Plate XI, 'Copy of a Lithographic Print',[26] is another copy, this time not of a printed page but of an engraving. He distinguishes this copy from the earlier facsimile in Plate IX by the fact that in

24

contrast with facsimile copies, photography is able to make copies much larger or smaller than the originals. Plate XXIII 'Hagar in the Desert', shows another application of photography: the multiplication of originals. Talbot writes: 'Fac-similes can be made from original sketches of the old masters, and thus they may be preserved from loss, and multiplied to any extent.'[27]

Plate XIII 'Queens College, Oxford', shows an architectural view. It is a frontal view of the building;[28] so, unlike his first depiction of Queen's College, the quality of linear perspective is not fully exploited in this image. But in his description of the plate Talbot makes clear that a photographic image enables perceptions that are different from perceptions of the real world:

> It frequently happens, moreover—and this is one of the charms of photography—that the operator himself discovers on examination, perhaps long afterwards, that he has depicted many things he had no notion of at the time. Sometimes inscriptions and dates are found upon the buildings, or printed placards most irrelevant, are discovered upon their walls: sometimes a distant dial-plate is seen, and upon it—unconsciously recorded—the hour of the day at which the view was taken.[29]

25

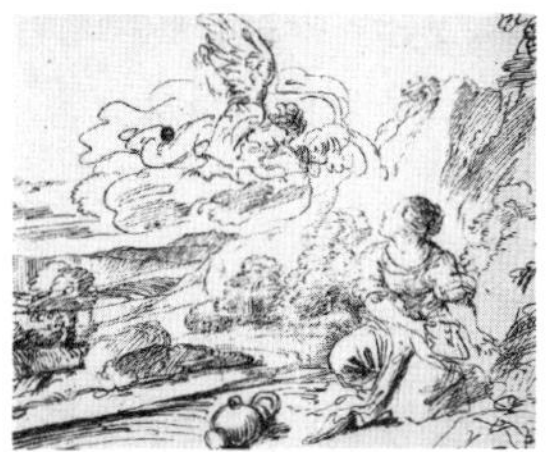

27　William Henry Fox Talbot, *The Pencil of Nature*, 1844, Plate XXIII: 'Hagar in the Desert'.

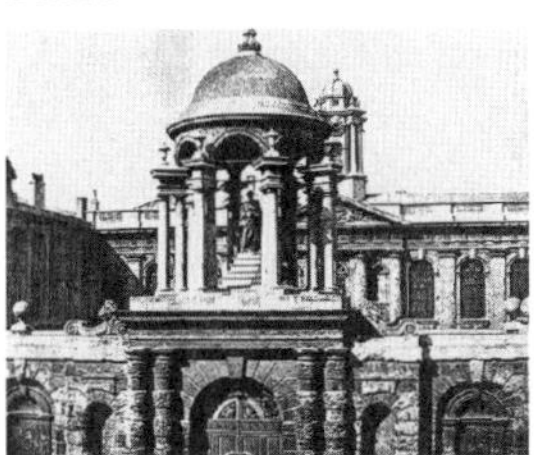

28　William Henry Fox Talbot, *The Pencil of Nature*, 1844, Plate XIII: 'Queens' College, Oxford'.

29　Talbot, *The Pencil of Nature*, n.p.

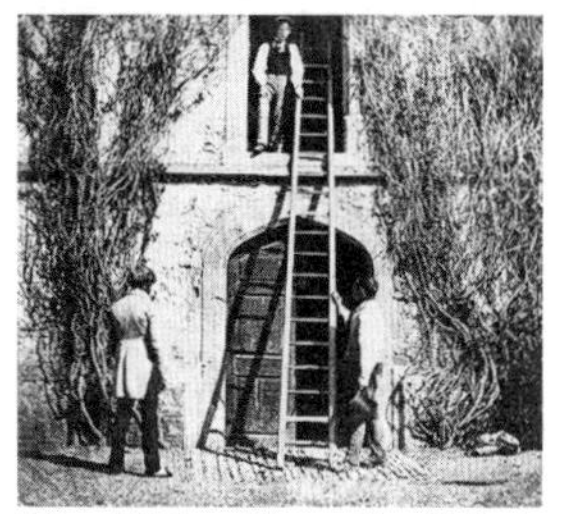

30 William Henry Fox Talbot,
The Pencil of Nature, 1844,
Plate XIV: 'The Ladder'.

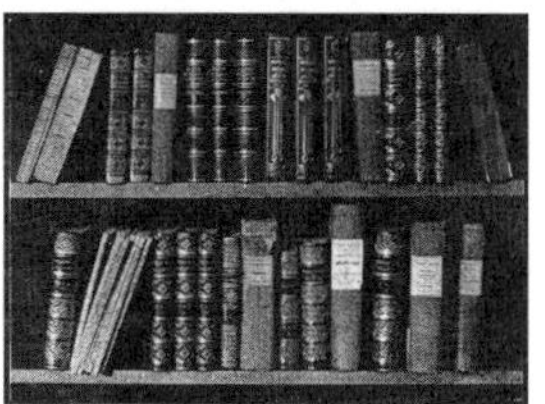

31 William Henry Fox Talbot,
The Pencil of Nature, 1844,
Plate VIII, 'A Scene in a
Library'

The fact that the camera does not select details in the visual field but includes all of them, shows that we discern more details in a photographic image then in our perception of the world.

It is noteworthy that Talbot did not include any portraits in his selection of images, for he begins his text accompanying Plate XIV with the remark that portraits and groups of figures form some of photography's most attractive subjects.[30] He promises the reader to present some portraits in the course of the work. But because he was never able to finish his project and present the fifty plates that he had planned, portraits or groups of human figures were not included in *The Pencil of Nature*. But not only the genre of portraiture is missing. As mentioned earlier, also the genre of landscape is absent. I will argue later that this is significant because both genres form a problem for the dominant notion of photography as snapshot of the world.

One of the most intriguing plates is Plate VIII, 'A Scene in a Library'.[31] The text that goes with this image is puzzling because it does not describe the image, at least not directly. It describes at length a 'rather curious experiment or speculation'. 'When a ray of solar light is refracted by a prism and thrown upon a screen, it forms a coloured band known by the name of the solar spectrum.' Even rays that are normally invisible because they are beyond the limits

26

of the spectrum, can be revealed. This experiment demonstrates that 'the eye of the camera would see plainly where the human eye would find nothing but darkness'. How does the description of the experiment relate to the plate which it accompanies?

In her essay 'Tracing Nadar' Rosalind Krauss is also puzzled by the question why Talbot included this photograph of books and by its relation to the accompanying text.[32] Whereas in most other cases the plates serve to illustrate the arguments in the text as demonstrations of them, the relation between text and plate is now more complicated. She presents the possibility that the role of the photograph of the books is conceptual insofar that it is the embodiment of a speculative projection. Whereas Talbot's text is a discussion of 'invisible rays', it ends with a reference to books which still have to be written:

> Alas! That this speculation is somewhat too refined to be introduced with effect into a modern novel or romance; for what a *dénouement* we should have, if we could suppose the secrets of the darkened chamber to be revealed by the testimony of the imprinted paper.[33]

Although for Talbot, books contain cultural signs and the pencil of nature produces natural signs, his reference to novels and romances suggests that the photographic trace is also a transcription of thought.

27

32 Rosalind Krauss, 'Tracing Nadar', *October* 5 (Summer 1978), pp. 29–47.

33 Fox Talbot, *The Pencil of Nature*, n.p.

34   Krauss, 'Tracing Nadar',
p. 42.

35   William Henry Fox Talbot,
introduction to *The Pencil of
Nature*, facsimile edition (New
York: Da Capo Press 1969), n.p.

The darkened chamber described by Talbot in the same text is not only a reference to the camera obscura but also to 'a wholly different region of obscurity: the mind'.[34]

Krauss' reading of Talbot is motivated by her interest in initial conceptions of photography. That is why she concentrates not only on Nadar, but also on an earlier generation of thinkers and practitioners of photography, to which Talbot belongs. Although Krauss' speculation on the relation between Talbot's text and the plate it accompanies is convincing as such, it does not consider the plate as a photographic image but as a representation of books. She only sees what the image shows: two shelves with books on them. A closer look at the photographic image reveals, however, more than just books. Many of the spines of the leather-bound books show reflections of light. The human eye does not see these reflections. We do not notice them because we just see the spines of books. The 'eye of the camera' reveals the 'invisible rays of light', and we see shiny spines of books in the photographic image. Krauss' conceptual reading of the image is all about light exerting, as Talbot wrote 'an *action* … sufficient to cause changes in material bodies', but she does not *see* that light in the image she is reading, although Talbot mentions this explicitly in the introduction to his book *The Pencil of Nature*.[35]

Although some of the plates can retrospectively be understood in terms of the dominant photographic approach of the snapshot, many plates are examples of totally different photographic practices. In order to de-naturalize the photographic approach and to get a better view of the photographic image, in what follows I will especially focus on the kind of photographic practices implied by those plates that deviate from the practice of the snapshot.

Medium Specificity and Photography

Like Talbot's *The Pencil of Nature*, the photographs by Kraijer are a good starting point for a critical reflection on the photographic approach. They go against the grain by complicating this approach. No one will question the fact, however, that Kraijer's images are photographs, although they do not comply with the prevalent notion of what this medium inherently is considered to be. To suggest that photography has an inherent nature or essence is, of course, tricky in itself. For there are opposing views of photography's ontological identity. As Geoff Batchen remarks, many postmodern critics have argued that photography does not have such an identity, because all meaning is determined by context and not by an inherent nature or essence.[36] The

29

36 Geoffrey Batchen mentions John Tagg, Allan Sekula, Victor Burgin and Abigail Solomon-Godeau as the main representatives of postmodern criticism in the field of photography. See Batchen, *Burning With Desire: The Conception of Photography* (Cambridge, MA: MIT Press, 1997), p. viii.

37   Clement Greenberg, 'Four Photographers' [review of Atget, Steichen, Feininger and Cartier-Bresson], in *Clement Greenberg: The Collected Essays and Criticism: Volume 4, Modernism with a Vengeance, 1957–1969*, ed. John O'Brian (Chicago: University of Chicago Press, 1993), p. 183.

meaning of photography, then, depends on the different contexts in which photography is being used and those contexts change over time, in history. The opposite view identifies and values photography according to its supposedly fundamental characteristics as a medium. It will be obvious that representatives of these opposing views focus on different photographic practices in support of their conviction.

To believe in the fundamental characteristics of the medium of photography implies a belief in the modernist notion of medium specificity. This is a contested notion. First of all, it is controversial because of the way it was proposed by critics such as Clement Greenberg. This critic has not written much on photography, but in his essay 'Four Photographers', Greenberg describes the medium specificity of photography by comparing it to literary prose:

> The art in photography is literary art before it is anything else: its triumphs and monuments are historical, anecdotal, reportorial, observational before they are purely pictorial. Because of the transparency of the medium, the difference between the extra-artistic, real-life meaning of things and their artistic meaning is even narrower in photography than it is in prose.[37]

The low status of photography among other artistic mediums is expressed by the fact that in photography, due to its transparency, there is almost no difference between real-life meaning and artistic meaning. Whereas other media such as painting are supposed to rely exclusively on technical, formal features for their medium's specificity, photography works best 'when it calls the least attention to itself and lets the almost "practical" meaning of the subject "come through"'.[38] Greenberg claims that as in prose, form in photography is reluctant to become content. His pejorative notion of photography (and of literary prose) relies heavily on photographic practices that come together in Kracauer's idea of the dominant approach to photography and in snapshot photo-graphy.

Rosalind Krauss has criticized such a formalist notion of medium specificity not by completely deconstructing and refusing it, but by complicating it. Medium specificity is always a combination of prevalent photographic practices and the technical features of the medium of photography. This implies that medium specificity is not an inherent essence, but that it can change over time when new practices come about and become prevalent. In the case of photography, it is Kracauer's account of the photographic approach, in other words the practice of snapshot photography, which for Krauss defines the medium specificity of photography.

Another complication of the idea of medium

38   Ibid.

31

39   Hal Foster, 'Re: Post', in
*Art After Modernism: Rethinking
Representation*, ed. Brian Wallis
(New York: New Museum of
Contemporary Art; Boston:
David R. Godine, 1984), p. 195.

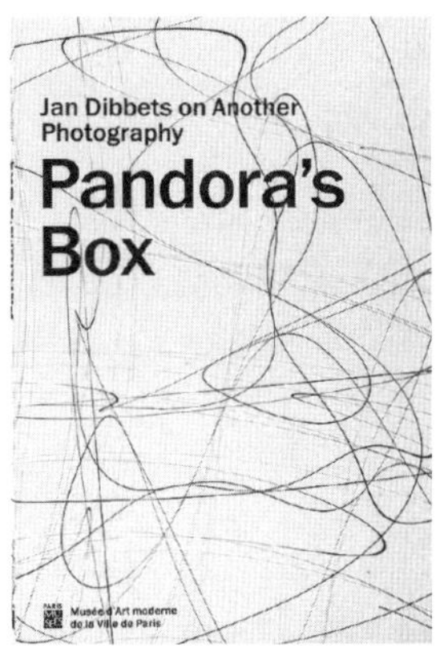

40   Catalogue Jan Dibbets,
*Pandora's Box: Jan Dibbets on
Another Photography*, Musée
d'Art Moderne de la Ville de
Paris / Paris Musées, 2016.

specificity is what George Baker has called, in a variation on Krauss' notion of 'sculpture in the expanded field', 'photography's expanded field'. Whereas Kraijer's images are still undoubtedly photographs, postmodern art practices started to use photography in such ways that it has expanded the field of what is considered to be photography. Hal Foster's discussion of Krauss' essay on sculpture also applies to photography: 'Though no longer defined in one code, practice remains within a *field*. Decentered, it is recentered: the field is (precisely) "expanded" rather than deconstructed.'[39]

A good example of the expanded field of photography is the 2016 exhibition in the Musée d'Art Moderne de la Ville de Paris curated by Jan Dibbets, 'Pandora's Box: Jan Dibbets on Another Photography'[40]. This exhibition included works by artists such as Liz Deschenes, Spiros Hadjidjanos, Seth Price and Kelley Walker, which are not photographs in the recognizable formal sense, but are based on processes that they have in common with photography. Dibbets' exhibition demonstrates postmodernism's challenge to photography adequately. In the words of Baker (elaborating on the idea of 'expanded field'): 'What we need in the contemporary moment are maps: we should not retreat from the expanded field of contemporary photographic practice, rather we should map its possibilities, but also deconstruct its potential closure and further open its multiple logics.'[41]

Although I fully agree with Baker's account of the expanded field of photography, I will for the moment focus on the medium, instead of the field of photography. I do that because the expansion of the field did not only take place in the beginning of the 1960s with postmodern art practices. There is also, what I would like to call, an 'inner field of expansion'. The dominant photographic approach has marginalized a diversity of photographic practices that were already performed since the inception of the medium. That is why a further reflection on photography's medium specificity can also contribute to '[opening] its multiple logics'.

So, let's for the moment take a step back from postmodern photographic practices and see how medium-specific accounts of photography have made features that also belong to it, invisible or marginal. The camera as the embodiment and producer of the technical features of the image is often considered to be an objective recording device. The images it produces are then objective. Many people held and still hold that photographs copy nature or reality faithfully. In the article of 1951 already mentioned, Kracauer objects to such a notion of photography as being objective or faithful. He is very much aware of the fact that the photograph fundamentally trans-

41   George Baker, 'Photography's Expanded Field', October 114 (Fall 2005), p. 138.

42 Kracauer, 'The Photo-
graphic Approach', p. 63.

forms the visual field that exists before the camera. In its failure, or one could also say its 'refusal', to match reality the photograph is revealed in its difference from reality:

> But it need scarcely be stressed that in actuality photographs do not copy nature but metamorphose it, by transferring three-dimensional objects to the plane and arbitrarily severing their ties with their surroundings—not to mention the fact that they usually substitute black, gray and white for the given colour schemes.[42]

These features, so different from the standard conception of what the camera does or stands for, result in a kind of image that enables a very specific mode of looking. Kracauer explains that the beholder of the photographic image will discern in photographs details ('minutae' in his words) that we tend to overlook in everyday life. This special quality of the photographic image also suggests that it cannot be conflated with the world of which it is supposed to be a faithful copy. But the beholder does not only see more things, but also sees them faster:

> … Photographs permit the spectator to apprehend visual shapes in a fraction of the time he would require for a similarly acute apprehension of the actual objects. There are three reasons for

this: photographs, by isolating what they present, facilitate visual perception; they transform
depth to one plane; and they usually also reduce
the angle of vision, thus enabling the eye to com-
prehend with relative ease whatever is
represented.[43]

Kracauer's account of the formal characteristics of
the photographic image and of the perception solic-
ited by that image suggests that the earlier notion of
medium specificity has to be relativized. The interaction between dominant practices in working with
a medium and technical and formal features, is relative because even the technical and formal features
are not objective features but a matter of notions
people hold or not. Still, Kracauer's account of the
technological transformation from world to photographic image seems to me much more precise than
the notion of the photographic image as faithful or
transparent.

In the early 1920s, the Hungarian artist László
Moholy-Nagy, living in Berlin, was well aware of
the fact that the camera differs in crucial aspects
from the eye in how it presents the visible world. But
for him the photographic image is much more faithful to the optical experience and objective than the
human eye. Visual experiences by the eye are not
objective because they continuously interact with

43 Ibid., p. 64

35

44 László Moholy-Nagy, *Painting, Photography, Film* (1925) (Cambridge, MA: MIT Press, 1969), p. 166.

45 Vilém Flusser, *Towards a Philosophy of Photography* (London: Reaktion Books, 2000). Originally published as *Für eine Philosophie der Fotografie* (Göttingen, 1983).

intellectual experience and perceived optical phenomena are supplemented by associations and imaginative patterns. He concludes that photographic images enable us to 'see the world with entirely different eyes'.[44] This difference does not derive from the claim that the camera is an objective recording device, but rather from the claim that the eye is doing the opposite of recording objectively. Important is that the photographic image has its own formal, optical characteristics, which differ from human vision.

The work of another German-speaking thinker on photography, the Czech-Brazilian Media theorist Vilém Flusser, can be read as a radicalization of Kracauer's ideas of the special features of the photographic image and its production. I will take his reflections on photography into account because his rather radical and oppositional thinking provides an effective framework for de-naturalizing the photographic approach and for an understanding of photography in its differing from the reality it shows. In his book *Towards a Philosophy of Photography* Flusser argues that 'technical images' such as photographs are usually seen as 'symptoms of the world'.[45] Viewers read the photographed world instead of the photographic image. This explains Flusser's use of the term 'symptom' instead of sign of the world, because it is the causal, indexical relation between the image and the world it shows that enables the viewer to approach the photographic image as a snapshot of the world. As a result, photographs have the reputation to be objective and non-symbolic. Viewers do not relate to photographs as images, but as specific ways of looking at the world. 'Their criticism is not an analysis of their production but an analysis of the world.'[46]

However, for Flusser, technical images do not offer a transparent view on the world. Photographic images are utterly symbolic, which implies that in photographs we do not see the world, but concepts of the world. In order to understand photographs adequately we have to consider them as conceptual, which means that we have to become aware of the translations that have taken place from world to image in the photographic technology. This technology, however, discourages awareness:

> The function of technical images is to liberate their receivers by magic from the necessity of thinking conceptually, at the same time replacing historical consciousness with a second-order magical consciousness and replacing the ability to think conceptually with a second-order imagination.[47]

For Flusser something like naïve, non-conceptual photography does not exist, since a photograph is by

46 Ibid., p. 15.
47 Ibid., p. 17.

48   Ibid., p. 34.

definition an image of concepts. These concepts, which Flusser also called 'categories', together form the programme of the camera. The following passage must be quoted at length because it encompasses an elaborate account of that programme.

> The categories of the camera are registered on the outside of the camera and can be adjusted there, as long as the camera is not fully automatic. These are the categories of photographic time and space. They are neither Newtonian nor Einsteinian, but they divide time and space into rather clearly separated areas. These areas of time and space are distances from the prey that is to be snapped, views of the 'photographic object' situated at the centre of time and space. For example: one time and space for extreme close-up; one for close-up, another for middle distance, another for long distance; one spatial area for a bird's eye view, another for a frog's-eye view; another for a toddler's perspective; another for a direct gaze with eyes open as in olden days; another for a sidelong glance. Or: one area of time (shutter speed) for a lightning-fast view, another for a quick glance, another for a leisurely gaze, another for a meditative inspection. The act of photography has its movement within this time and space.[48]

This quotation demonstrates well the great diversity of the camera's concepts or categories. They determine how photographic images look; awareness of them challenges the notion of photography as transparent or objective. Flusser writes:

> On the hunt, photographers change from one form of space and time to another, a process which adjusts the combinations of time-and-space categories. Their stalking is a game of making combinations with the various categories of their camera, and it is the structure of this game—not directly the structure of the cultural condition itself—that we can read off from the photograph.[49]

It is especially the current fully-automatic camera that makes the programme of the camera completely invisible. With the digital revolution, photographic concepts or categories have become part of the unconscious of the photographic image. It is the task of photography criticism to bring the programme of the photographic image to light again. Besides the aesthetics of the photographer—a coding in the second degree according to Flusser—the concepts of the camera also have to be 'decoded'.[50] But it is not only photography criticism that should understand and reveal the programme of the photographic image. It is first of all the task of the photographer

39

49 Ibid., p. 35.
50 Ibid., p. 48.

51   Ibid., p. 36.

VILÉM FLUSSER

Into the
Universe of
Technical
Images

Translated by Nancy Ann Roth
Introduction by Mark Poster

52   Vilém Flusser, *Into the Universe of Technical Images*, introd. Mark Poster (Minneapolis: University of Minnesota Press, 2011). Originally published as *Ins Universum der technischen Bilder* (Göttingen, 1985).

or other 'functionaries of the camera':

> In choosing their categories, photographers may think they are bringing their own aesthetic, epistemological or political criteria to bear. They may set out to take artistic, scientific or political images for which the camera is only a means to an end. But what appear to be their criteria for going beyond the camera nevertheless remains subordinate to the camera's programme.[51]

When Flusser refers to the cultural condition, he means the cultural condition created and determined by the rise of technical images. Photography is the first example of technical images but cinema and computer technology are other examples. Especially in his book *Into the Universe of Technical Images*, Flusser discusses the new cultural condition called into life by technical images.[52] Technical images are not just a new sort of traditional images; they differ from them fundamentally, that is ontologically; and they are completely new media. Traditional and technical images arise from completely different kinds of distancing from concrete experience. Traditional images, like figurative paintings and drawings are observations of objects; technical images, which owe their existence to technical apparatuses, are compositions of concepts. Traditional images are the result of depiction, whereas technical images come from visualization. According to Flusser, those functions are fundamentally different and should not be confused with those of traditional images.

Technical images are not the phase or step of mediation and abstraction that comes after traditional images; traditional images were followed by linear texts, and technical images are the step after linear texts. Technical images are 'envisioned surfaces'. 'When we look at a photograph with a magnifying glass, we see grains. When we get close to the television screen, we see points.'[53] That explains why technical images can only be considered as images at all only if they are seen superficially: the viewer should keep his distance from them. Producers of technical images (photographers, cameramen, video makers) are those who 'envision'; they handle the apparatuses and visualize. The images they visualize are not produced by cameramen but by the apparatus. Envisioners differ from writers because they do not need deep insight into what they are doing. 'They are freed from the pressure of depth and may devote all their attention to constructing images.'[54] The apparatus has condemned the envisioner to 'superficiality' in the figurative sense of the word. This unleashes a wholly unanticipated power of invention, a power which is hallucinatory and has recently become 'real' in the form of 3D technology. The position of this new cultural condition is

53 Ibid., p. 33.
54 Ibid., p. 36.

41

55   Ibid., p. 37 (emphasis added).

56   Ibid., p. 38.

57   Ibid.

58   Vilém Flusser, *Writings* (Minneapolis: University of Minnesota Press, 2002), p. 63.

fundamentally contradictory: 'Envisioners stand at the most *extreme edge of abstraction* ever reached, in a dimensionless universe, and they offer us the possibility of again experiencing the world and our lives in it *as concrete*.'[55]

The power to envision is the power of drawing the concrete out of the abstract.[56] Although we are not enough aware of this, the rise and fall of technical images implies a cultural revolution. All vision, imagination, and fiction of the past must pale in comparison to our images: 'We are about to reach a level of consciousness in which the search for deep coherence, explanation, enumeration, narration, and calculation is being surpassed by a new, visionary, superficial mode of thinking.'[57] Flusser distinguishes technical images not only from traditional images, but also from writing. Writing concerns a higher step in abstraction than traditional images based on depiction. His notion of writing is intimately related to a specific notion of temporarility, which is history. History is, according to him, not possible without writing. 'With the invention of writing, history begins, not because writing keeps a firm hold on processes, but because it transforms scenes into processes: it generates historical consciousness.'[58] The temporality implied by photographic practices and images will be an important issue in this book. I will elaborate on Flusser's distinction between the temporality called into life by writing and by technical images. Writing, he claims, creates awareness of time as linear movement because it performs the function of transforming 'scenes into processes'. The linearity of writing demands a progressive reception, which results in a very specific experience of time, namely linear time: 'Linear codes demand a synchronization of their diachronicity. They demand progressive reception. And the result is a new experience of time, that is linear time, a stream of unstoppable progress, of dramatic unrepeatability, of framing, in short, history.'[59] As Mark Poster points out, historians have other reasons for assuming a close relationship between history and writing. It is only when writing begins to offer a material, objective basis for memory of the past that one can begin to speak of history.[60]

The linear mode of consciousness (history) related to writing is in crisis, according to Flusser, because writing is being supplanted by technical images. The culture of technical images begins with photography. These images encourage a non-linear form of reading and composition. Photographs are 'dams placed in the way of the stream of history, jamming historical happenings'.[61] The temporality of photographs is one of instantaneousness, of an all-at-once-ness. Images are read with no sense of movement: 'In pictures we may get the message first, and

43

59 Ibid., p. 39.

60 Mark Poster, 'An Introduction to Vilém Flusser's *Into the Universe of Technical Images* and *Does Writing Have a Future?*', in Flusser, *Into the Universe of Technical Images*, xiv.

61 Flusser, *Writings*, p. 127.

62   Ibid., p. 23.

63   Flusser, *Into the Universe of Technical Images*, p. 48.

then try to decompose it. … This difference is one of temporality, and involved in the present, the past and the future.'[62] It is especially Flusser's distinction between traditional images and technical images that is not convincing for everyone. He argues that they require an inversion of interpretation:

> Traditional images are mirrors. They capture the vectors of meaning that move from the world toward us, code them differently, and reflect them, recoded in this way, on a surface. Therefore it is correct to ask what they mean. Technical images are projections. They capture meaningless signs that come to us from the world (photons, electrons) and code them to give them a meaning. So, it is incorrect to ask what they mean. … With them the question to ask is, what is the purpose of making the things they show mean what they do? For what they show is merely a function of their purpose.[63]

A photograph of a house can look very similar to a painting or drawing of the same house. This suggests that they are the same kind of images and that there is only a difference in degree. But the photograph succeeds better in representing the house than the other kind of images, because it is more realistic. 'But it is exactly the task of an inverted interpretation, a criticism suited to technical images, to show that this apparent "objectivity" of technical images is merely a function of the purpose their meaning serves.'[64] The critical project of photography (and other technical images) is to show that in defiance of common sense, photographs are not mirrors but 'projections that are programmed to make common sense appear mirror-like'.[65]

Because technical images are projections, they must be decoded not as representations of things out there in the world but as signposts directed outward. To continue the idea of the projector, the object of criticism should concentrate on the projector, not on the image that is produced by it. The projector is the 'programme' of the camera, responsible for how the image looks. The conclusion that Flusser then draws is indebted to that other famous theorist of media, Marshall McLuhan:

> Technical images do not show us their meaning; they show us a way we may be directed. It is not what is shown in a technical image but rather the technical image itself that is the message. And it is a significant, commanding message.[66]

This means that we must criticize technical images such as photographs not on the basis of what they show, but on the basis of their programme. He elaborates the conventional metaphorical imaginary of 'shooting images' to emphasize this point: 'We must

64 Ibid., pp. 48–49.

65 Ibid., p. 49.

66 Ibid.; he is implicitly referring to Marshall McLuhan's well known *Understanding Media: The Extensions of Man* (1964).

start not from the tip of the vector of meaning but from the bow from which the arrow was shot.' In other words, criticism of photographs requires an analysis of their trajectory and their intention behind it.[67]

What is striking about Flusser's philosophy of photography is that the indexical causality underlying the photographic image, so central in almost all reflections on photography of the last forty years, plays no role in it. He refers a few times to 'the magic' by means of which receivers of technical images are liberated from the necessity of thinking conceptually and to understand and 'see' the translations that bring the image to life. This liberation is the main function of technical images and it creates the illusion that these images are 'symptoms of the world'. But what kind of process is he referring to when he speaks of magic by means of which receivers of these images are liberated? Is it the indexical imprinting of light that produces the image? Or is the iconicity of the photographic image which strikes viewers even when they are not aware of the process that produced it? The iconicity is so perfect that we can even speak of an analogy between image and world instead of a representation of the world in or by the image. However, when Flusser raises the issue of the magic of technical images, he is not discussing the technical image's production, but its reception. This suggests that the magic he talks about concerns the perfect iconicity of the technical image, not its indexicality.

It is precisely this repressed element of photography, its perfect iconicity, that Kaja Silverman focuses on in her recent book, *The Miracle of Analogy*.[68] Silverman re-evaluates classical nineteenth-century theories of photography and repudiates the idea of the indexicality of photography as being responsible for the effect of magic it has on the viewer. She sketches an alternative history and theory of photography proceeding form the idea of photography as analogical. Photography is, in her words, 'an ontological calling card. It helps us to see that each of us is a node in a vast constellation of analogies, each linked to another, it to another, and so on'.[69] Photography can be seen then as an analogical transfer, representing a 'second becoming of the world'.[70] Flusser's philosophy can be read as an attempt to dispel the magic or miracle of photography as a second becoming of the world.

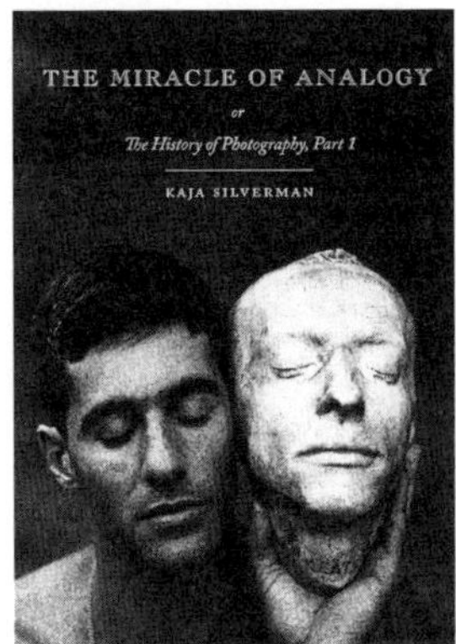

68   Kaja Silverman, *The Miracle of Analogy, or the History of Photography, Part 1* (Stanford University Press, 2015).

69   Ibid., p. 11.

70   Ibid., p. 33.

Transparency and Remediation

The reflections on photography by Kracauer and Flusser have in common that they both try to understand photography in how it differs from the reality it shows. Therefore, their thinking can be understood

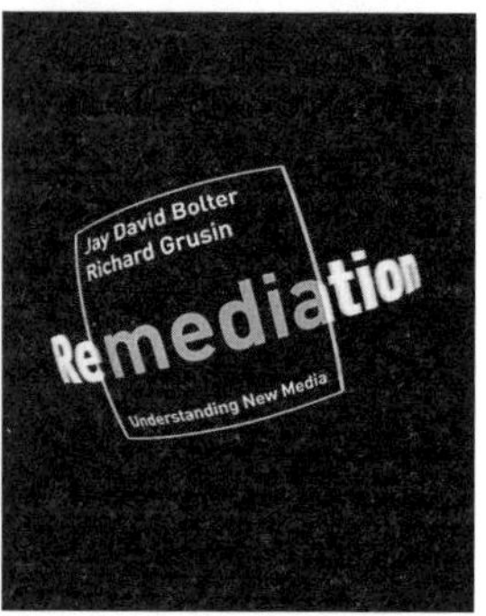

71b Jay David Bolter and
Richard Grusin, *Remediation:
Understanding New Media*,
paperback edition (Cambridge,
MA: MIT, 2000).

as a deconstruction of the prevalent tendency to read photographs as symptoms of the world (Flusser) or of the photographic approach or attitude (Kracauer). They both see as the task of the criticism of photography to analyse the different ways the photograph transforms that which exists before the camera.

In recent years, another media theory has been proposed, however, of which the main assumption points in the opposite direction: it assumes that the main reason to develop or even invent new media, a process that is called 'remediation', is to make them more transparent. Although it goes completely against the grain of the present book, and against the work of Kracauer and Flusser that inspired it, I will devote some thoughts on it in this introduction, because in this new theory the medium of photography is taken as exemplary for demonstrating the main goal or inspiration behind any remediation. As at first sight the assumption of a desire for transparency seems to be completely convincing, because it is so ubiquitous in many Western theories of representation, this assumption invites some scrutiny.

In their book *Remediation: Understanding New Media*, published in 1999, Jay David Bolter and Richard Grusin understand the process of remediation as based on a double logic, namely on the two contradictory imperatives for immediacy and hypermediacy.[71] They articulate the contradiction between

48

the two imperatives as follows: 'Our culture wants both to multiply its media and to erase all traces of mediation: It wants to erase its media in the very act of multiplying technologies of mediation.'[72] This kind of personification of culture is needed in order to project onto culture and its media a phantasmatic dimension. Culture has desires and fascinations, more concretely, a desire for immediacy and a fascination for hypermediacy. The desire for immediacy is a desire for a transparent medium and a desire to deny the mediated character of technologies and media. It is the 'desire to get past the limits of representation and to achieve the real'.[73] This real should not be understood in a metaphysical sense, but in terms of the viewer's experience: 'it is that which evokes an immediate (and therefore authentic) emotional response'.[74]

The fascination with hypermediacy, in contrast, concerns a specific representational practice, a cultural logic, and a visual style. They quote W.J.T. Mitchell to explain it: It is a visual style 'that privileges fragmentation, indeterminacy, and heterogeneity and that emphasizes process or performance rather than the finished art object'.[75]

Although immediacy and hypermediacy stand for opposite conditions, it is clear that they are not equally strong. Libidinal desire determines the direction of historical processes of remediation much

49

72 Jay David Bolter and Richard Grusin, 'Remediation', *Configurations* 4, no. 3 (1996), p. 313.

73 Ibid., p. 343.

74 Ibid.

75 Ibid., p. 327.

76 Ibid., p. 330.

77 Ibid.

78 Ibid.

more powerfully than the more self-conscious and distant fascination for hypermediacy. For Bolter and Grusin the fascination for hypermediacy is the historical counterpart to the desire for immediacy. It can be recognized in diverse forms and media, such as illuminated manuscripts, Renaissance decorated altarpieces, Dutch painting, Baroque cabinets, and modernist collage and photomontage.[76] Sometimes hypermediacy 'has adopted a playful or subversive attitude both acknowledging and undercutting the desire for immediacy'.[77] At the end of the twentieth century, the psychodynamic condition or function of hypermediacy has become even more oppositional: 'we are in a position to understand hypermediacy as immediacy's opposite number, an alter ego that has never been suppressed fully or for long periods of time'.[78]

The transparency for which the desire for immediacy longs, seems to be satisfied by the medium of photography. So, it is far from surprising that photography is staged several times in their treatise on remediation to exemplify the object of desire. The medium of photo collage is then the counterpart of photography, challenging the immediacy of photography by consisting of heterogeneous spaces:

> When photomonteurs cut up and recombine 'straight' photographs, they discredit the notion

that the photograph is drawn by the 'pencil of nature', as Fox Talbot had suggested. Instead photographs themselves become elements that human intervention has selected and arranged for artistic purposes.[79]

The photo collage as an arrangement for artistic purposes results in a medium we look *at* instead of *through*.

In view of the double logic of remediation, a few words should be said about the difference between remediation and mediation. For Bolter and Grusin all mediation is remediation because each act of mediation 'depends upon other acts of mediation. Media are continually commenting upon, reproducing and replacing each other'.[80] This is not a side-effect of remediation; they even call it the goal of remediation to refashion or rehabilitate other media. In the case of photography, Fox Talbot justified his invention because of his dissatisfaction with the device of the camera obscura for making accurate perspective drawings by hand.[81] Almost explicitly, he presents photography as a remediation of the medium of the camera obscura. So far, the meaning of mediation and remediation seems to be clear. But in the course of Bolter and Grusin's argumentation, remediation as a process broadens its object: it does not only refashion other media, but also social

79 Ibid.

80 Ibid., p. 346.

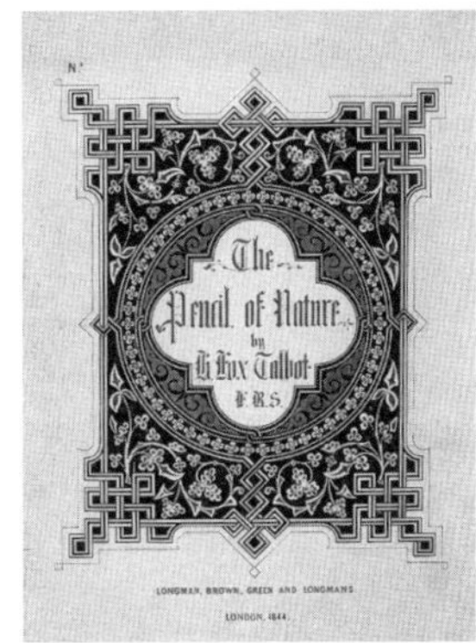

81 William Henry Fox Talbot, *The Pencil of Nature*, (London: Longman, Brown, Green & Longmans, 1844).

82 Ibid., p. 357.

arrangements and material practices. This becomes clear when they discuss photography as a remediation of the medium of painting:

> And although photography remediates painting, it was a more complex historical case. In their rivalry with painting, some photographers (such as Henry Peach Robinson) sought to be regarded as artists, while 'straight' photographers (such as Lewis Hine, Edward Weston, and August Sander) promoted themselves not as artists, but rather as social historians or even natural scientists. Their internal disagreements were both over the material basis of their medium and over the social and formal nature of the remediation that photography undertook. Whatever their differences, in each of these cases, the remediation of the social and the remediation of the material go hand in hand.[82]

Whereas at first the process of remediation seemed to be rather specific and limited to the refashioning of other media, it now dissolves into transformations of which the scope is no longer limited to media. Remediation becomes then the equivalent of transformation, whatever the object of transformation is.

Another slippage in the theory of remediation concerns the ambiguous role of culture and of the subject, or the self. When explaining the double

logic of immediacy and hypermediacy, I pointed to
the awkward personification of culture. Our culture
'wants', has 'desires' and 'fascinations'. In the section
'Remediation of Self', the authors claim that the
desire for immediacy and the fascination with hypermediacy also has a psychological dimension and that
the double logic 'can also refer to the attitude of the
subject toward the act of representation'.[83] This
results in assigning the desire for immediacy and the
fascination with hypermediacy to the subject. The
subject is defined as:

> ... a succession of relationships with various
> applications or media. She oscillates between
> media (moves from window to window, from
> application to application), and her subjectivity
> is determined by those oscillations. In the first
> case, the subject is assured of her existence by
> the fact that she can enter into immediate rela-
> tionships with the various media or media forms
> that surround her.[84]

The desire of immediacy seems to originate in the
subject and appears to be fulfilled 'by technologies
that deny mediation: Straight photography, live television, three-dimensional, immersive computer
graphics, and so on'.[85] But because these technologies never fully satisfy that desire (because they
never succeed in fully denying mediation), the

53

83   Ibid., p. 353.
84   Ibid., p. 355.
85   Ibid.

technologies that fail in denying mediation give rise to the fascination with hypermediacy in the subject: 'As this strategy always fails, a contrary strategy emerges, in which the subject becomes fascinated with the act of mediation itself.'[86]

It seems that desire and fascination form a dialectic: desire originates in the subject, whereas fascination originates in the technology or medium at the moment that it fails to satisfy the subject's desire for immediacy. In the chapters that follow, I will challenge this double logic of remediation by focusing on several counter practices in photography. Not through straight photography, but through blurred photography, staged photography, under- and over-exposed photography and archival photography, I will rethink the desire for immediacy and the fascination for hypermediacy. I will argue that the practices of the medium of photography as such are not at all the embodiment of the desire of immediacy. Important photographic practices in the history of the photographic medium emphasize the medium's hypermediacy in order to demonstrate that the photographic image is not a 'symptom of the world' but a construction.

Reflective Images

As already argued, the reflections on photography by Kracauer and Flusser have in common that both try to understand photography in how it differs from the reality it shows. Their ideas can be understood as a deconstruction of the customary tendency to read photographs as transparent. They both set as task for the criticism of photography to analyse the different ways the photograph transforms that which exists before the camera.

The photographic image transforms transparency into visibility when it reflects on its own features. As David Green remarks, the notion of reflexivity, whether one is concerned with film or photography or painting or whatever, has been central to theories of the medium, especially to ideas about medium specificity.[87] The idea is that it is only through reflexivity that it is possible to identify those properties and characteristics that are peculiar and unique to a medium, in other words, to define its so-called essence. So, reflexivity is in fact self-reflexivity. Green uses the example of the device of the freeze frame as a reflexive device of film. This device does not belong to film because it runs counter to common assumptions about the medium as being based in movement. When we apply this to photography it means, for example, that blurred images are

87 David Green, 'Marking Time: Photography, Film and Temporalities of the Image', in *Stilness and Time: Photography and the Moving Image*, ed. David Green and Johanna Lowry (Brighton: Photoworks, 2006), p. 19.

88 Philippe Dubois, 'Photography Mise-en-Film: Autobiographical (Hi)stories and Psychic Apparatuses', in *Fugitive Images: From Photography to Video*, ed. Patrice Pedro (Bloomington, IN: Indiana University Press, 1995), pp. 152–153; quoted by David Green, 'Marking Time: Photography, Film and Temporalities of the Image', in *Stillness and Time: Photography and the Moving Image*, ed. David Green and Johanna Lowry (Brighton: Photoworks, 2006), p. 20.

89 At first sight, Clément Chéroux's book *Fautographie: Petite histoire de l'erreur photographique* seems to address the same issue as my book *Failed Images*. Chéroux deals, however, with real photographic failures, whereas I consider failure as photographic practices taking place outside the dominant approach: they fail to conform to this approach.

self-reflexive. They are so because the blur is usually the result of movement, which counters the idea of the instantaneousness of the photograph. A blur can also be the result of a long time of exposure. The duration of time that causes a blur counters the conventional temporality of the snapshot as catching one single moment.

Philippe Dubois argues as follows for the importance of reflexivity for an understanding of medium specificity:

> I think we have never been in a better position to approach a given visual medium by imagining it in light of another, through another, in another, by another, or like another. Such an oblique, off-center vision can frequently offer a better opening onto what lies at the heart of the system. The thing is to practice this kind of oblique, sideways approach deliberately. We might begin with this simple idea: that the best lens on photography will be found outside photography.[88]

In the chapters that follow I will not focus on media outside photography, but on what I call 'failed images'. By failed images I mean photographs that are the result of photographic practices outside the practice of snapshot photography or the photographic approach.[89] These images fail to comply with the dominant notion of photography. Failed images

are the other within, instead of the other outside,
in another medium that is. Blurred images are, of
course, a good example, but also over- and under-
exposed images are. Another rather common photographic practice that does not fit comfortably in the
photographic approach is staged photography. One
of the problems of staged photography is, for example, the fact that the photographic image is supposed
to continue outside the frame. A staged photograph
only exists within it. And last but not least, I will
also devote a chapter to photographic practices that
consider photographic images as inventories, in other
words, as archival. These practices do not exhaust
the possibilities of photography's other-within, in
other words, of the mediums' rich palette of possible
modes of image-making. But I hope the analyses
that follow will make a convincing case for a different approach to photography, so that we can finally
let go of that alleged standard that has never really
been one.

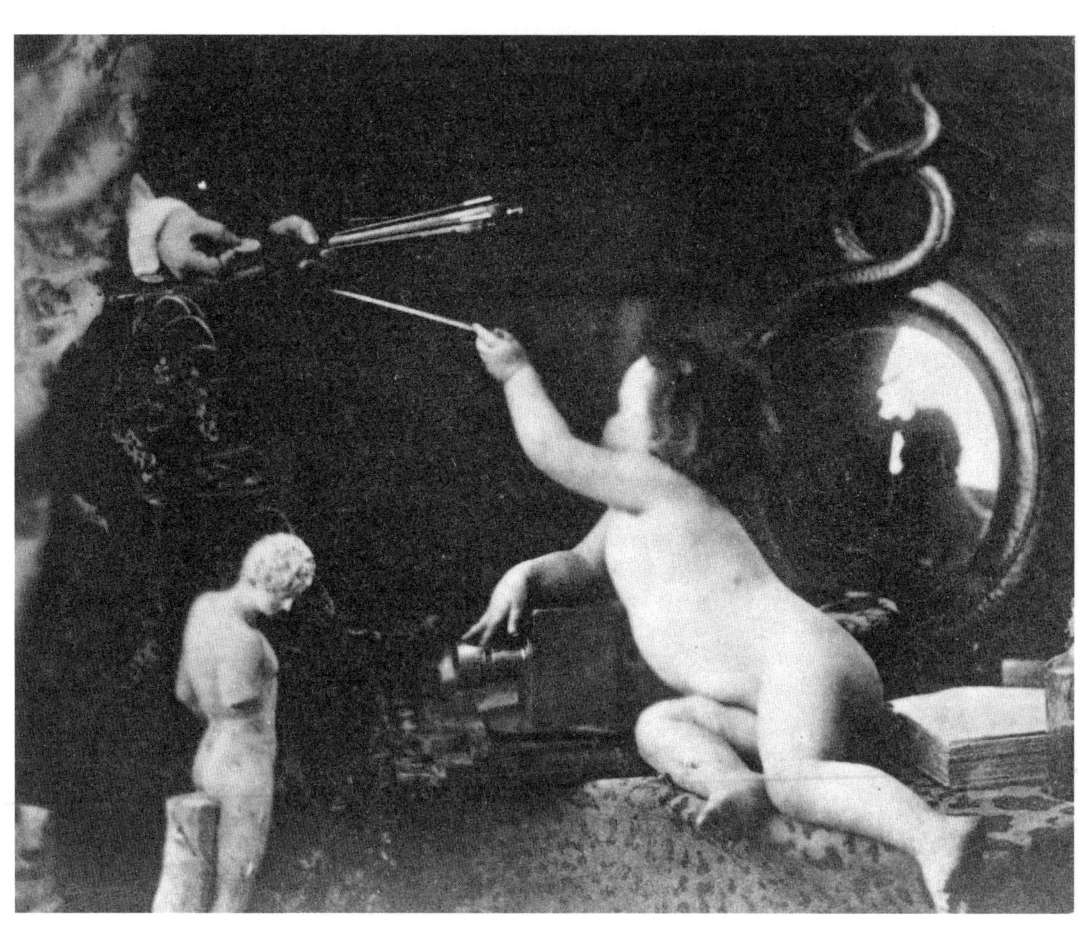

Oscar Gustave Rejlander,
*The Infant Photography Giving
the Painter an Additional Brush,*
1856.

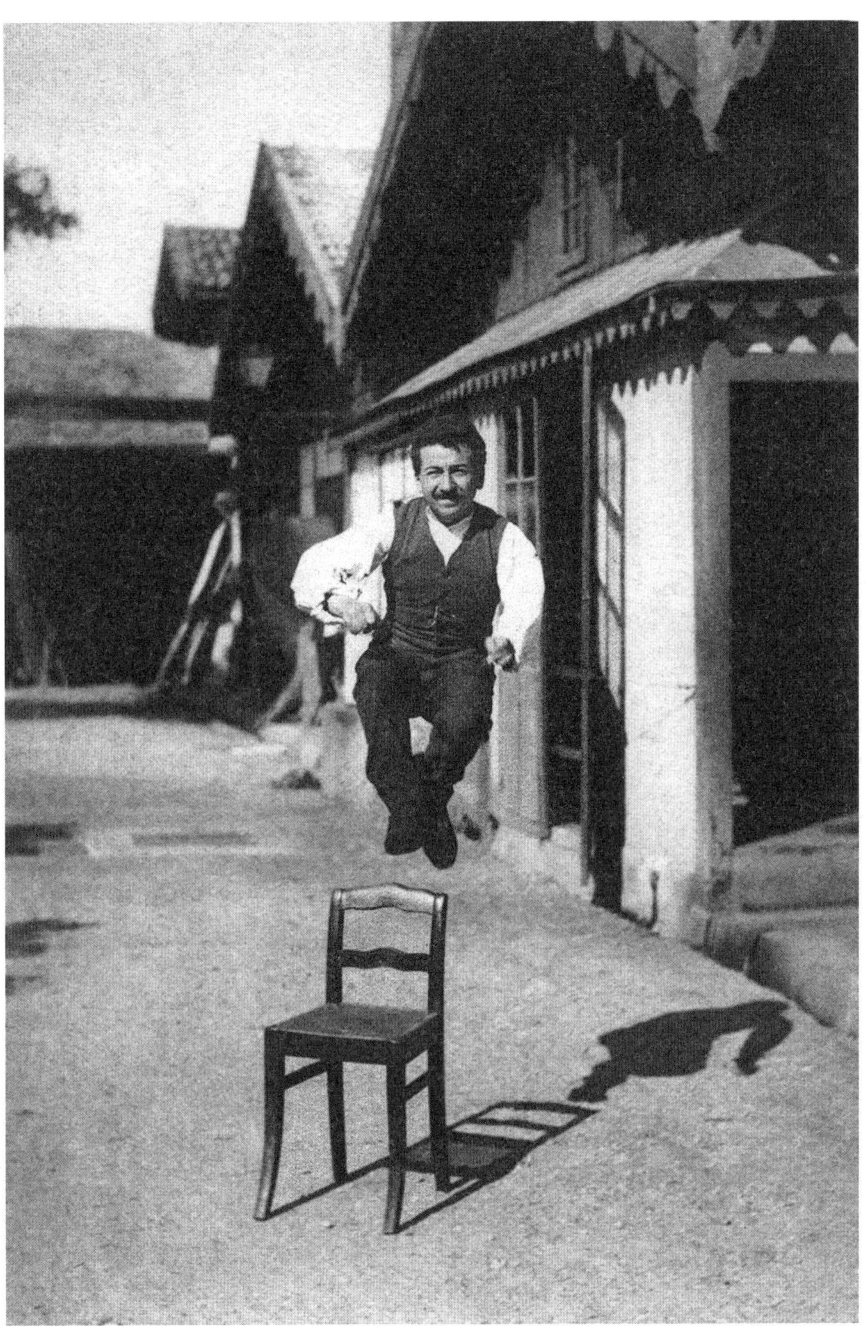

Louis Lumière, *Auguste Lumière
jumping over chair*, c. 1888.

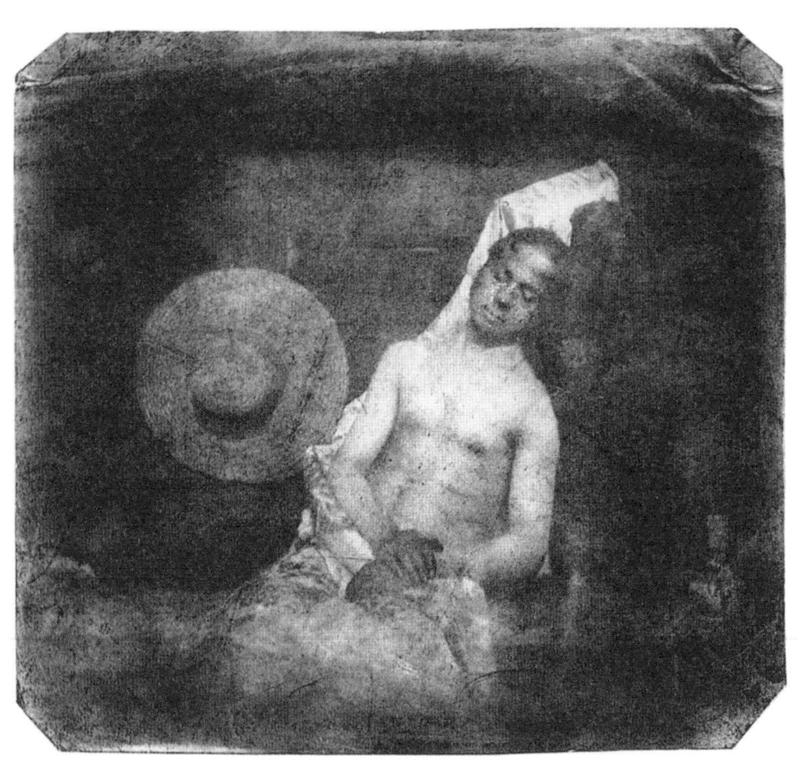

Hippolyte Bayard, *Self-Portrait as a Drowned Man*, 1840.

Staged Photography

At the end of the twentieth century, saying that images do not refer to the world but only to each other has become a truism. The postmodern society of the simulacrum has radically changed old debates and oppositional positions on photography and art. In the world of photography there has always been controversy surrounding the issue of allowing staged scenes or manipulated negatives and prints. Should one embrace and defend either straightforward (naturalist, straight, pure) photography or what is called 'un-straight' photography as a viable position and practice? When in the 1980s Cindy Sherman became one of the most celebrated artists, this question suddenly started to look dated. All of her photographs are staged. Whereas in the nineteenth century staged, un-straight photography was contested but widely practised, in the course of the twentieth

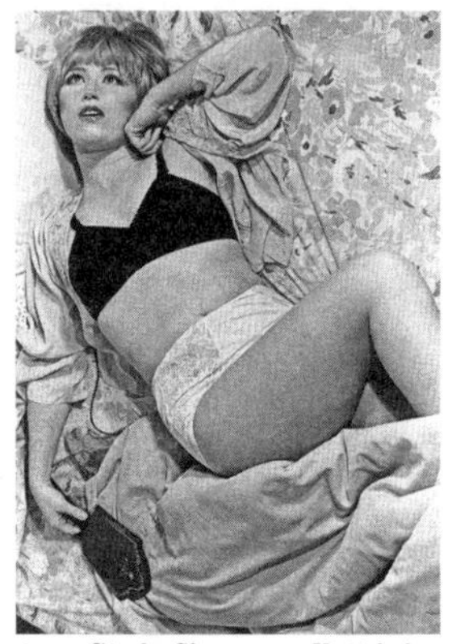

1a   Cindy Sherman, *Untitled Film Still #6*, 1977.

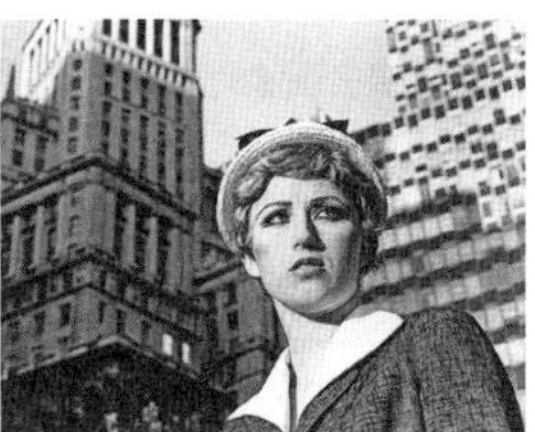

1b   Cindy Sherman, *Untitled Film Still #21*, 1978.

century it had withdrawn into the margins of the worlds of art and artistic photography. Sherman radically overturned this marginal position of staged photography. She does not only stage her images, but also draws attention to the act of staging itself. Her work demonstrates that the ontology of the photographic image can no longer be considered with trust in the straight image without construction or manipulation.

Sherman's photographs are always an explicit mixture of the real and the artificial. The *Untitled Film Stills* that established her reputation in the 1980s looked at first sight like snapshots taken from the real world. But the titles openly proclaimed a different truth. These images were taken from other images; they suggested stills taken from 1950s movies. So, was the woman in these images posing or acting? Was it a woman posing for a fictional film still or was she acting in a film, during which a snapshot was taken?[1]

It turns out that Sherman masqueraded in all her photographs. All staged scenes showed Sherman herself with a different hairstyle and outfit. Still, these images could not be called self-portraits; Sherman's subjectivity could not be traced in any of these images. Instead, she used photography to undermine the idea of subjectivity and of self-expression. Sherman did not have an authentic subjectivity that could be expressed because the portraits of/with herself were simulacra and did not have an authentic original. Her point is that female subjectivity is always modelled on images of femininity circulating in our culture. And those images are stereotypical instead of unique or individual. The same conclusion could be drawn about masculinity, if male masquerading had been her topic. What is important to notice is that staging and masquerading are not just tools that she uses to make her images, they are the topic of her images. In our postmodern world, staging has become the most fundamental condition, which organizes subjectivity and representation.[2]

The series of images Sherman made after the *Film Stills* continue to stage Sherman masquerading, but in each series, she models herself on a different kind of feminine imaginary, from everyday American suburban to wildly grotesque. An exception to this principle is the series of abject images, in which subjectivity is safeguarded by abjecting everything that threatens the subject's borders. The abject is what the subject-in-becoming must get rid of in order to become an I. What we get to see in this series is not the safeguarded self, but everything that had to be abjected in order for the subject to establish and maintain distinct, safe borders. Since the abject is or was also part of the self, these images still stage Sherman.

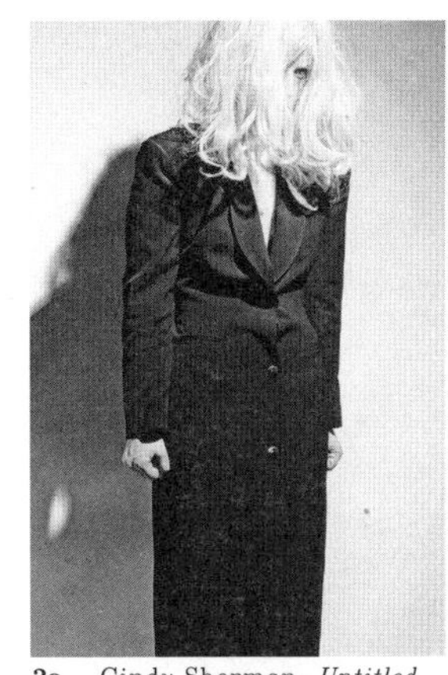

2a Cindy Sherman, *Untitled #122*, 1983.

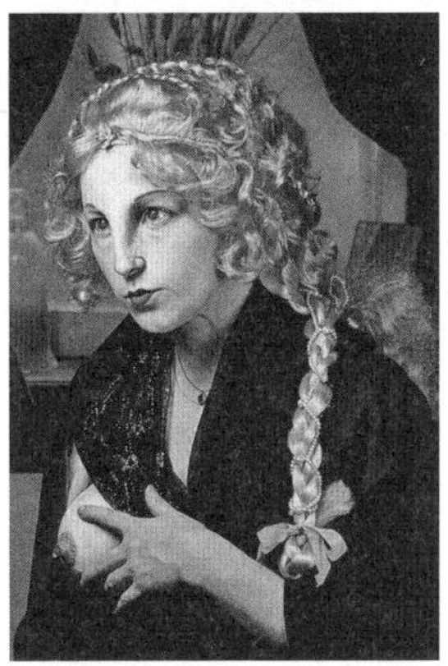

2b Cindy Sherman, *Untitled #225*, 1990.

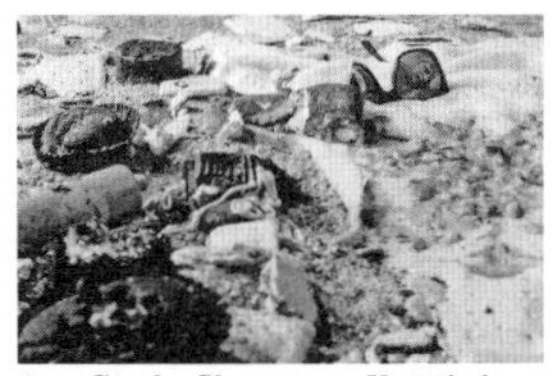

3   Cindy Sherman, *Untitled #175*, 1987.

4   For a discussion of abjection, see Julia Kristeva, *Powers of Horror: An Essay on Abjection* (New York: Columbia University Press, 1982), and Ernst van Alphen, 'Skin, Body, Self: The Question of the Abject in the Work of Francis Bacon', in *Abject Visions: The Power of Horror in Art and Visual Culture*, ed. Rina Arya and Nick Chare (Manchester: Manchester University Press, 2016), pp. 119–129.

5   See Jean-François Lyotard, *The Postmodern Condition: A Report on Knowledge* (Minneapolis: University of Minnesota Press, 1984).

The anxieties triggered by the abject are first of all anxieties resulting from the end-products and by-products of the body, such as body fluids, blood, urine and faecal matter. What defines these end- or by-products of the body is that they are neither subject nor object. They embody the transition between the body and what is outside it. In her photograph *Untitled #175* we see a scene filled with vomit, taking the process of abjection most literally.[3] In the glasses in the upper right of the image we see a reflection of Sherman in masquerade. It is only in the image of vomit, that her image can emerge.[4]

After Sherman established herself as a canonical artist, it is hard to maintain that staged photographic images are failed images. Postmodernism can no longer be dismissed. But powerful as 'the postmodern condition', as the French philosopher Jean-François Lyotard has termed it, may be, it does not mean that the photographic approach as defined by Kracauer has lost its meaning.[5] The ideological nature of this dominant notion manifests itself more explicitly by contradicting prevalent insights into our present condition. Staged and other forms of un-straight photography are still met with uncomfortable responses. They are still seen as failed images, failing to understand the true nature of photography. In order to understand according to what kind of thinking staged photography is supposed to be a violation of the photographic image, I will highlight some key moments in the trajectory of staged photography.

Ann Thomas has distinguished three forms in the trajectory of staged photography.[6] The first is the arranging of models to compose narrative tableaux. This form emerged in the mid-nineteenth century in Victorian contexts; the main practitioners then were Henry Peach Robinson and Oscar Gustave Rejlander.[7] The second form of staged photography features the artist as primary actor or model and concerns individual role-playing concentrating on identity issues. Well-known practitioners of this form are surrealist artists such as Man Ray, Claude Cahun and Marcel Duchamp;[8] but also one of the first photographers in early photography, Hippolyte Bayard, has made images in this format. The third type Thomas distinguishes is more emphatically performance-based, meaning that the photographers themselves act out sequences of choreographed actions for the camera. Especially in the 1970s, photography was used for this staged practice, e.g. by the artist Pierre Molinier.[9] However, in her trajectory of staged photography Ann Thomas only takes into consideration the staging of models, be it the artists themselves or not. I will use a more general notion of staged photography in this chapter.

65

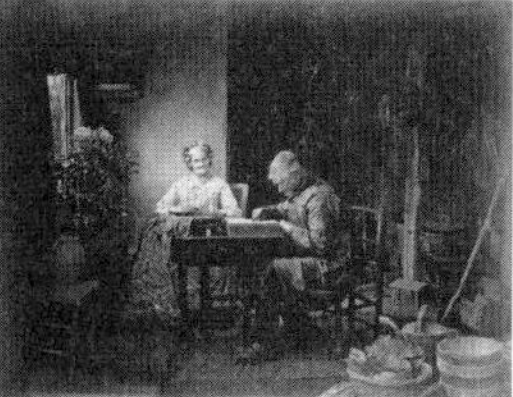

6 Ann Thomas, 'Modernity and the Staged Photograph, 1900–1965', in *Acting the Part: Photography as Theatre*, ed. Lori Pauli (London: Merrell Publishers, 2006), p. 102.

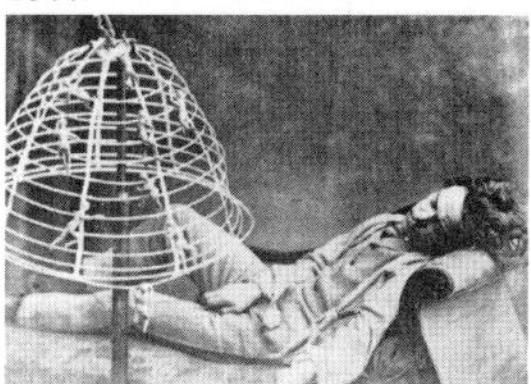

7a Henry Peach Robinson, *When The Day's Work Is Done*, 1877.

7b Oscar Gustave Rejlander, *The Dream*, 1860.

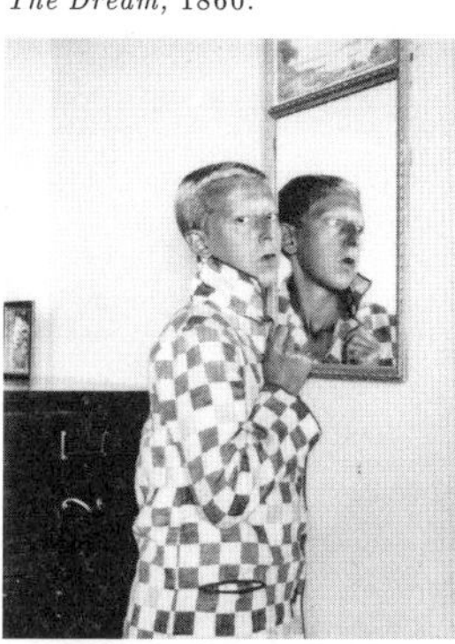

8a Claude Cahun, *Self-Portrait*, 1927.

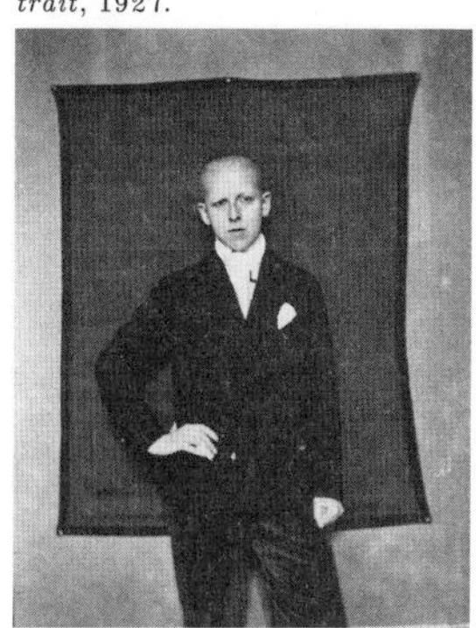

8b Claude Cahun, *Self-Portrait*, 1920.

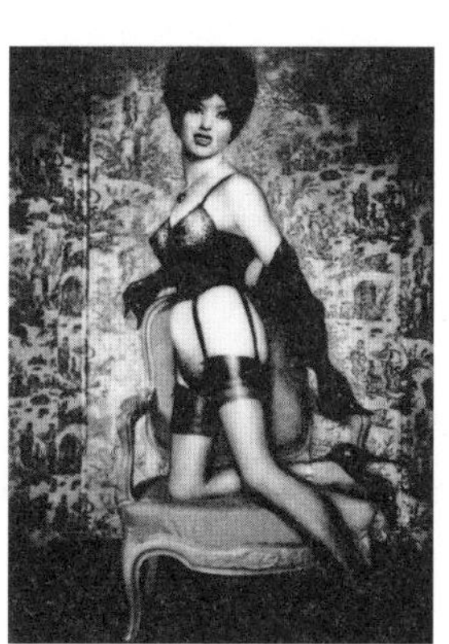

9 Pierre Molinier, *Effigy*, 1970.

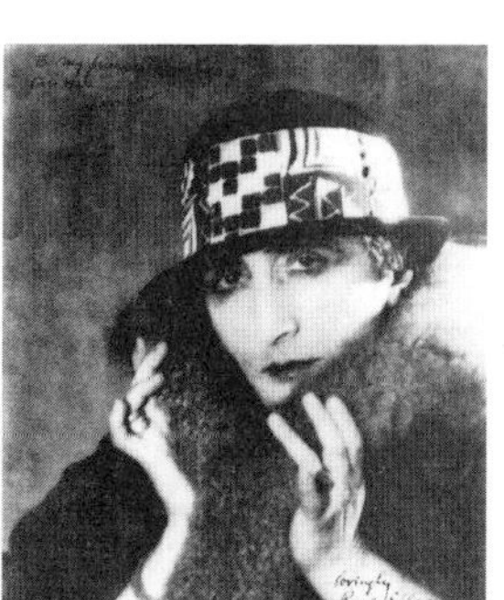

8c Man Ray, *Portrait of Rrose Selavy (Marcel Duchamp)*, 1920.

Staged photography is usually understood as images of posed figures and constructed scenes. Not the image is staged, but the world of which the image is taken. In what follows, in contrast, I argue that staged photography also includes other means of constructing and determining the photographic image, such as combination printing, painterly gum processes, and other handwork on negatives or prints. All these different means of manipulating the resulting image counter the idea of straight photography or snapshot photography. According to this notion of staging, the staging of the photographic image takes place before and after the image is taken, not at the moment the image is taken.

Sitting, Posing and Self-Possession

The main properties Kracauer assigned to the standard approach to photography are an outspoken affinity with un-staged reality and the tendency to stress the fortuitous. These properties are embodied in instantaneous snapshots. But in the early photography of the nineteenth century the staging of reality was a necessary condition for the making of a photograph. The long exposure time needed for a daguerreotype portrait required posing for quite a while. The iodized silver plates exposed in the camera obscura needed a long exposure to light before a pale image would appear. The sitter whose portrait was being made had to remain frozen for as long as possible. This long exposure resulted in a very peculiar kind of image showing staring gazes and motionless poses. The long exposures sitters had to endure in those days inscribed an experience of duration and a haunting presence into the image. It was the technology behind the daguerreotype image that resulted in a very specific kind of photographic sign with a specific temporality that is almost the opposite of the un-staged snapshot.

The required extended posing had both negative and positive effects. In Henry James' short story 'The Real Thing' (1893)[10] an artist complains about a woman who sits for him to have her portrait drawn:

> I could see she had been photographed often, but somehow the very habit that made her good for that purpose unfitted her for mine … . I began to find her too insurmountable stiff; do what I would with it, my drawing looked like a photograph or a copy of a photograph.[11]

But the long posing did not only result in a stiffened sitter, it also bestowed a very special temporality on the image. In his essay 'Little History of Photography' Walter Benjamin gives a beautiful account of the intimate relationship between the extended

THE REAL THING

AND OTHER TALES

BY

HENRY JAMES

New York
MACMILLAN AND CO.
AND LONDON
1893
All rights reserved

10 Title page Henry James, *The Real Thing and Other Tales* (New York / London: Macmillan & Co., 1893).

11 Quoted by Brian Lukacher, 'Powers of Sight: Robinson, Emerson, and the Polemics of Pictorial Photography', in *Pictorial Effect: Naturalistic Vision: The Photographs and Theories of Henry Peach Robinson and Peter Henry Emerson*, ed. Ellen Handy (Norfolk Virginia: The Chrysler Museum, 1994), p. 30.

12   Walter Benjamin, 'Little History of Photography', in *The Work of Art in the Age of Its Technological Reproducibility and Other Writings on Media*, ed. Walter D. Jennings, Brigid Doherty and Thomas Y. Levine (Cambridge, MA: Harvard University Press, 2008), p. 276.

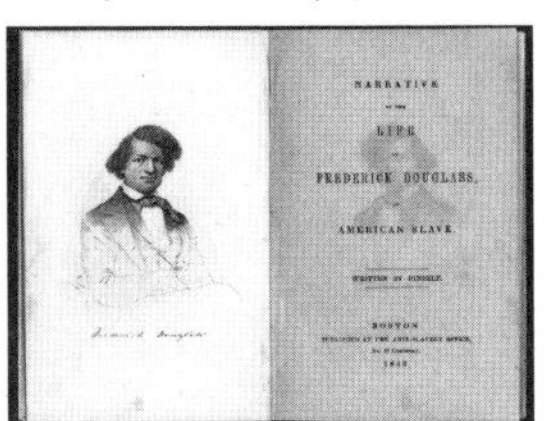

13   Frederick Douglass, *Narrative of the Life of Frederick Douglass, an American Slave* (Boston: Anti-Slavery Office, 1845).

pose technically required for daguerreotype images and the kind of temporality produced by those images. He describes the photographs of a Newhaven fishwife by David Octavius Hill:

> In Hill's Newhaven fishwife, her eyes cast down in such indolent, seductive modesty, there remains something that goes beyond testimony to the photographer's art, something that cannot be silenced, that fills you with an unruly desire to know what her name was, the woman who was alive there, who even now is still real and will never consent to be wholly absorbed in 'art'.[12]

In this description Benjamin recognizes the past, the present and the future as if these were all absorbed into one continuous duration.

The long posing for daguerreotype images also requires presence of mind and composure. One should be in control of one's emotions and actions. American abolitionist and former slave Frederick Douglass (1818–1895) understands this required composure as a form of self-possession, symbolically announcing freedom and the end of slavery. Today especially known for his autobiography *Narrative of the Life of Frederick Douglass, an American Slave* (1845) he has also written several speeches in which he explains the social importance of photography, especially of daguerreotype images.[13] For him there

68

is a vital link between art in general and reform, and more specifically between photography and freedom. Photography is important for achieving freedom and uprooting racism. Also, there is no other figure in American history of the nineteenth century of whom so many photographs exist, especially daguerreotype images. He frequented photographers' studios and sat for his portrait whenever he could.[14] There remain now 160 photographs of him, all with distinct poses, including nine daguerreotypes and four ambrotypes. In the nineteenth century only members of the British royal family had more photographic portraits taken of themselves. The main reason why Douglass appreciated these images so much has little to do with the image as such, but with the fact that they were relatively inexpensive so that people from all classes could have their image made: 'The ease and cheapness with which we get our pictures has brought us all within range of the daguerreian apparatus.'[15] Daguerre has converted the planet into a picture gallery, he claims. 'Daguerreotypes, ambrotypes, photographs and electrotypes, good and bad, now adorn or disfigure all our dwellings.'[16] This has the effect that 'Men of all conditions may see themselves as others see them', because it was only in mirrors that one could see oneself through the eyes of others. Photography makes people independent of other

69

14 John Stauffer et al., eds., *Picturing Frederick Douglass: An Illustrated Biography of the Nineteenth Century's Most Photographed American* (New York: Liveright, 2015), p. ix.

15 Frederick Douglass, 'Lecture on Pictures', in John Stauffer et al., *Picturing Frederick Douglass*, p. 128.

16 Ibid., p. 127.

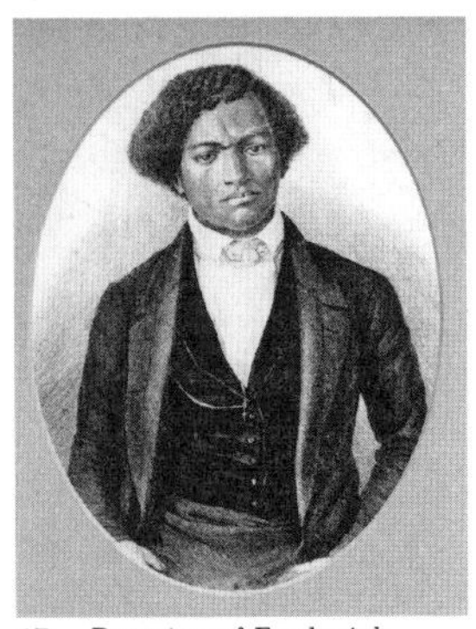

17   Drawing of Frederick Douglass as a young man.

18   Frederick Douglass, 'A Tribute for the Negro', *The North Star*, 7 April 1849. Quoted in Stauffer et al., *Picturing Frederick Douglass*, p. xv.

people's gazes, and as a consequence, of their prejudices. It enables people to look at themselves and free themselves from those prejudices.

Photography made one independent from other people's gazes, whereas engraving and painting did not. When an engraver had made a portrait of him with a slight smile, Douglass was outraged. His portrait had 'a much more kindly and amiable expression than is generally thought to characterize the face of a fugitive slave'. Although no longer a slave, he wanted the look of a defiant but respectable abolitionist. For a painted or engraved portrait one depended completely on the maker of such portraits.[17] He explained as follows why it would never work for a black person to have his portrait made in painting or engraving:

> Negroes can never have impartial portraits at the hands of white artists. … It seems to us next to impossible for white men to take likenesses of black men, without most grossly exaggerating their distinctive features. And the reason is obvious. Artists, like all other white persons, have adopted a theory respecting the distinctive features of Negro physiognomy.[18]

Because of preconceived ideas about what black people look like, it is impossible for white people to draw or paint them with 'impartial' likeness. Photography's assumed faithfulness should afford impartial likeness. But more important is that the required posing gave the sitter control over the resulting portrait. Photographic portraits provide dignity to the sitters for these portraits. When someone's picture is taken 'there is even something statue-like about such men':

> See them when or where you will, and unless they are totally off guard, they are serenely sitting or rigidly standing in what they fancy their best attitude for a picture.[19]

Douglass suggests that posing for a portrait performatively produces dignity. The image is not seen in terms of its likeness to the sitter, but as actively producing a truth about the sitter that results from his posing and other aesthetic elements of the image.[20] The sitter of the portrait discovers this truth of having dignity when he sees the image taken of him. In Douglass' own portraits the dignity is not only bestowed on him by his statue-like pose, but also by his bourgeois middle-class outfit. He considers this production or revelation of truth the social force of pictures. This makes it understandable that he gives this long lecture on daguerreotypes and other photographic portraits in a speech which is supposed to be about the abolition of slavery.

Douglass literally performed for the photographer and determined many formal features of the

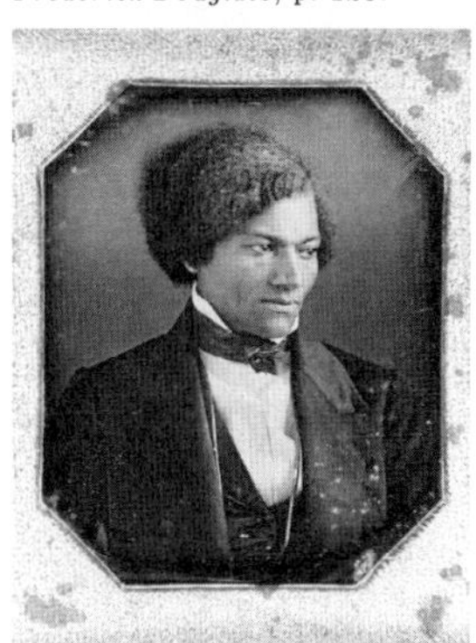

19 Frederick Douglass, 'Lecture on Pictures', in John Stauffer et al., *Picturing Frederick Douglass*, p. 128.

20 Daguerrotype of Frederick Douglass, 1848.

71

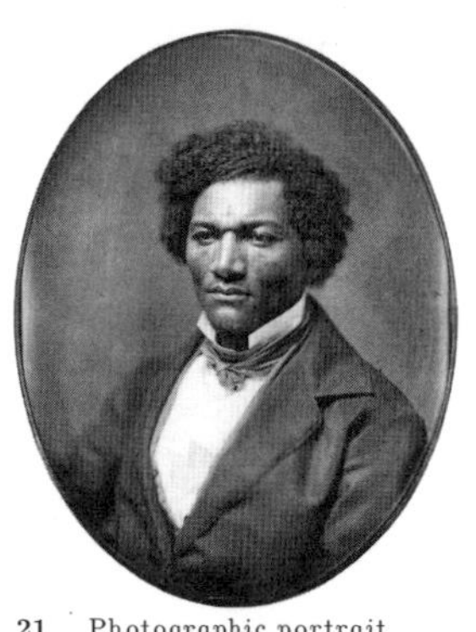

21   Photographic portrait
Frederick Douglass, 1843.

22   John Stauffer et al.,
Picturing Frederick Douglass,
p. xxvii.

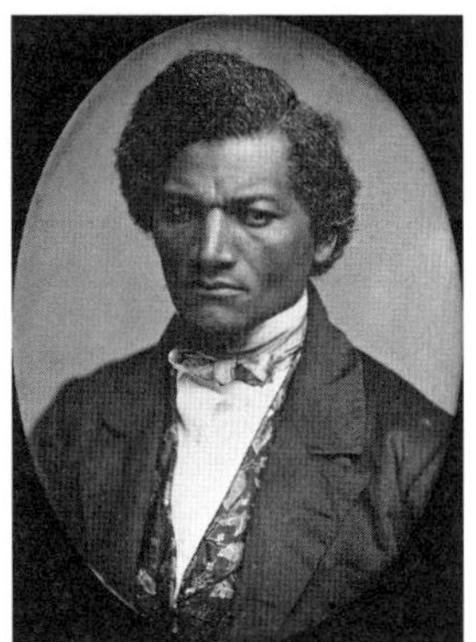

23   Samuel J Miller, *Frederick
Douglass*, 1847/52.

image. Although he had his image taken by a great number of different photographers, his images have many formal features in common, which suggests that Douglass himself had outspoken ideas about what the image should look like. The vast majority of his portraits are closely cropped or vignetted.[21] This draws all attention to Douglass himself, not to the context of the studio in which the photograph was taken. Compared to other studio portraits of that time there are almost no props to distract the viewer. Elaborate backdrops like painted scenes of landscapes are missing. The images should completely concentrate on the portraiture of black masculinity and citizenship. The only variations in the vast number of portraits taken of him concern different angles, different gestures and the adjusting of his clothing, hairstyle and facial hair. 'The changes in his appearance indicated his status as a "self-made man".'[22] This status of self-made man was performatively produced by the images he had taken of him, by his posing, and by how he himself determined what his image would look like. That is why his portraits are in fact self-portraits, although taken by someone else, a photographer.[23]

Because it is performative, the act of posing is also political. As Stauffer remarks, for Douglass posing marked a break from his experience as a slave. In a speech from 1847 he confesses the following:

72

... dissatisfaction was constantly manifesting itself in the looks of a slave. [I have] been punished and beaten more for [my] looks than for anything else— for looking dissatisfied because [I] felt dissatisfied—for feeling and looking as [I] felt at the wrongs heaped upon [me].[24]

His stern, dignified facial expressions when posing for his many portraits give him the power he did not have when he was still a slave.

They also throw an interesting light on the many daguerreotypes and other kinds of photographic portraits he had made of himself. He confesses that vanity is part of it: 'A man is ashamed of seeming to be vain of his personal appearance, and yet who ever stood before a glass preparing to sit or stand for a picture without a consciousness of some such vanity?'[25] But this embarrassing vanity is the price one has to pay for the 'gratification of the innate desire for self-knowledge' which can be fulfilled through sitting for a daguerreotype portrait. In that sense, his portraits are all his own making. Although he was not the photographer, he is the author of his own portraits. Having these portraits made of him is 'a process of soul-awakening self-revelation'.[26] As a former slave, Douglass needed this self-confirmation through portraiture repetitively.[27]

24 Douglass, 'American Slavery is America's Disgrace' (1847), quoted in John Stauffer et al., *Picturing Frederick Douglass*, p. xxiv.

25 Douglass, 'Pictures and Progress', in Stauffer et al., *Picturing Frederick Douglass*, p. 166.

26 Ibid., p. 169.

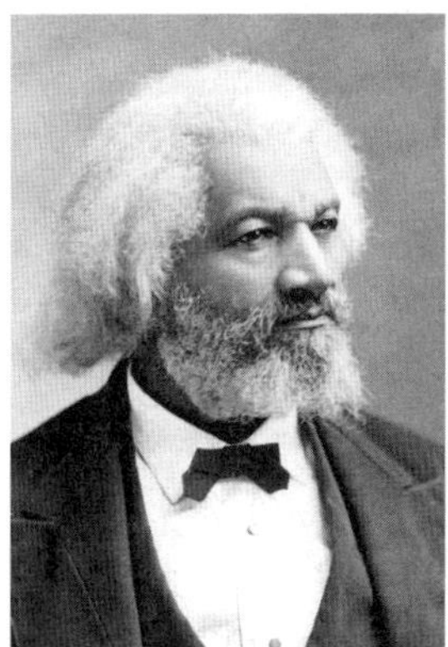

27 Frederick Douglass, c. 1876.

When in the 1880s, in France, Louis and Auguste Lumière developed a new form of photographic dry-plate process, it transformed photography's relation to time and to the spectator. Thanks to this new process, exposure time was reduced dramatically. It enabled the photographer to catch a moving object in full flight, without creating a blur. As a result, viewers started to see photography as a revelatory practice. A world of phenomena that had been hitherto hidden from the human eye revealed itself in photographs. From now on, it is not the human subject sitting for a portrait to be taken who looks frozen, but it is time itself that is frozen. The instantaneous image became a new reality thanks to this newly developed photographic technology. Staged tableau photographs were from then on the sheer opposite of the instantaneous photograph. The image that is at the beginning of this new, but still prevalent photographic discourse is probably a photograph of 1887, in which we see Auguste Lumière jumping over a kitchen chair in his courtyard.

The instantaneous photograph catches not only the jumping ancestor of photography, but also his ghostly shadow. The context in which this happens is far from staged; it is the courtyard where this experimental event took place. Soon Étienne-Jules

Marey's analyses of movement and those of
Eadweard Muybridge in his famous locomotion
series of animals and human figures would follow.[28]
This development in photographic technology seems
to imply the end of staged photography, but that is
not really true. Although the instantaneity of the
photographic image became the dominant paradigm,
staged photography remained an ongoing practice,
but from now on marginalized and met with doubt
or suspicion.

Tom Gunning has argued that the new instantaneous photograph offered a completely new discourse of the body in its relationship to space and
time. These images of instantaneity are not only pre-
cursors of the moving images of the cinematograph,
they prefigure also 'a new modern self image, a casual self presentation diametrically opposed to the
formal, almost allegorical poses of studio portraiture'.[29] Bodies no longer look as posed and disciplined as they were represented in the photographic
studios. From now on they look more casual, represented in play and leisure.

This new discourse of the body did not make an
end to the posing of bodies in staged photography.
While becoming a more marginal practice it also
opened up new horizons with new meanings for
posing and staging. At first, before it became the
common, dominant approach to photography, the

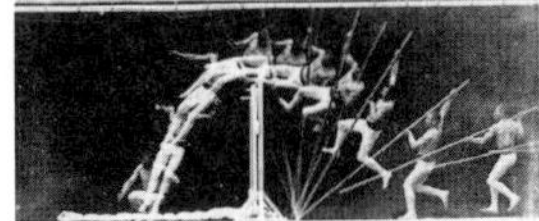

28a   Étienne-Jules Marey,
Chronophotographic study of
man pole vaulting, 1890.

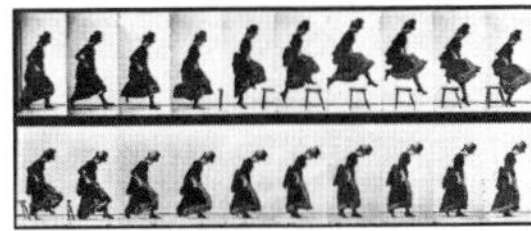

28b   Eadweard Muybridge,
Woman Jumping Over Chair,
1887.

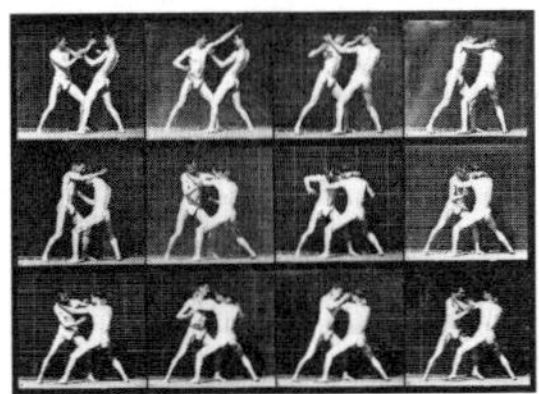

28c   Eadweard Muybridge,
Human Locomotion, Men Box-
ing, 1887.

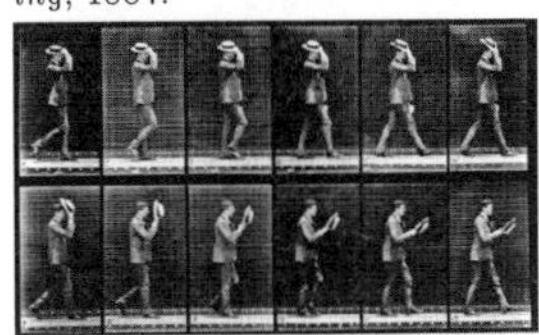

28d   Eadweard Muybridge,
*Human Locomotion, Man Taking
Off His Hat*, 1887

29   Tom Gunning, 'New
Thresholds of Vision: Instanta-
neous Photography and the
Early Cinema of Lumière', in
*Impossible Presence: Surface and
Screen in the Photogenic Era*, ed.
Terry Smith (Sydney: Powers
Publications, 2001), p. 90.

instantaneous image offered possibilities for scientific uses of photography. The work of Muybridge and Marey are good examples of this because it enabled them to achieve a scientific analysis of motion. But the new photographic technology also provided people who were suspicious of the artistic value of photography with a new argument: now, more than ever, the photographic image was the result of a technology for which the agency of the photographer was of little importance. The moment the photograph came to be seen as a revelation, it also seriously questioned the intentionality of the photographer as artist. Although this lack of intentionality undermined the notion of photography as a new art, it also opened up new possibilities for staging and posing in photography. For staging increased the modest intentionality in photography. The hand of the photographer could be recognized in his staging of a scene and in his handwork on negatives and prints. Pictorialist photographers especially, who tried to elevate the medium of photography to the aesthetic domain of art, would continue the practice of staged photography.

The Staging of Narrative: The Photographic Tableau

The temporality of duration was evoked by photographic portraits, especially daguerreotype portraits. A major staged genre in the mid-nineteenth century is the photographic tableau. In the genre of the tableau photograph the world is staged literally and elaborately, and often technically. This photographic genre relates to history painting and genre painting in art but also to the world of theatre and amateur dramatic pastimes of the nineteenth-century bourgeois class. One or more actors posed with props in a natural or artificial setting for one moment out of a narrative scene. The image showed what one, since German philosopher Gotthold Ephraim Lessing's *Laocoon* (1766), calls the 'pregnant moment' of a narrative: one moment out of a narrative sequence, embodying the entire narrative in a nutshell.[30] The represented action was framed by the borders of the picture itself. Although such tableaus were narrative, because of the staged and constructed nature of the scenes, the overall effect was one of stillness. Many tableaus produce a sense of theatrical display, which orients the staged scenes toward the viewer. They are staged in front of the camera, which gives the images a sense of frontality. This frontality seemingly speaks to the viewer directly in the mode of second person address.

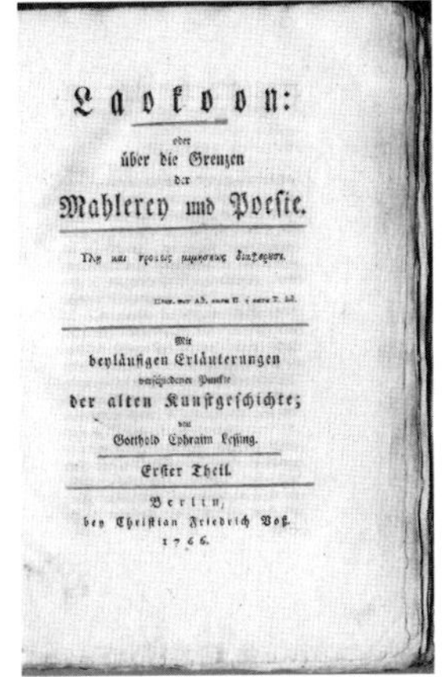

30   Gotthold Ephraim Lessing, *Laocoon* (Berlin: Christian Friedrich Boß, 1766).

77

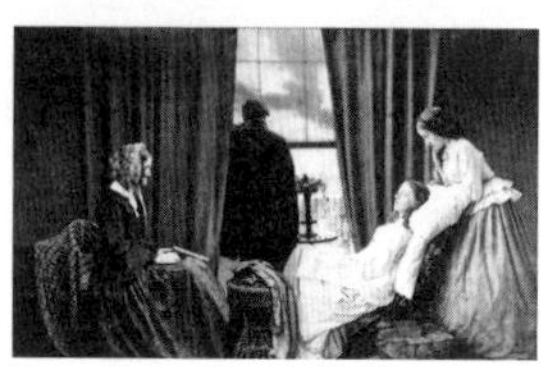

31 Henry Peach Robinson,
Fading Away, 1858.

The best-known photographers who staged tableau images are the Swedish Oscar Gustave Rejlander, living in the UK, and his British follower Henry Peach Robinson. Robinson's tableaus are especially frontal, which positions his viewers, as it were, in front of a stage. A good example is Robinson's staged photograph *Fading Away*.[31]

The theatrical scene suggests an elaborate narrative history of a family drama. The daughter is dying, and whereas her mother and sister support her by being present at her deathbed, the father is not able to do this. He isolates himself in his own grief. Such complex, intricate histories are evoked by the stillness of this narrative image, requiring prolonged contemplation and meditation. The stillness of Robinson's tableau seems to be out-of-sync with the narrative it opens up. It looks literally like a *tableau vivant*; although very narrative, the scene looks frozen. The nineteenth-century public was well aware of this uneasy fit of image and meaning. According to Marta Weiss:

> Victorian audiences recognized that Robinson had photographed a model acting a part, not an actual dying girl. The overtly theatrical nature of the composition, with its frieze-like arrangement of figures framed by parted curtains, signalled that this was a staged scene. The quotation from

a poem by Shelley that accompanied the exhibition print further reassured viewers that this was not an unmediated representation of reality.[32]

The responses to this kind of photographic staging and artistry were not enthusiastic. The photographic genre quickly fell out of fashion, consigning its proponents to the margins of photographic history.[33]

Marta Weiss distinguishes different practices of staged photography in the Victorian times of which Henry Peach Robinson was part, 'ranging from those in which the photographer poses a hired model in accordance with his or her vision, to those in which the subject initiates the sitting, as in the case of a guest at a fancy-dress ball, who commissions a photographer to document his or her costume'.[34] In-between those almost opposite practices there is a practice in which the initiating roles of photographer and model are more ambiguous and in which neither the photographer nor the subject has sole control. These kinds of staged photographs were usually made by the middle and upper classes for whom the taking of and posing for photographs was a form of social interaction, similar to the staging of *tableaux vivants*.

The pictorialist photographers H.P. Robinson[35] and O.G. Rejlander[36] did more than just stage the world they photographed. In addition to the staging

32 Marta Weiss, 'Staged Photography in the Victorian Album', in *Acting the Part: Photography as Theatre*, ed. Lori Pauli (London: Merrell Publishers, 2006), p. 82.

33 Joanna Lowry, 'Modern Time: Revisiting the Tableau', in *Time and Photography*, ed. Jan Baetens, Alexander Streitberger and Hilde van Gelder (Leuven: Leuven UP, 2010), p. 53.

34 Weiss, 'Staged Photography in the Victorian Album', p. 84.

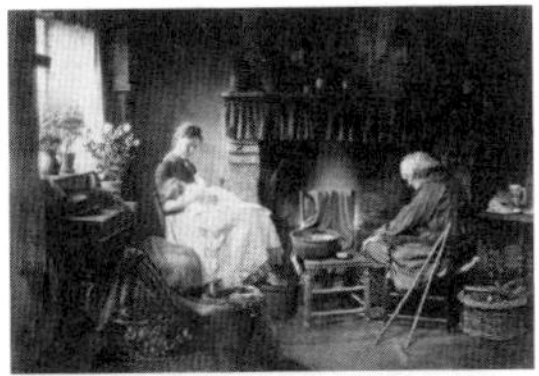

35 Henry Peach Robinson, *Morning and Evening*, c. 1902.

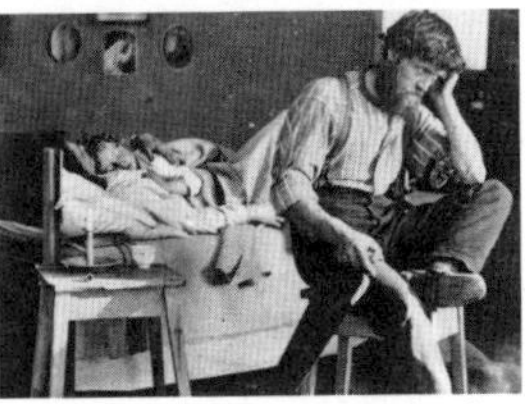

36a Oscar Gustave Rejlander, *Hard Times*, c. 1860.

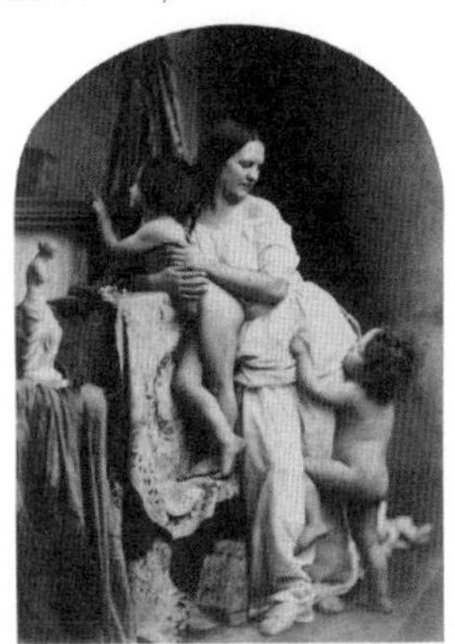

36b Oscar Gustave Rejlander, *The Madonna and Child with St. John the Baptist*, 1860.

37 Henry Peach Robinson, *Pictorial Effect in Photography* (London: Piper and Carter, 1869; Reprint, Pawlett: Helios, 1971), p. 37.

of a scene, they added another constructed layer to the image. By means of what is called 'combination printing', multiple negatives were used to generate a self-consciously composed and composite image. The resulting image consists in fact of a multitude of separate photographic fragments. Their photographs undermine the so-called referentiality or indexical contingency of the images in puzzling ways. Often, preliminary sketches in pencil and watercolour were made before the photographic image was put together. By using this artistic approach to composing the image, the photographer could be sure that almost every detail in the image was intended instead of the result of indexical causality. In the words of Robinson: 'Everything must have a meaning, and the meaning must be *the object* of the picture; there must be nothing "to let"'.[37] Robinson's remark is clearly inspired by his competitive ambition to elevate photography to the aesthetic domain of art. Especially painters were unconvinced about photography as a medium for making narrative tableaus, which were until that moment exclusively executed in the medium of painting, especially in history painting and genre painting. French painter Eugène Delacroix, well-known for his historical tableaus, made sceptical remarks about the narrative possibilities of photography when he imagined a photograph of a scene round the bedside of a dying woman and saw it as a total failure: 'The reason is that according to the liveliness of your imagination [in painting] you will find the subject more or less beautiful; you will be more or less the poet in that sense where you are also an actor; you see only what is interesting, whereas the camera records everything.'[38] Delacroix put the finger on the sore point of the photographic medium. Whereas the painter as intentional agent is present in every detail of his work, the photographer is not, because it is the camera that records everything automatically. According to this notion of art as fundamentally intentional, a photograph cannot contain any poetry or other artistic qualities.

But it is precisely staged photography, especially when the staging is doubled by means of combination printing and forms of retouching, that compensates for this deficiency of intentionality. If photography succeeds in infusing intentionality in all details of the image, photography has even something to add to the traditional artistic domains of painting, sculpture and drawing. In the following photograph titled *The Infant Photography Giving the Painter an Additional Brush* of c. 1856, Rejlander represents photography's ambition to be one of the artistic practices in the most classical way imaginable.[39] This allegory is not only staged but also the result of combination printing and handwork like painterly gum

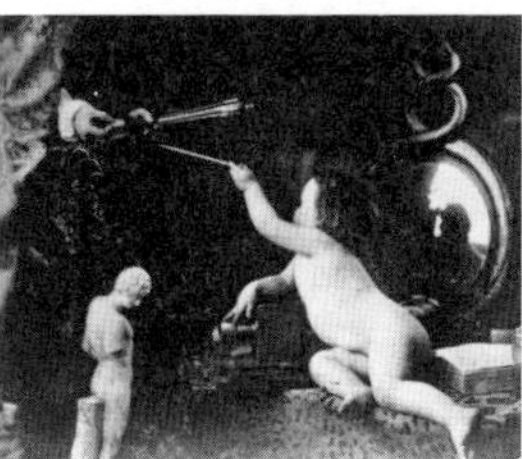

38   Journal entry of Delacroix from 1853, quoted in Lukacher, 'Powers of Sight', p. 32.

39   Oscar Gustave Rejlander, *The Infant Photography Giving the Painter an Additional Brush*, 1856.

40   Robinson, *Pictorial Effect in Photography*, p. 109.

41   Shelley Rice, 'Parallel Universes', in *Pictorial Effect: Naturalistic Vision: The Photographs and Theories of Henry Peach Robinson and Peter Henry Emerson*, ed. Ellen Handy (Norfolk Virginia: The Chrysler Museum, 1994), p. 61.

processes. The then-new medium of photography is represented by the naked infant as a classical putto in the centre of the image. Behind the putto in the mirror we see the reflection of the photographer behind the camera busy creating the image, revealing the meaning of the classical allegory.

Robinson articulates his position on photography clearly in his book *Pictorial Effect in Photography*:

> A great deal can be done and beautiful pictures made, by the mixture of the real and artificial in a picture. It is not the fact of reality that is required, but the truth of imitation that constitutes a veracious picture.[40]

In the words of Shelley Rice: 'as long as something *looks* real, it doesn't have to *be* real'.[41] In the days he was writing this, this notion was widely shared, especially by pictorialists whose discursive paradigm was the one of aesthetics.

The fabrication of pictures of models who were dressed up by using combination printing methods by photographers such as Rejlander and Robinson also incurred a lot of scepticism and critique. These kinds of photographic images were seen as the opposite of naturalist photography. The American photographer Peter Henry Emerson put forth his critique of non-naturalist photography in his 1889 book *Naturalist Photography*. Emerson contended that photography should be as pure as possible and he is considered to be the forefather of what later became known as 'straight' photography. Straight or pure photography rejects combination printing and the staging of scenes, because, according to Emerson, it turned photography into a hybrid form of painting.[42] The issue is not that all manipulations of the image are seen as aberrations from the ideal of straight photography. The point is that a photographic image should serve what is considered a truth. The debate between Robinson and Emerson concerned the nature of that truth. Both men defended their techniques by constantly referring to 'truth', but Robinson legitimized his technique by referring to aesthetic truth, whereas Emerson referred to scientific truth. Both photographers made use of soft focus technique.

Robinson used a lens that slightly softened the focus in order to avoid a strong proliferation of facts and details. For Robinson, such a proliferation precluded photography from being an art. In that respect Robinson's deployment of soft focus can be compared to Julia Margaret Cameron's use of it, for whom it was a pictorialist issue.[43] I will discuss her images in more detail in the next chapter, on blurred photography. Emerson, however, legitimized soft focus by claiming that we actually see in soft focus, which is a truth of another kind.[44] Although

83

42   For a good reading of Emerson's writings in relation to his own photographs, see Charles Palermo, 'The World in the Ground Glass: Transformations in P.H. Emerson's Photography', *The Art Bulletin* 89, no. 1 (March 2007), pp. 130–147.

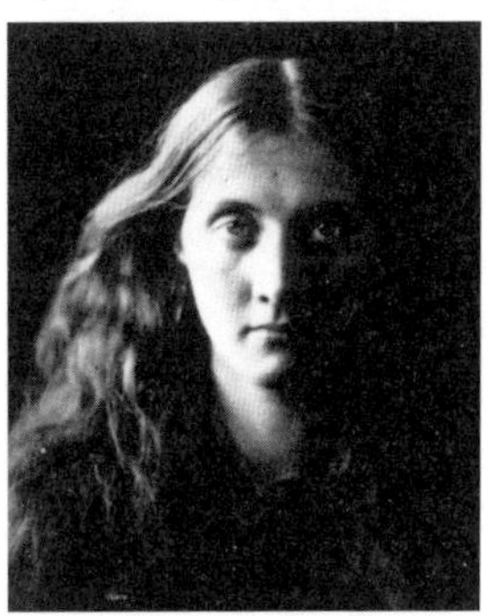

43   Julia Margaret Cameron, *Portrait of Mrs. Herbert Duckworth*, 1867.

44   For the debate between Robinson and Emerson, see Rice, 'Parallel Universes', pp. 60–63.

45   See Nancy Newhall, *P.H. Emerson: The Fight for Photography as Fine Art* (New York: Aperture, 1975).

Emerson legitimized his position on naturalist photography with reference to scientific truth, this does not imply that he considered the medium of photography only of scientific importance, as a tool for scientific research. On the contrary; Emerson became one of the most effective combatants in the fight for photography as a fine art. Photography could, however, only be taken seriously as a fine art, if it would be naturalist and pure and not make use of the aberrations of staged, and of what was later to be called un-straight photography.[45] The different notions of truth used by Robinson and Emerson foreshadow the fundamental difference between nineteenth- and twentieth-century notions of photographic art. As Rice puts it:

> For Robinson, artistic truth aspired toward a fixed and immutable Ideal, expressed through rules of composition that could be judged right and wrong. This Ideal ultimately transcended Nature, as long as it did not violate her principles. Emerson on the other hand, was seeking something more imminent, less conceptual; he sought not to express the Ideal but his own vision of nature. For him *perception* was individualized, subjective, necessarily fragmented, impossible to conventionalize. With Emerson, art became an internal state, and photography

the medium qualified to turn that state inside out.[46]

Although Emerson used some techniques that we now consider manipulation of the image, in general he was in favour of naturalist, straight photographs of what he considered real characters in real nature. His ideas where at first, however, less influential than one would expect. Although Alfred Stieglitz and other young photographers of those days became fans of Emerson's plea for straight photography, Robinson's ideas remained very influential. Especially those who wanted to liberate photography from the scientific and technical contexts in which it was then usually seen, continued to use the staging of scenes, combination printing, painterly gum processes, or handwork on their pictures. According to Rice the ideal of straight photography became dominant only much later. Emerson's ideas only became institutionalized in the 1930s. And even then, they hardly managed to wipe out combination printing or handwork in the subsequent work of the photographers considered avant-garde.[47] The staging of scenes continued but was from then on a practice by means of which photographers placed themselves in the margins of the artistic as well as the photographic world.

46   Rice, 'Parallel Universes', pp. 62–63.

47   Ibid., p. 61.

48   Thomas, 'Modernity and the Staged Photograph, 1900–1965', p. 108. She quotes Mortensen from his book *The Model: A Book on the Problems of Posing* (San Francisco: Camera Craft, 1948), p. 141.

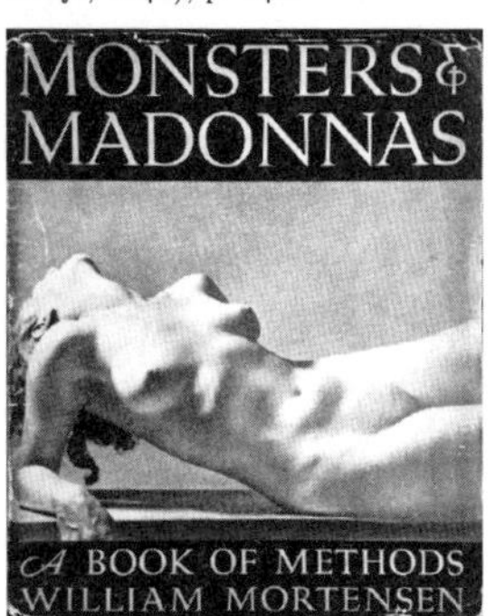

49   William Mortensen, *Monsters & Madonnas: A Book of Methods*, 1936

Although in the US the debates about straight and un-straight photography seem to have turned to the advantage of straight photography, in the 1930s a strong and articulate proponent of un-straight photography set the stage with his photographs and with his books. Living in California and running a school in Laguna Beach, William Mortensen was internationally known and attracted students from all over the world. He taught his students to stage scenes for making pictures, to hand-work their pictures and combination printing. He published nine books with his images and his ideas about un-straight photography. In his publications he issued elaborate instructions on posing, costume and make-up and he insisted on the importance of significant gesture and narrative. 'In creating such tableaux, Mortensen believed that photographers should not consult fashion plates but the work of great painters of the past.'[48] His plea for this marginalized photographic practice is extremely compelling to us now, since we are used to post-modern photographic practices.

Mortensen's best-known book is *Monsters & Madonnas*, which he published in 1936.[49] In this book, he expresses his contempt for the obsession with photographic technique in the field of amateur and professional photography:

86

In photography we see the threat of the Machine come to pass. The Monster is in control. Thousands of potential artists are ruled brain and hand by the dictates of the Machine. The Machine manifests itself in many ways. It appears in the form of a multiplicity of cameras.[50]

Instead, he actively defends the role of the imagination in photography, realized by whatever technical means. 'With the Monster brought to heel, there remains the problem of releasing and putting to work that creative urge, that emotional drive', which Mortensen refers to as the imagination. The imagination is for him an 'active power that demands creative outlet'.[51] In the process of making pictures it is necessary always 'to seek ways to strengthen and give confidence to the imagination, and to free it from the officious interference of the conscious mind', meaning, of the Monster of the camera. To have confidence in the imagination implies that one should use all the means of un-straight photography. These means enable the photographer to make pictures:

> Cameras do not make pictures. Emulsions do not make pictures. Developers do not make pictures. Processes do not make pictures. Gammas, factors, and the abracadabra of the technician do not make pictures. Yet all that eventually counts

87

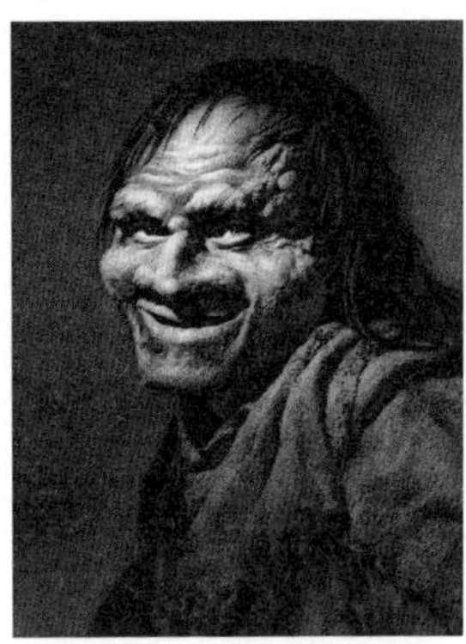

50   William Mortensen, *Monsters & Madonnas* (New York: Arno Press, [1936] 1973), n.p.

51a   William Mortensen, *Belphegor*, 1930.

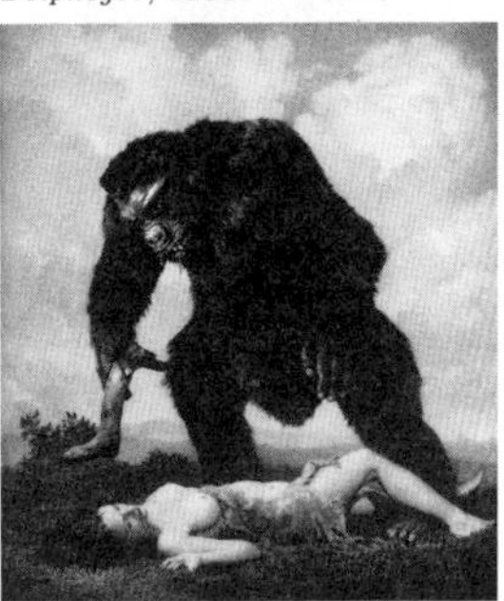

51b   William Mortensen, *L'Amour*, 1935.

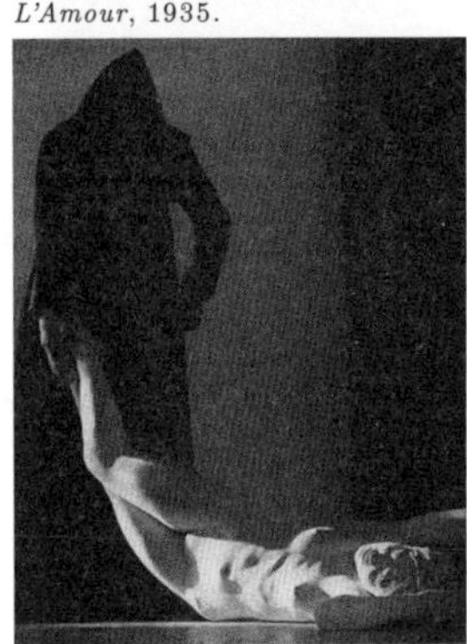

51c   William Mortensen, *Death of Hypatia*, c. 1930.

52 William Mortensen, *Monsters & Madonnas* (New York: Arno Press, [1936] 1973), n.p.

53 In his *L'art poétique* (1674) Nicolas Boileau privileged verisimilitude in the following famous words: 'Jamais au spectateur n'offrez rien d'incroyable. Le vrai peut quelquefois n'être pas vraisemblable.' [Never offer the viewer anything incredible. The truth can sometimes not be probable.]

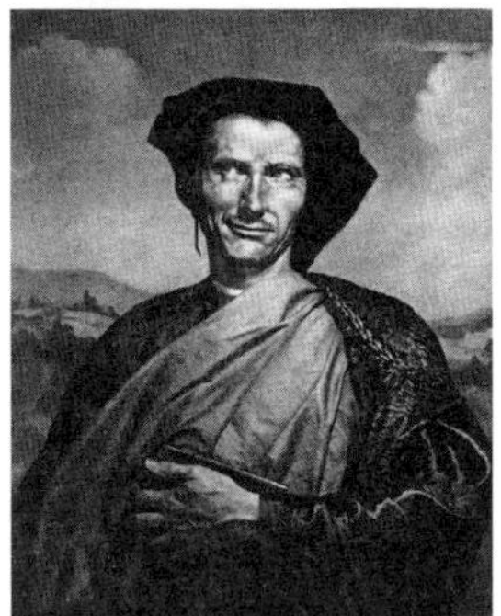

54 William Mortensen, *Machiavelli*, 1936.

with a photographer is whether he makes pictures.[52]

After his introduction, in which he explains the role of the imagination in picture making and the means to do this, he demonstrates it through his own images. In three parts, Characters, Nudes, and Grotesques, he explains all the devices he has used to make the images he shows. As Cameron did almost a century earlier, he explains why likeness is not at all important in picture-making. In the text accompanying his character study *Thunder*, he argues that likeness is only of interest to those who are acquainted with the models. If one pursues ideals of wider significance than likeness, realistic representation is of very limited interest. In his text with the image *Woman of Languedoc* he explains that the costume the woman is wearing makes no pretence to authenticity. 'An authentic costume is nearly always bad pictorially.' The only criterion that counts is how elements work pictorially. In his text accompanying the image *Machiavelli*, he evokes the classical, literary distinction between truth and verisimilitude.[53]

Whereas the stakes of the debate between Robinson and Emerson were different notions of truth, artistic versus scientific, Mortensen opts for the alternative to verisimilitude.[54] The devices and means he used to make this portrait do not pursue

88

likeness with other existing portraits of Machiavelli;
verisimilitude is the pursued quality to make it a
good picture. He also made use of combination
printing: 'The landscape background was accom-
plished by a montage of two additional negatives,
one of hills and one of clouds. The principal negative
was printed first.' Mortensen does not describe his
means as tricks that had better remain hidden, but as
the necessary tools to make a good picture.

Mortensen's approach to the photographic image
is, in fact, conceptual *avant la lettre*. The photographed object is never an end in itself, but it contributes to the mental conception he has of the image
he wants to make. With his outspoken ideas about
non-straight photography he does not only continue
the tradition established by photographers such as
Cameron, Rejlander and Robinson, but in his writings he also pays homage to one of the first photographs ever made. Already around 1840 the French
Hippolyte Bayard made an image of himself as a
drowned man.[55] He made this self-portrait out of
frustration and anger, because he was never given
any credit for the invention of photography.

This is not just a story about this image; Bayard
wrote the following on the back of the image:

> The corpse which you see here is that of M.
> Bayard, inventor of the process that you have

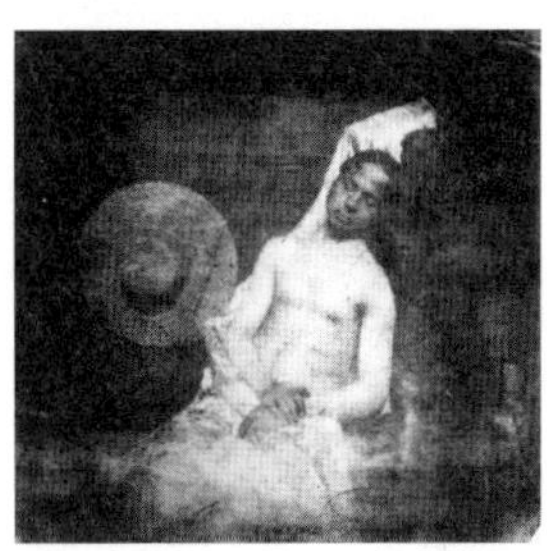

55   Hippolyte Bayard, *Self-Portrait as a Drowned Man*, 1840.

56   Quoted in Jillian Lerner, 'The Drowned Inventor: Bayard, Daguerre, and the Curious Attractions of Early Photography', *History of Photography* 38, no. 3 (2014), p. 220.

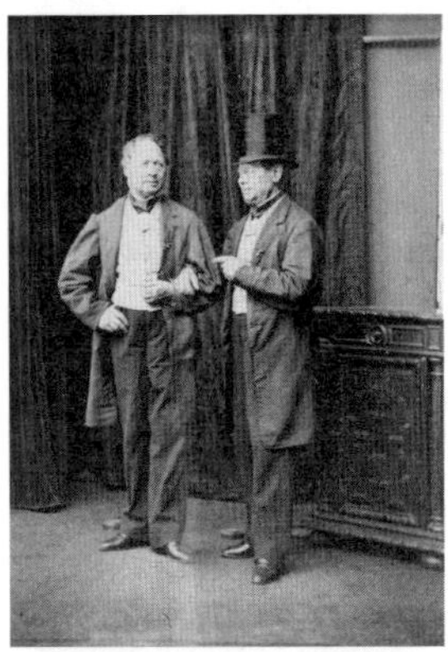

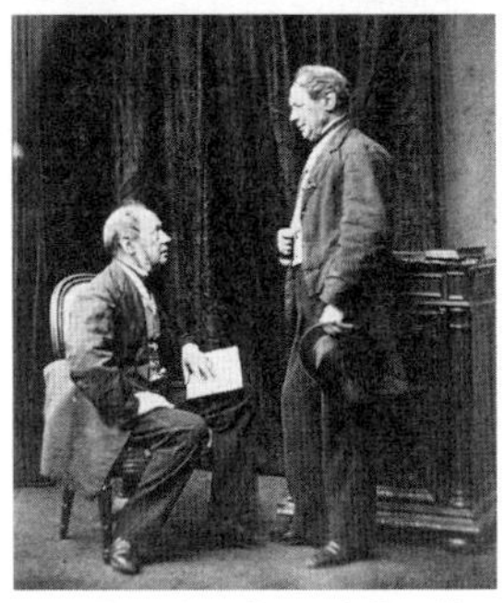

57   Hippolyte Bayard, Double auto-portraits, c. 1865.

just seen … . To my knowledge this ingenious and indefatigable experimenter has been working for about three years to perfect his invention. … The government having given too much to M. Daguerre, said it could do nothing for M. Bayard, and the unhappy man drowned himself. Oh! The fickleness of human affairs! Artists, scholars, journalists were occupied with him for a long time, but here he has been at the morgue for several days, and no-one has recognized or claimed him. Ladies and Gentlemen, you'd better pass along for fear of offending your sense of smell, for as you can observe, the face and hands of the gentleman are beginning to decay. H.B. 18 October 1840.[56]

Bayard shows a photograph, the proof of his invention, showing his body as a macabre visual attraction. He staged his suicide by drowning, made an image of it and underlines the decomposition of his body. His body will soon be illegible, as the invention of photography already is. Bayard did not only play his own suicide; he also acted a part in many of his images. In his *Bayard attending a Patient* (c. 1840) he holds the wrist of a child as if playing the part of a physician. Two other self-portraits stage Bayard himself as if in conversation with his double.[57] It is clear that immediately at the beginning of the history of photography Bayard understood the potential of the photographic image 'as a kind of virtual stage'.[58]

Mortensen followed a tradition that already started with one of the inventors of photography. But later in the twentieth century there are several artists who take up the tradition of un-straight, staged photography and for whom Mortensen is a role model. The best-known ones are the American artists Duane Michals, Jerry Uelsmann, Joel-Peter Witkin, and the Dutch artist Erwin Olaf.[59] Michaels described the tensions between straight and un-straight photography in the 1960s and 1970s as follows: 'I am a short story writer: Most other photographers are reporters. I am an orange. They are apples.'[60] His distinction between oranges and apples suggests that both groups of photographers represent different worlds that cannot be compared although using the same medium of photography. While the differences are major and incompatible, the opponents and proponents of straight photography have one thing in common: straight or un-straight, embellished or plain, photography was used as a medium through which an individual sensibility is expressed. The means and devices which are allowed for the expression of this sensibility differ radically, but the ultimate goal does not.

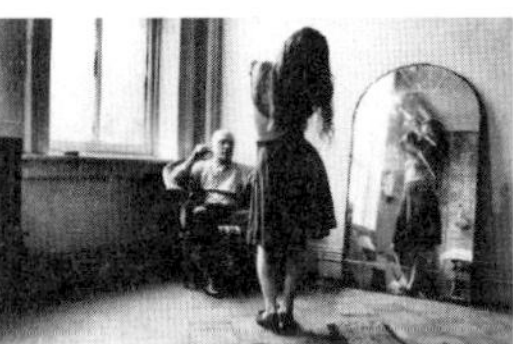

58 Lori Pauli, 'Setting the Scene', in *Acting the Part: Photography as Theatre*, ed. Lori Pauli (London: Merrell Publishers, 2006), p. 20.

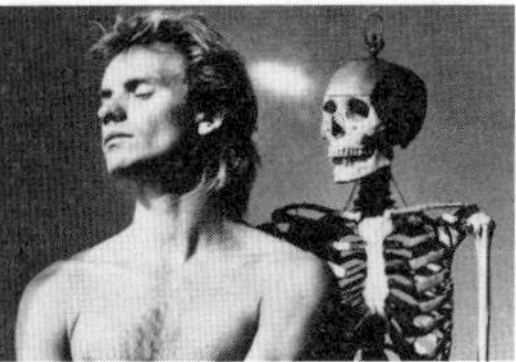

59a Duane Michals, *For Balthus*, 1969.

59b Duane Michals, *Sting Looking Like A Young Danny Kaye*, 1982.

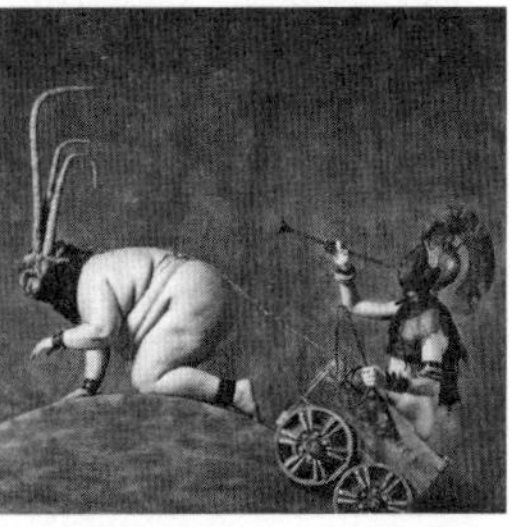

59c Erwin Olaf, *Chessmen*, 1988.

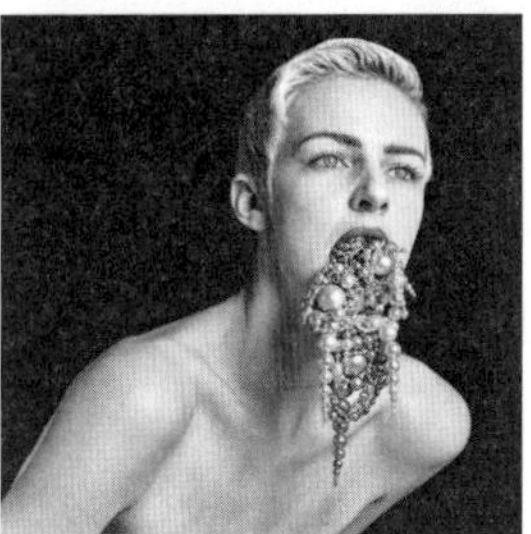

59d Erwin Olaf, *Pearls*, 1988.

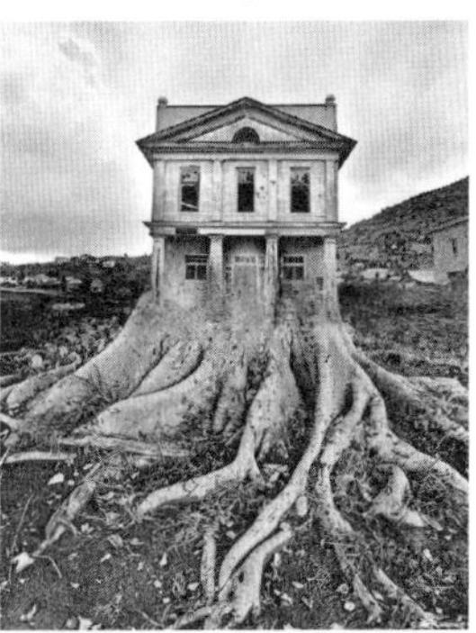

59e Jerry Uelsmann, *Untitled*, 1982.

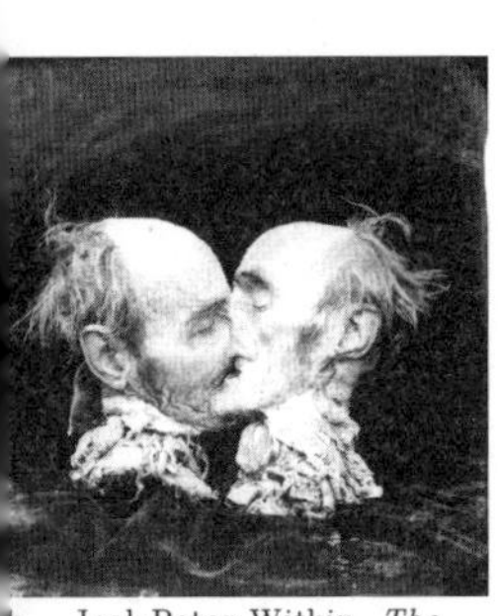

h Joel-Peter Witkin, *The ss [Le Baiser], New Mexico*, 82.

91

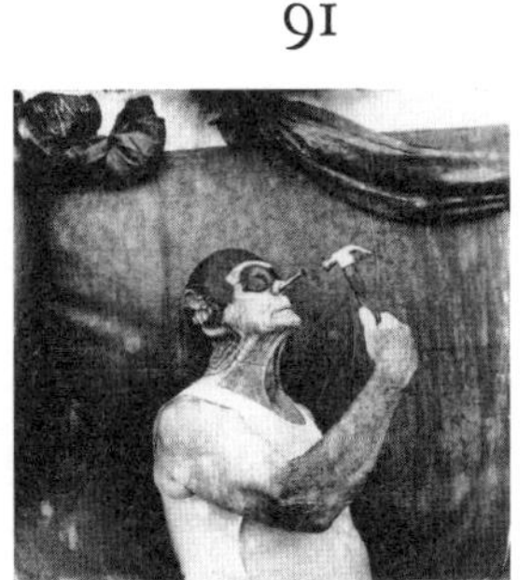

59g Joel-Peter Witkin, *Melvin Burkhart—Human Oddity, Florida*, 1985.

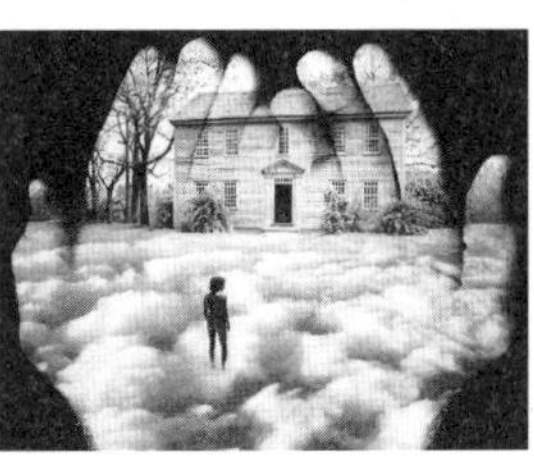

59f Jerry Uelsmann, *Untitled*, 1989.

60 Quoted by Rice, 'Parallel Universes', p. 68.

Sensibility Hollowed Out:
The Postmodern Parodies of Thomas Demand

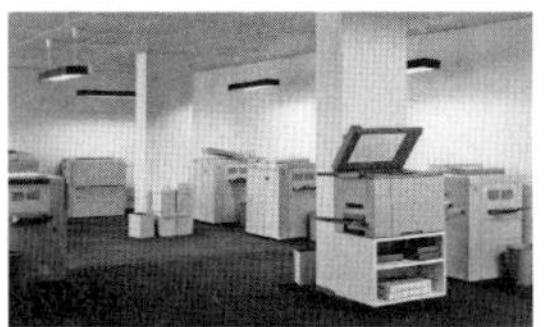

61a Thomas Demand, *Copyshop*, 1999.

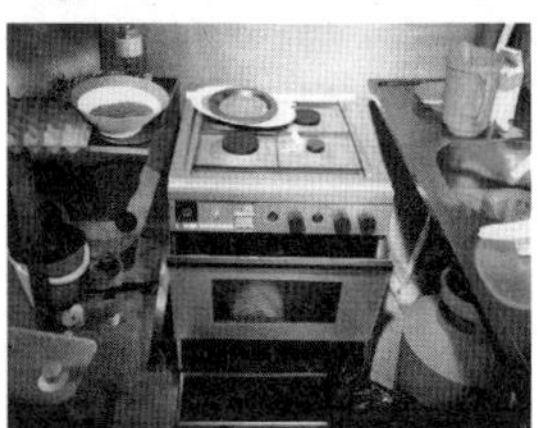

61b Thomas Demand, *Kitchen*, 2004.

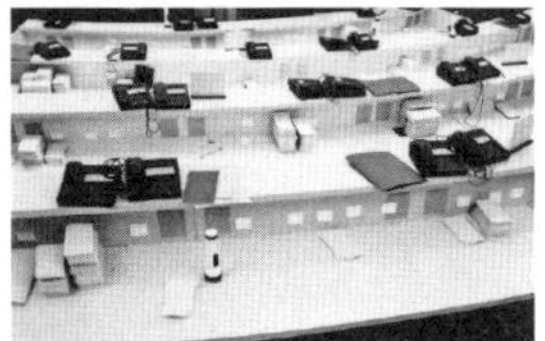

61c Thomas Demand, *Poll*, 2001.

In the 1990s German artist Thomas Demand amazed the art world with photographs that were completely staged. At first glance, his images look like photographs of bleak, dull interiors of offices, corridors, or apartments. There are never human figures in them. Nothing staged so far. A closer look reveals, however, that his images show paper worlds. Although radically realistic, some details that should be present in an indexical, referential image, are missing. Telephones have no buttons or numbers on them; bottles, tubes, and boxes have no logos on them; all interiors look too clean and new and show no indications of use. Human beings are not only literally absent; there are no traces of them either. It turns out that all his images are photographs of paper models.[61]

Demand's procedure to make these images is as follows. He chooses a photograph, usually from internet, newspapers or other media. The image refers to a highly charged scene of politics and crime. On the basis of such an image of an actual place, he then makes a life-size paper model of that place. Finally, he makes a large-scale photograph of the paper model. The social and political meaning of the original scene that underlies the paper model and the image taken of that model is absent but implied, or implied by its absence.[62] His images are not only feats of illusionary perfection, they are also ontologically puzzling. Conventional staged photography remains indexical, although not in the pure and literal sense of that term. They are 'the result of a physical imprint transferred by light reflections onto a sensitive surface'.[63] Staged images still bear an indexical relationship to the world, albeit a staged world. In staged photography the indexicality is partly displaced from world to artist. Staging is the result of the artist's intentionality. His or her intentionality is indexically present in the staging of the world. In conventional tableaus, photography staging is the means to diminish unintentional details in order to demonstrate artistic intentionality. The staged photographic image as a whole is then the expression of the artist's sensibility.[64]

Demand's images are staged in every detail, which means that they are one hundred percent intentional. The artist's control is present all over. This is a reason for Michael Fried to consider his images as allegories of intentionality:

> Demand's aim is not to make a wholly intended object—in this case, a wholly digitized photograph—but rather to make pictures that *represent or indeed allegorize intendedness as such,*

62 Karen Henry, 'The Artful Disposition: Theatricality, Cinema, and Social Context in Contemporary Photography.' In *Acting the Part: Photography as Theatre*, ed. Lori Pauli (London: Merrell Publishers, 2006), p. 152.

63 Rosalind Krauss, 'Notes on the Index: Part 1', in *The Originality of the Avant-Garde and Other Modernist Myths* (Cambridge, MA: MIT Press, 1985), p. 203.

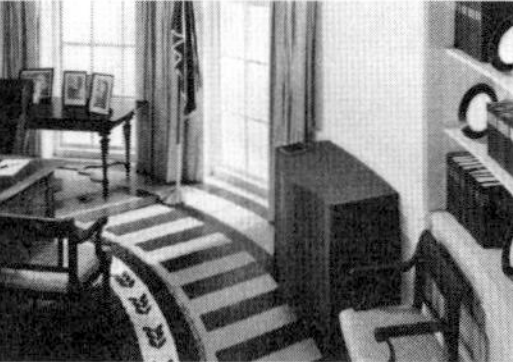

64a   Thomas Demand, *Presidency II*, 2008.

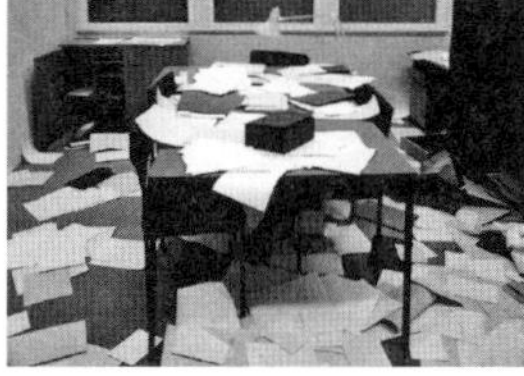

64b   Thomas Demand, *Office*, 1995.

65   Michael Fried, *Why Photography Matters as Art as Never Before* (Haven: Yale University Press, 2008), p. 272 (emphasis in text).

and this turns out to require exploiting the 'weakness' of the traditional photographic image precisely in that regard.[65]

I do not know about Demand's aims nor do I consider those decisive for an understanding of his work, but it is indeed important to understand Demand's foregrounding of intentionality. In the history of photography, showing the photographer's intentionality, for example by means of staging, functions as proof of the artistic. The image's indexicality to the world is reduced and reoriented towards the photographer as artist. On the basis of a re-oriented index we read in the image the sensibility of the artist. And true enough, for Fried Demand's allegories of intentionality prove that photography matters as art, more than ever before.

However, to read Demand's bleak paper worlds as expressions of the artist's sensibility is rather hilarious. His images are not the intentional expression of a sensibility to the world; they are images of paper models of images. If they partake of a sensibility it is not the artist's but the postmodern sensibility according to which images only refer to other images. Definitely, the work of Demand has much in common with the work of Cindy Sherman. By saturating his images with intentionality, Demand is not embracing the idea that photography matters as art when it is provably intentional. On the contrary; he is extending intentionality into the absurd, and hollowing out the connection between intentional sensibility and art. The target of his postmodern parodies is, however, not photography, but art; and staging is his means.

Allegories of Staging, Allegories of Photography

Staging increases the image's intentionality. However, the staged scenes of Hiroshi Sugimoto lack this effect completely. His series of black-and-white photographs of Dioramas and Wax Museums show utterly staged worlds but the staging has not been done by the photographer. His intentionality is not responsible for it, and his photographs are as straight as one could wish.[66] On his website Sugimoto describes his dioramas as follows:

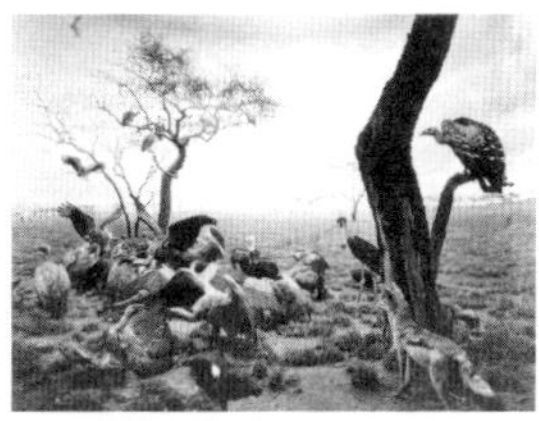

66a   Hiroshi Sugimoto, *Hyena—Jackal— Vulture*, 1976.

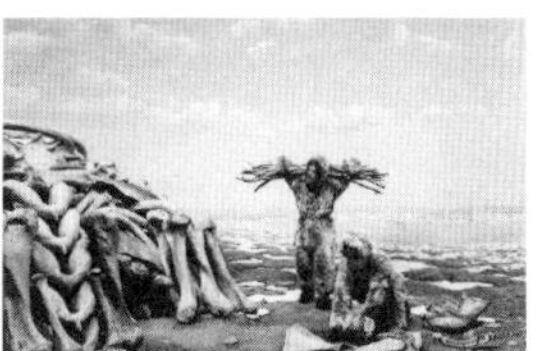

66b   Hiroshi Sugimoto, *Cro-Magnon*, 1994.

> When I [was] first in New York in 1974, I visited many of the city's tourist sites, one of which was the American Museum of Natural History. I made a curious discovery while looking at the exhibition of animal dioramas: the stuffed animals positioned before painted backdrops looked utterly fake, yet by taking a quick peek with one eye closed, all perspective vanished, and

95

67 www.sugimotohiroshi.com (last accessed 2 October 2017).

68 Nancy Spector, 'Reinventing Realism', in *Sugimoto Portraits*, ed. Tracey Bashkoff and Nancy Spector (New York: Guggenheim Museum, 2000), p. 18.

suddenly they looked very real. I'd found a way to see the world as a camera does. However fake the subject, once photographed, it's as good as real.[67]

The transformation from diorama to photograph is one of fake into real and of colour into black-and-white. The media of dioramas and wax museums belong to the nineteenth century and have a very historical aura. Their staged artificiality pursues a maximum of lifelikeness and verisimilitude. But it is their stillness and frozen nature that belies their artificiality and fakeness. Strangely, when those characteristics are displaced to the photograph taken of such a diorama or wax museum, the same characteristics do no longer qualify as fake but as real. The frozen state and the illusion of stillness is now an effect of the camera's technique. Sugimoto's reproductions of reproductions invert the effects of stillness: scenes that aspire to a condition of suspended time but fail to do so and that look dead, are brought to life. 'Inverting the logic of photography's unavoidable alliance with death, its capacity to entomb its subject in a moment that will never recur, Sugimoto gives breath to the wax statues.'[68]

The paradoxical effect of transforming death into life is first of all caused by translating artificial colours into black-and-white. Although the colours of the dioramas are as realist as possible, the chemical colours are not able to create a perfect impression of reality.[69] But because of the fact that black-and-white preserves a boundary between itself and the world of colour, they seem more alive than the dioramas in natural history museums.[70] This is also the case with the lightning of the dioramas; this is clearly artificial light. In the black-and-white photographs the light seems to be natural. Another metamorphosis takes place with the seam between the stage and its painted background. In the real dioramas, the seam between the three-dimensional world and the two-dimensional plane is clearly visible. In the photographs the two worlds continue almost seamlessly.

Sugimoto's diorama photographs do not only relate to the real dioramas, but also to the kind of images of wildlife photography. As Brougher remarks, wildlife photographs generally have a similar look, especially those of dangerous animals. They are usually in colour and have a blurred background. This is because of the photographer's position at a safe distance and the use of telephoto-lenses as well as the attempt to capture animals in motion. A second transformation concerns the three-dimensionality of the dioramas as well as wax museums, which is reorganized into a perspectival flat image with a wide tonal range and super-real clarity. The blurred background that one would expect is missing. The

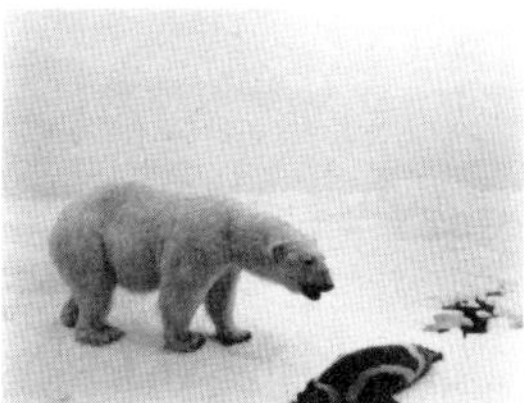

69a   Hiroshi Sugimoto, *Polar Bear*, 1976.

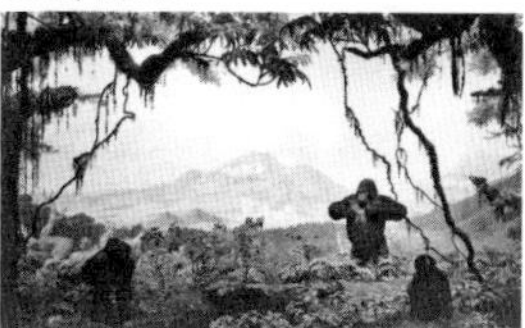

69b   Hiroshi Sugimoto, *Gorilla*, 1994.

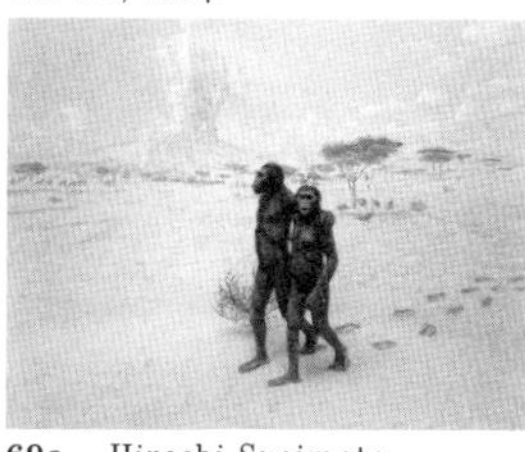

69c   Hiroshi Sugimoto, *Earliest Human Relatives*, 1994.

70   Hans Belting, *Looking through Duchamp's Door: Art and Perspective in the Work of Duchamp, Sugimoto, Jeff Wall* (Cologne: Walther König, 2009), p. 83.

71   For a very good account of allegory, see Craig Owens, 'The Allegorical Impulse: Toward a Theory of Postmodernism', in *Beyond Recognition: Representation, Power, and Culture* (Berkeley CA: University of California Press, 1992).

72   Kerry Brougher, 'Impossible Photography', in Kerry Brougher and Pia Müller-Tamm, *Hiroshi Sugimoto* (Ostfildern: Hatje Cantz Verlag, 2010), p. 20.

photographic images resulting from these transformations are not snapshots of temporal moments, but fixations of a timeless or suspended state. The photographic instants these images present are prolonged indefinitely. Like daguerreotype portraits and photographic tableaus, Sugimoto's dioramas and wax museums are intensely durational. But his images are not the result of long posing or the staging of scenes, his images are straight. By taking artificial, staged scenes of the world as the object of his camera, he turns staging into an allegory.[71] His allegories of staging the world are allegories of photography; but not photography as instantaneous snapshots of punctual time, but of a photography that is durational and that indefinitely prolongs time.

Although the staged scenes look extraordinarily realistic, there is something in these images that indicates that they are not showing the real thing but a staging of the real:

> The result is a photograph that 'feels' inherently wrong to us. A disconnection exists between the content and the presentation, between what we see and our knowledge of photography's vocabulary, which is acquired through processing countless images in our media-saturated culture.[72]

It is because of this feeling that there is something wrong with the image that they can begin to work as allegories of photography.

Staging as Unintentional Sensibility

When, in the twentieth century, photography became more and more a medium for the expression of an individual sensibility, by the same move it found an answer to the criticism that it was not intentional enough. In contrast to a real artist, a photographer could never have complete intentional control over all the details present in the photographic image. It was the mechanical apparatus of the camera that was in charge of most of that. But when the image as such, in its totality, was the result of an expression by an individual subjectivity in charge of the camera, then somehow the photographer is alleged to be present in all details and aspects of the image taken.

This logic enabling the medium of photography to be taken seriously as art depends on a notion of subjectivity as intentional and on a notion of art as being the result of individual expression. Although the twentieth century is in many respects the century in which the entanglement of this notion of subjectivity and of art became standard, it is at the same

73   André Breton, 'Manifesto of Surrealism' (1924), in *Manifestoes of Surrealism* (Ann Arbor: University of Michigan Press, 1969), p. 31.

74   André Breton, *Surrealism and Painting* (New York: Harper & Row, 1972).

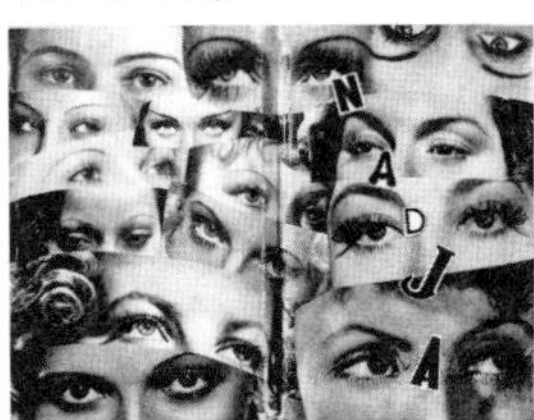

75a   Cover of the 1928 Gallimard edition of *Nadja*, collaged over by Marcel Mariën, 1938.

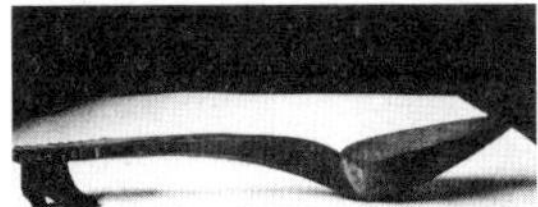

75b   Man Ray, Illustration for *l'Amour fou* by André Breton, 1937.

time the century in which both notions were challenged. But challenging them does not contradict their prevalence. Instead, it confirms it. Surrealist photography represents a major undermining of the idea of intentional subjectivity; it is rather focused on making present an unconscious interiority, which is by implication unintentional. One would expect that surrealism has little affinity with photography, because, in the words of its main spokesman of programmatic statements, André Breton, it has an aversion of 'real forms of real objects'.[73] But paradoxically, Breton is very tolerant towards the medium of photography, and in 'Le surréalisme et la peinture' he wonders when, finally, important books are going to be illustrated with photographs instead of with drawings.[74] As a consequence, after he made this remark, his own books are illustrated with photographs: his novel *Nadja* of 1928 mainly with those by Boiffard, and *L'amour fou* with images by Man Ray and Brassaï.[75]

As Krauss has argued, the kind of photographs that can be found in surrealist journals and books are very diverse. Many of these are conventional, straight photographs. Boiffard's images, with which Breton illustrated *Nadja,* are good examples. But there are images that are less conventional because they show unexpected 'found objects', such as Boiffard's photograph of a big toe in close-up, which

100

he made to go with an essay by Bataille.[76] Bizarre as this photograph may be, it is straight. But subsequently, there are many photographs of artists like Hans Bellmer and Man Ray that are utterly staged, for which objects and scenes were constructed. These images cannot be seen as straight images documenting the world. Other examples of un-straight photography are Man Ray's solarisation images or images of negatives. Although not literally staged, the negatives or prints have been worked upon in various ways. The variety of surrealistic photographic images covers the whole spectrum of straight and un-straight photography. What they all have in common, however, is a very specific poetics, according to which the world is not shown as the result of the expression of an inner sensibility (of the photographer), but as 'written representation'.[77] Although many images are un-straight and staged, it is not the image itself that should attract attention. The photographic world is like an automatically written text full of unexpected and unknown signifiers that need to be read, deciphered in order to be understood. Whereas the image is transparent, the world we see in the image is not.

The photographs of dolls by Hans Bellmer are most obviously staged. The frightening, torturous and tortured dolls are artificial constructions made of body parts of dolls. The scene in which they are

101

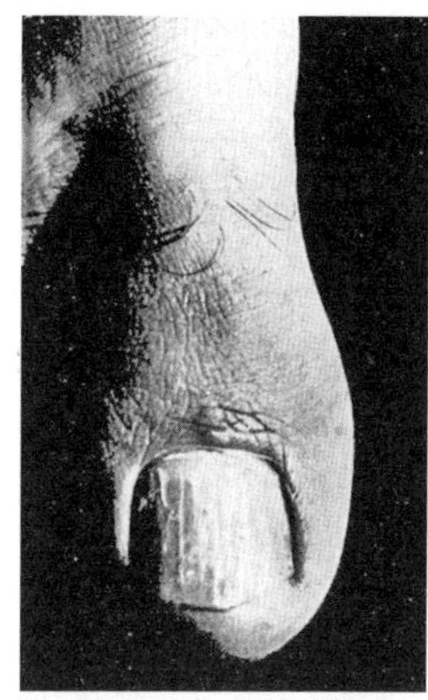

76 Jacques-André Boiffard, *Big Toe*, 1929.

77 For a brilliant analysis of surrealist poetics and surrealist photography, see Krauss, *L'Amour fou.*

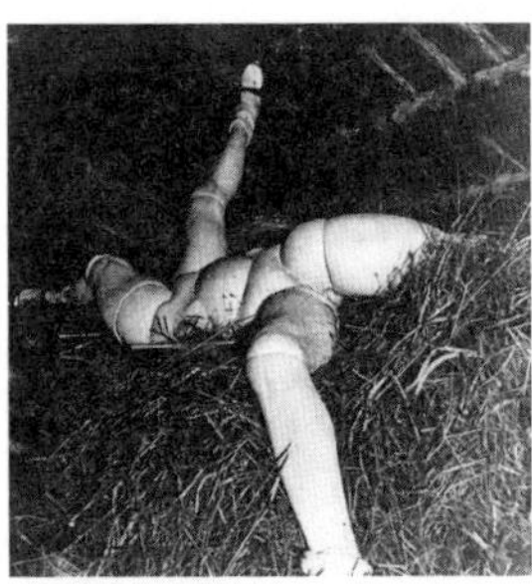

78a Hans Bellmer, *Poupée in Hayloft*, 1935–1936.

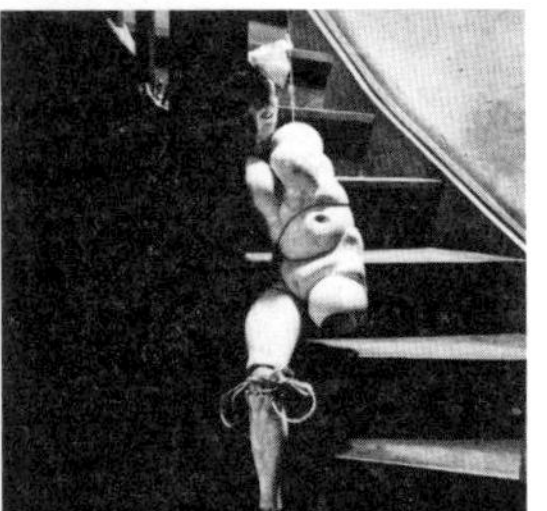

78b Hans Bellmer, *La poupée*, 1935.

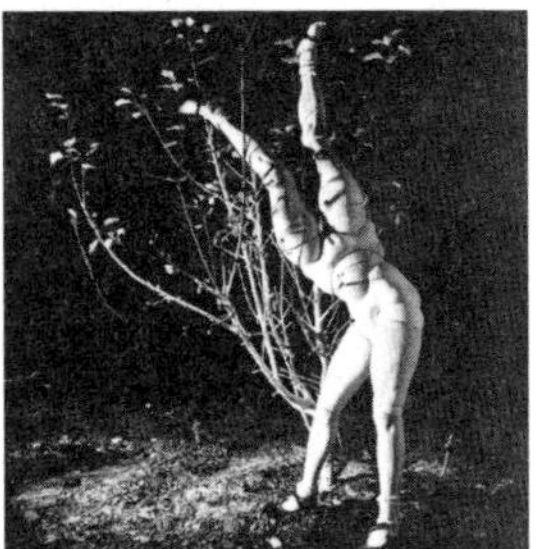

78c Hans Bellmer, *Deux demi-soeurs*, 1933–1935.

placed is not very specific and rather abstract. But the scene fills the whole image, suggesting that it is part of a world that continues outside the frame of the image, and as a result, is part of that world. This is the paradox of this kind of staged photography: although the staged scene only exists within the frame of the image, it creates the illusion to continue outside of it, which is a feature of the image.[78]

Although projected onto the world, one could wonder if this staged world is not the projection of a subjectivity that is no longer in control of itself. The world as a written text full of puzzling signifiers is then the unconscious world of the subject projected outwards. It is hard to claim that such surrealist worlds are the expression of an inner sensibility. But the problematic element in this conventional way of describing and characterizing images is the idea of 'expression', not 'inner sensibility'. The photographed world the viewer gets access to is rather like an unintentional projection of an unconscious inner sensibility. For in surrealism, it is not only the world which presents itself as automatically written signifiers, but also the inner world of the unconscious. The subject, squeezed in between the unconscious and the world, lacks intentional agency to control and understand either of them. Surrealist photographs are not the photographer's intentional, subjective visions, but projections of worlds that are

102

automatically written and mechanically produced by the camera. This is one of the reasons why surrealist photography is much more convincing and powerful than surrealist painting. Also, when painted, surrealist worlds have to be actively read and deciphered, but in this case, they are the product of a fully intentional expressed inner vision of the artist. The subjective visions of surrealist photographers, staged or not, are confrontations with worlds that are not expressed, but are found or bumped into. Not subjective perception is the basis of these photographic images, but the unintentional, accidental revelation of worlds.

Staging Visionary Images

The images of Juul Kraijer with which I started out the introduction to *Failed Images* have a surreal quality. They are also clearly staged, as many surrealistic photographs are; the images of dolls by Bellmer just mentioned are a good example. Still, instead of understanding them within the framework of a surrealist poetics, I will discuss them as another, distinct manifestation of staged photography.[79] I contend that Kraijer's images are best understood as visionary. When I say visionary, I am suggesting that it belongs to a different ontology than the one of

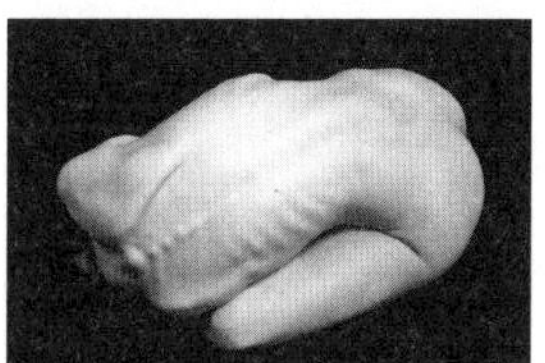

79a Juul Kraijer, *Untitled (L.P. #8)*, 2014–2015.

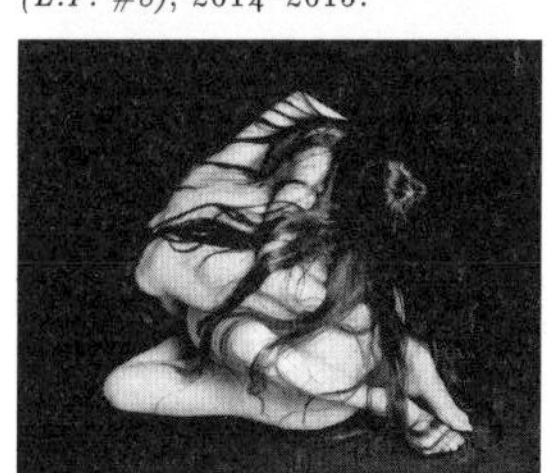

79b Juul Kraijer, *Untitled (L.P. & C.M. #1)*, 2016–2017.

103

80 For a more elaborate reading of Juul Kraijer's work, see my essay 'Visionary Images', in *Juul Kraijer: Werken 2009–2015* (Zwolle: WBOOKS, 2015), pp. 82–86.

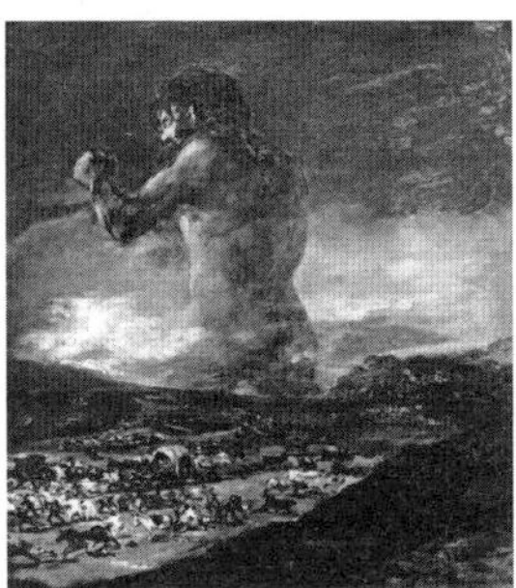

81a Francisco Goya, *El Coloso*, 1808–1812.

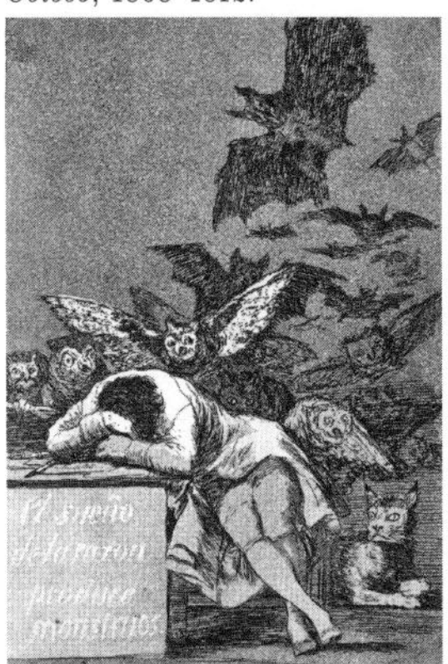

81b Francisco Goya, *The Sleep of Reason Produces Monsters*, 1797–1799.

surrealism, which can be understood as an ontology of the unintentional unconsciousness.[80]

The visionary involves an artistic paradigm that exists not only in the visual arts but in literature as well. Although major artists such as Grünewald, William Blake, Francisco Goya, William Turner, Odilon Redon, Antonin Artaud, and in literature writers such as Gustave Flaubert, Joris-Karl Huysmans, Franz Kafka and James Joyce belong to it, this paradigm has never been well established or dominant.[81] It is only once in a while that it manifests itself through the work of idiosyncratic artists or writers, who do not really fit in the conventional artistic paradigms of their time, even if this is not limited to the visionary only. The author of not only *Madame Bovary*, but also and especially of *The Temptation of Saint Anthony*, Gustave Flaubert, called the visionary approach to art 'artistic hallucination'. By calling it artistic he distinguishes it from hallucinations resulting from drugs or from certain psychological conditions. In 1866, in a letter to the literary scholar Hippolyte Taine he describes the phenomenon of artistic hallucination as follows:

> In artistic hallucination the tableau is not *clearly delimited*, however precise it may be. Thus, I can *perfectly* see a piece of furniture, a figure, a bit of a landscape. But it wavers, it is suspended,

it can be anywhere. It exists alone, without relation to the rest, while in reality, when I look at an armchair or a tree, I see at the same time the other pieces of furniture in my room, the other trees in the garden, or at least I am vaguely aware they exist. Artistic hallucination cannot not bear on large spaces, move in a very large frame. Then one falls into a dreamy state and becomes calm again. It even always ends like that.

You ask me if it interlocks for me with the surrounding reality? No.—The surrounding reality has vanished. I don't know anymore what is around me. I belong exclusively to that apparition.

In contrast, in pure and simple hallucination it is quite possible to see a false image with one eye and the real objects with the other. That is precisely the torture.[82]

For Flaubert, these artistic hallucinations were the basis for the writing of *The Temptation of Saint Anthony*. These visionary scenes prefigured his writing. Or, with his writing he records what he has hallucinated first. The spatial dimension of artistic hallucination Flaubert mentions is also literally at stake in Kraijer's images, in her photographs as well as drawings: they never bear on large spaces, they never move in a very large spatial frame. The staged

82   Gustave Flaubert, *Correspondance*, ed. Bernard Masson (Paris: Gallimard, 1998), p. 499 (emphasis in text; my translation).

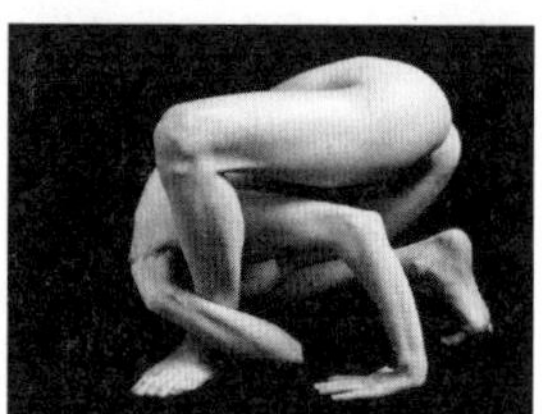

83 Juul Kraijer, *Untitled (L.P. #2)*, 2014–2015.

scenes do not seem to have any surrounding reality. That makes them differ from surrealist images.[83]

The paradox of staged surrealist photography is that although the staged scene only exists within the frame of the image, it creates the illusion to continue outside of it. Bellmer's images of dolls are good examples of this principle. The scenes fill the whole image, suggesting that it is part of a world that continues outside the frame of the image, and as a result is part of that world. This is never the case in Kraijer's images. To quote Flaubert once more: 'You ask me if it interlocks for me with the surrounding reality? No.—The surrounding reality has vanished. I don't know anymore what is around me. I belong exclusively to that apparition.' The posed bodies in the two illustration images here do not have any context or background. They are framed by a black spatial vacuum. The first image shows a body that consist of a knot of arms and legs, limbs without centre. The pose of the female model is such that her head and body almost become invisible. This body has no centre anymore; head and body are gone and a pattern of limbs remains. The second image is the exact opposite; it has only a torso, but no limbs or head. The torso looks armoured, like the shell of a turtle. These staged worlds present themselves as visionary hallucinations or apparitions, because a contiguous world is radically absent.

In his essay 'The Doors of Perception', Aldous Huxley describes the visions he had after experimenting with mescaline.[84] Although these visionary perceptions are not artistic in Flaubert's sense, they have the same spatial and temporal characteristics.

> The really important facts were that spatial relationships had ceased to matter very much and that my mind was perceiving the world in terms of other than spatial categories. At ordinary times the eye concerns itself with such problems as Where?—How far? How situated in relation to what? In the mescalin experience the implied questions to which the eye responds are of another order. Place and distance cease to be of much interest. The mind does its Perceiving in terms of intensity of existence, profundity of significance, relationships with a pattern. ... Space was still there; but it had lost its predominance. The mind was primarily concerned, not with measures and locations, but with being and meaning.[85]

Huxley's indifference to space was accompanied by an even more complete indifference to time. There was plenty of it, but 'exactly how much was entirely irrelevant'. 'My actual experience had been, was still, of an indefinite duration or alternatively of a perpetual present made up of one continually changing

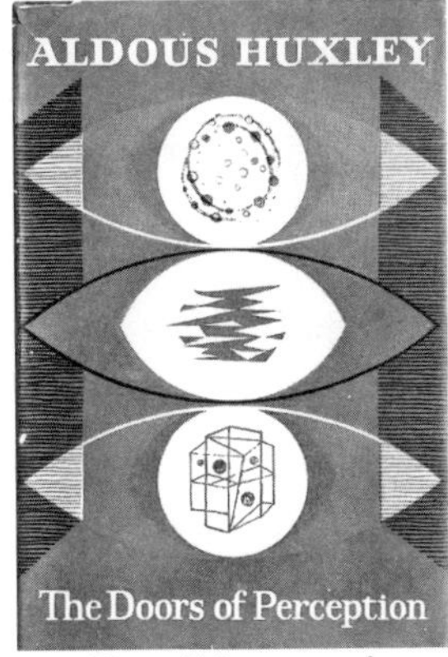

84   First edition cover of Aldous Huxley, *The Doors of Perception*, 1954.

85   Aldous Huxley, 'The Doors of Perception', in *The Doors of Perception and Heaven and Hell* (London: Vintage Classic, 2004 [1954]), p. 9.

apocalypse.' His visual impressions are intensified although interest in space is diminished and interest in time almost disappears. A bit further he writes: 'the eye recovers some of the perceptual innocence of childhood, when the sensum was not immediately and automatically subordinated to the concept.'[86]

In the Introduction I described Kraijer's photographic images in 'negative' terms, in qualities they do not or barely embody. I phrased the reasons why her works do not correspond to Kracauer's conception of the photographic approach in terms that closely resemble Huxley's and Flaubert's descriptions of their visions. Her images suspend time and the spatial dimension is reduced to an absolute minimum. The indistinct light or dark backgrounds reduce our orientation in space to that of an almost vacuum. The visions of the two writers, but also Kraijer's, are certainly not perceptual although utterly visual. They were perceived by what is usually called 'the inner eye'. These visionary experiences present themselves *as if* they are perceptual. But they are not; or better said, they are perceptions without an object.

Although the expression 'the inner eye' refers to the visual sense, to sight, these visions of the inner eye cannot be reduced to the visual. Kraijer's photographic works with snakes, scorpions or lizards are good examples. Although it is at first the extraordinary sight of a human face covered by a frightening reptile that strikes the eye, other senses partake in this uncanny experience.[87]

In a horizontal photograph of 2014 we see a big lizard on top of the face of a woman. Its tongue sticks out of its muzzle. Whereas the movements of reptiles' tongues are extremely fast, so fast that the human eye can almost not register them, the lizard's tongue is caught by the camera without showing any movement. It is sharp and in focus. The visual image of this tongue foregrounds the other activated senses; we feel the weight of the lizard's belly on the woman's face and we taste and smell its skin.

Another series of photographs of 2014–2015 shows a head covered with snakes. These images remind us immediately of the mythological figure of Medusa, especially Caravaggio's painted rendering of her head on a shield. The killing power of the mythological Medusa resides in her eyes. Her powerful eyes petrify any person who faces her gaze. The petrifying effect of the poison produced by the snakes on her head is shifted, displaced to Medusa's eyes. But the eyes of Kraijer's Medusa-like heads are always covered by the snakes, which conventionally adorn Medusa's head but do not cover her face. Consequently, even Medusa's gaze is turned inwards. When her petrifying gaze has been transformed into an inner eye, its fixating power does not

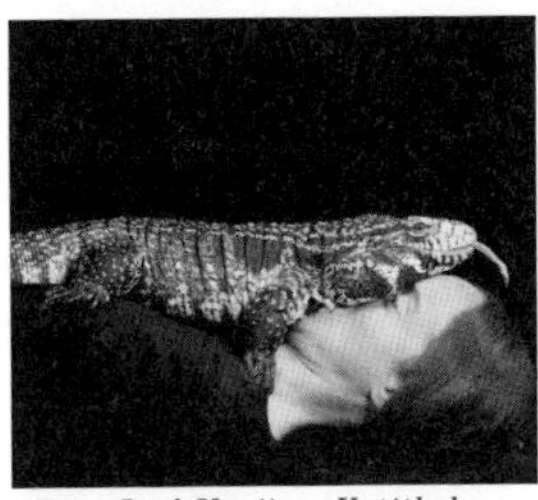

87a   Juul Kraijer, *Untitled*, 2014.

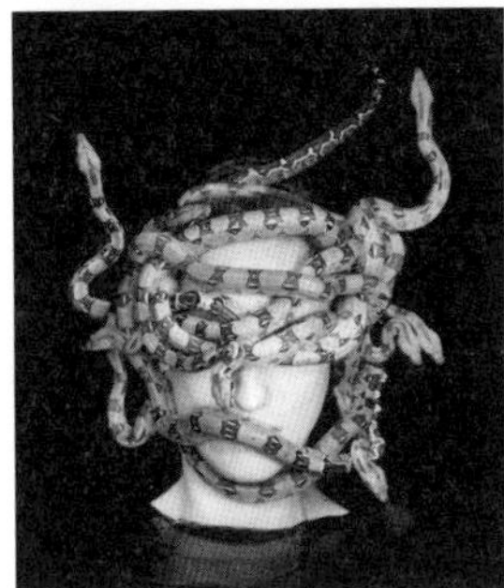

87b   Juul Kraijer, *Untitled*, 2014–2015.

88   In 2007 Kraijer made a video with the significant title *Inner Eye*. Whereas her photographs never have titles, her video works do. It is a 24-minute loop. It shows close-ups of an eye that looks inward. That eye clearly sees without an object in front of it. The vision is inner or, in other words, visionary. The video has no sound, which enhances the impression that this vision is inner. The inner eye is not only cut off from the perceptual but also from the aural and other sensorial experiences of the outer world. The video can be seen as a mise-en-abyme, a mirror image, of the rest of her work in photography; all her works are the result of what was first seen by the inner eye. For the term mise-en-abyme, see Mieke Bal, *Narratology: Introduction to the Theory of Narrative* (Toronto: University of Toronto Press, 2009).

89   Huxley, 'The Doors of Perception', p. 9.

90   Flaubert, *Correspondance*, p. 495. Quoted in: Jean-François Chevrier, *L'hallucination artistique de William Blake à Sigmar Polke* (Paris: l'Arachnéen, 2012), p. 19 ref.

result in a hallucinatory image, but in a photographic image. Medusa's gaze turned inwards as mirror image for visionary photography.[88]

When Huxley described the kind of universe he had entered after taking mescaline, he did that in terms of a 'continually changing apocalypse'.[89] It was the indefinite duration of time and the perpetual present that was experienced as an ongoing apocalypse. Flaubert used similar terms for his understanding of artistic hallucination. Whereas pathological hallucinations produce joy, artistic hallucination results in terror, he argued. The terror is the effect of 'the head that empties itself', of 'life that disappears from it'.[90] The joy resulting from other hallucinations is the effect of the opposite of emptiness, namely of absorption and plenitude. The transformations taking place when entering this new universe are not experienced as negative, although terms like apocalyptic and terror at first suggest as much. The terror is caused by entering a dimension in which everything is new and unexpected. Like the universe one is supposed to have access to after the apocalypse, it is the unknown one is confronted with that produces terror, a terror that can be seen as positive because as open and not yet defined. It is the kind of terror that also defines experiences of the sublime.

The 'continually changing apocalypse' is evoked in Kraijer's images by means of a motif that is as mythical as the apocalypse, namely metamorphosis. In fact, her images always show figures in a process of metamorphosis. When a photograph shows the face of a woman covered with little insects or embraced by a snake, it is not a narrative like the one of Hitchcock's film *The Birds* that is evoked.[91] The event that is alluded to is not an attack by dangerous or frightening animals, although the anxiety raised by such narratives is not completely beside the point. The event concerns transformations or metamorphoses, in other words: becomings. The boundaries between individual and animal, or individual and plant are absorbed into a pattern that makes it difficult to distinguish the one from the other. This explains also why references to classical mythology, like the one to Medusa, are abundant in Kraijer's work. Her photographic works can now be defined as inner visions of metamorphoses.

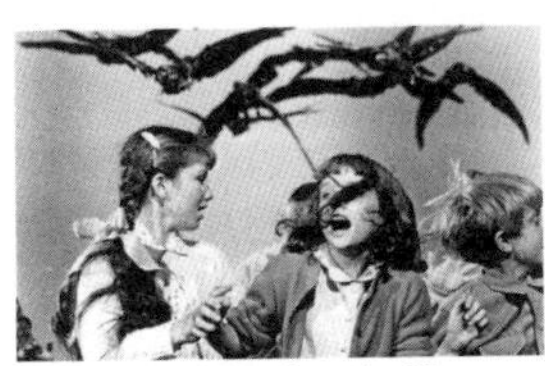

91 Alfred Hitchcock, *The Birds*, film still, 1963.

Because of the fact that the camera work of photography is almost automatically understood in terms of perceptions of the outer world, or as expressions of an inner sensibility, Kraijer's photographs position themselves as the radical negation of that assumption. It is because photography raises different expectations that her images work so eminently as going against the grain of that medium. This is so because the medium of photography assumes an analogy between what we see in the photographic image and what was present before the camera even if that was staged or if the image was worked upon. In the case of Kraijer's photographs the analogy with the external world is transposed to the world seen by the inner eye. She replaces outer visions by inner visions. But this transposition depends on the photographic principle of analogy. Without this principle, the transposition could never be established as convincingly.

The Common Ground of Staged Photography: From Requirement to Provocation

92   Mary Ann Doane, 'Real Time: Instantaneity and the Photographic Imaginary, in *Stillness and Time: Photography and the Moving Image*, ed. David Green and Joanna Lowry (Brighton: Photoworks, 2006), p. 25.

In the early history of photography staging was a necessity, especially in portraiture. When Douglass had had his first daguerreotype image taken of himself in 1841, his posing for it still required several minutes. This explains his statue-like look in that image. But photographic technology developed fast and his posing for images in later years required only a few seconds. Still, it was only around 1880, with the introduction of gelatine-silver bromide plates, that staging was no longer a necessity. These plates allowed for snapshots with an exposure time of 1/25 of a second, reorienting photography towards the instantaneous. Those very short moments of time were not really available to the naked eye.[92] For

Walter Benjamin it is the action of the snapping of the camera that related the medium of photography to modernity and the experience of the shock that defines that culture:

> Of the countless movements of switching, inserting, pressing, and the like, the 'snapping' of the photographer has had the greatest consequences. A touch of the finger now sufficed to fix an event for an unlimited period of time. The camera gave the moment a posthumous shock, as it were.[93]

Although it was around 1880, with the introduction of the silver-bromide plates, that the now prevalent photographic approach was established, it did not make different practices of staged photography completely disappear. The distinction between so-called straight and un-straight photography was viable after Peter Henry Emerson's debate with Henry Peach Robinson at the end of the nineteenth century. From now on, straight photography was the accepted standard from which un-straight photography was the aberration. But especially art-oriented photographic practices just continued to make staged photographs by staging scenes, combination prints or handwork on negatives and prints. The photographic practices of European avant-garde movements in the first half of the twentieth century demonstrates that well.

113

93   Walter Benjamin, 'On Some Motifs in Baudelaire', *Illuminations* (New York: Schocken, 1969), pp. 174–175.

In the twenty-first century the distinction between straight and un-straight seems at first to be hopelessly dated. Not only because of the postmodern condition according to which images only refer to other images and a snapshot of the world has theoretically become a naive idea. Also because of the relatively recent technology of digital photography, which enabled photo-shopping to become the latest practice of staging photographic images. But although the large majority of photographic images that we are now faced with are photo-shopped images, and are in that respect un-straight, it has not seriously challenged the expectations people have of a photograph, to be a pure and straight snapshot of the world. Photography's ontology has not fundamentally transformed with the technological developments of digital photography.

This also explains why visionary, hallucinating photographic images, like those of Kraijer, are not the confirmation of the recent victory of staged photography; on the contrary, her replacement of outer visions by inner visions still goes against the grain. She even needs the idea that vision is a perception of the outer world as differential background for the staging of inner visions.

From Sherman to Kraijer, and all the other un-straight photographers discussed in this chapter, these artists demonstrate that without the dominance of the photographic approach, the provocations of staged practices of photography would not work. Straight and un-straight need each other; there cannot be provocation without something to provoke. And due to being provocations these images can make us see.

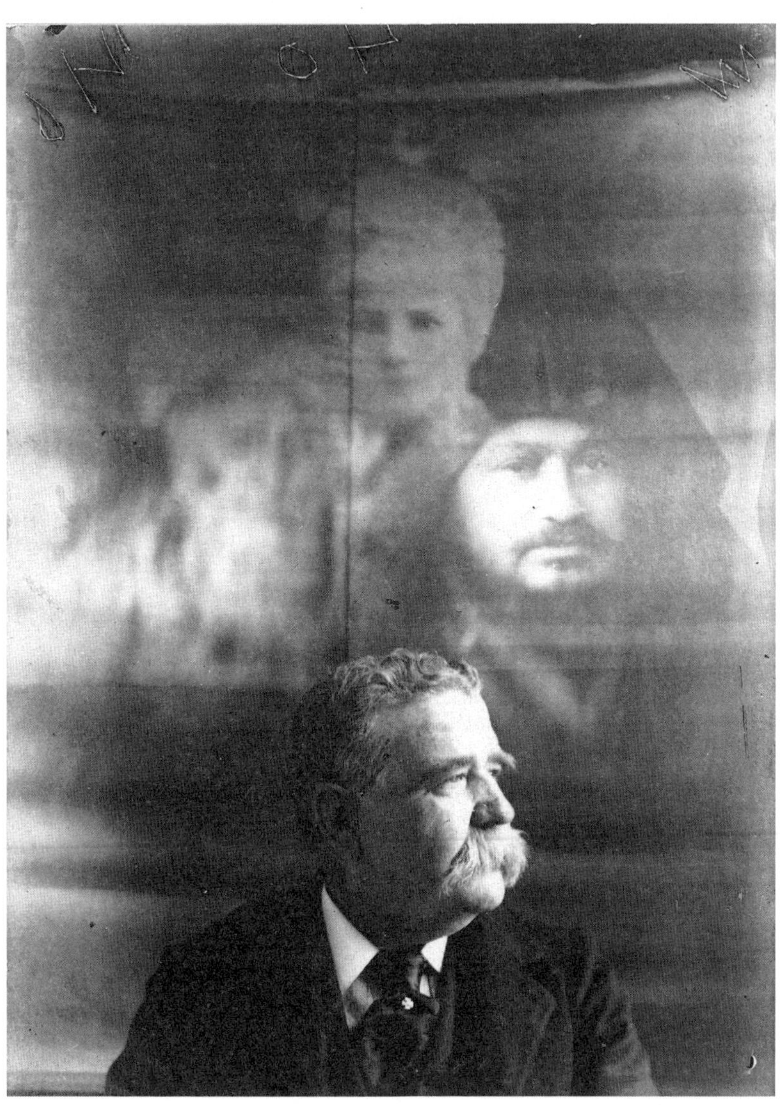

Richard Boursnell, *Spirit
Photography–John Watt Beattie,*
c. 1900.

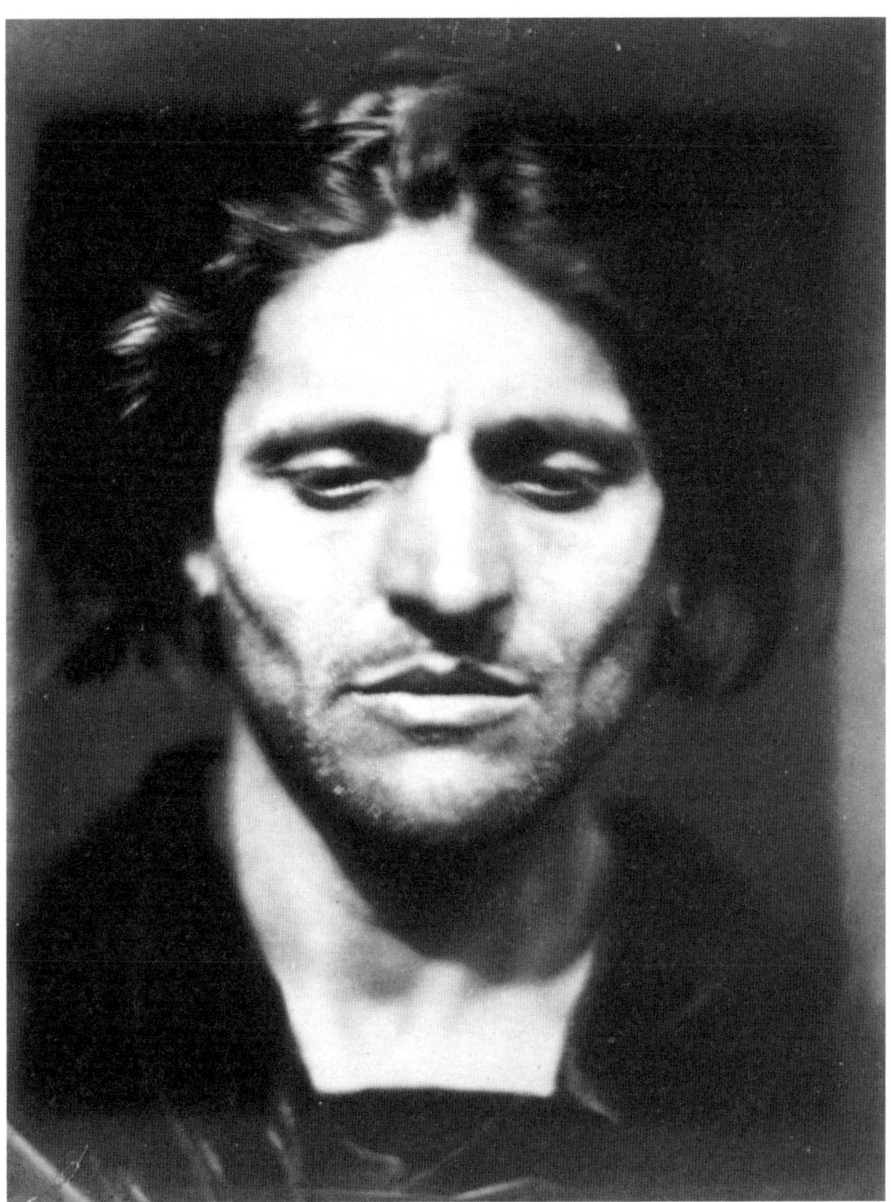

Julia Margaret Cameron, *Iago,
Study from an Italian,* 1867

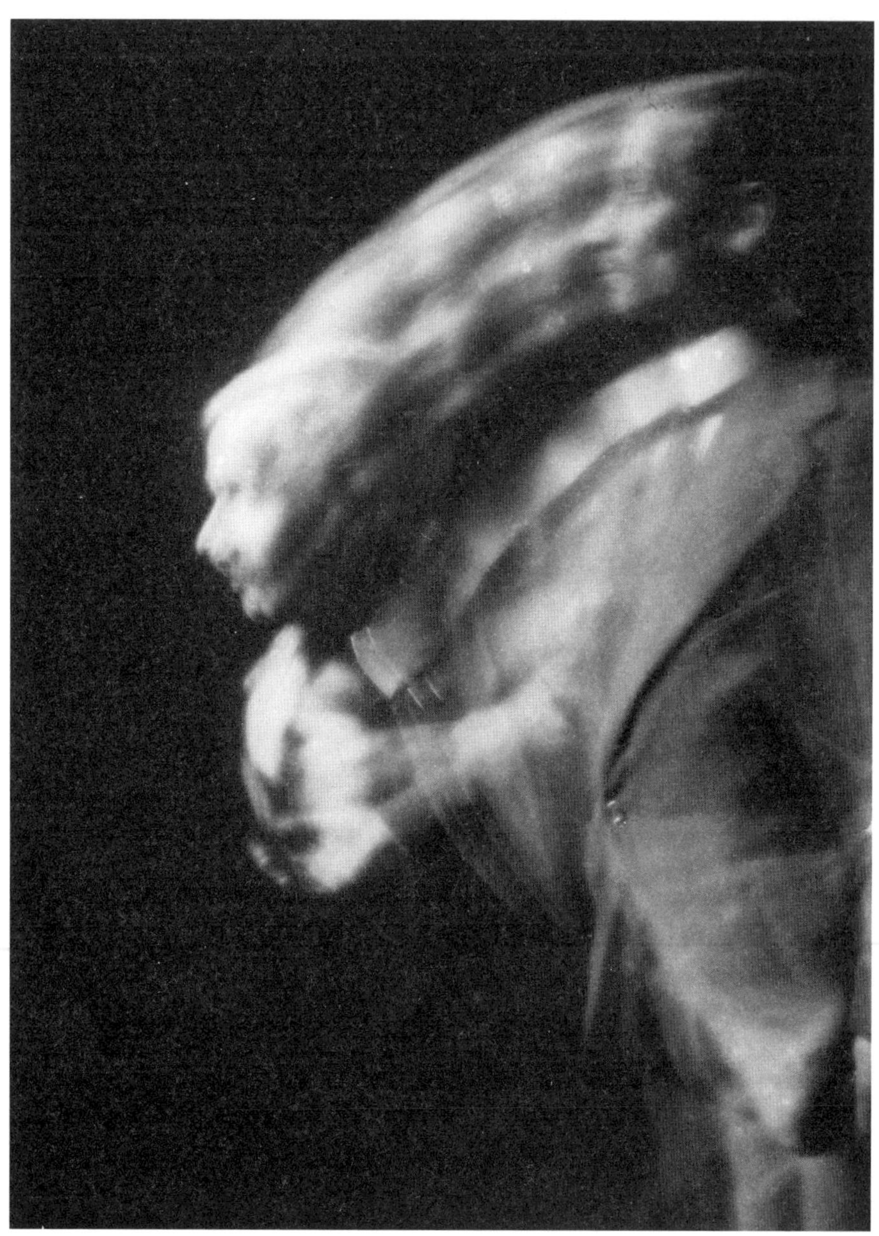

Arturo Bragaglia, *The Bow—*
Anton Giulio Bragaglia, 1911.

Blurred Images

We know very well how to distinguish an image from reality. This is a matter of common sense. But as Thierry de Duve somewhat hyperbolically remarks: 'Why does common sense vanish in front of a photograph and charge it with such a mythical power over life and death?' Common sense does not vanish because viewers are naïve or indoctrinated by ideological notions of photography, but because 'reality does indeed wedge its way into the image. The referent is not only that to which the sign refers, but also that upon which it depends'.[1] Still, the difference between image and referent is undeniable when the image is blurred or contains a blur. The blur indicates a condition of the image, not of the referent. Even if the blur is the result of motion, the movement of the camera, or the movement of the photographed subject, the blur implies the failure of

1   Thierry de Duve, 'Time Exposure and Snapshot: The Photograph as Paradox', *October* 5 (Summer 1978), p. 114.

the image to capture that movement. This implies that the blur offers possibilities to better understand the condition of the photographic image, even if, or precisely because it visualizes its limits or failures. In this chapter I will examine some of the various significations of blurred conditions of the photographic image. But, as I will argue, the blur does more than just that. It also visualizes dimensions, especially temporal ones, that are supposed to be invisible.

In the article quoted, in which he formulates the temporal paradox of photography, De Duve explores the specificity of photographic temporality and the variegated photographic practices in which it results. In an attempt to unravel that temporal specificity, he distinguishes two separate categories of photographs that both usually inform our experience and understanding of any photograph. As separate, almost opposed categories the paradox of photography seems to be resolved into an opposition. Contrasting the two as radically different, he distinguishes them as the snapshot and the time exposure. In its punctual suddenness and instantaneousness, the snapshot is 'event-like'. It is exemplified by the press photograph. The time exposure, in contrast, freezes the past tense of the photograph in a sort of infinitive. Although any photograph can evoke this temporal experience, De Duve considers the genre of the funerary portrait as exemplary of the time exposure.

Although the subject is dead, it is forever present in the funerary image. This kind of image is not 'event-like', but 'picture-like'.[2] The picture-like photographs are (literally) superficial in the sense that they generate photographs as semiotic objects. They are abstracted from reality and they require attention for the surface of the photograph. The event-like images are reality-producing, insofar as the only reality to be taken into account is the one framed by the act of taking a photograph. He calls these event-like images referential; they refer to a singular event.[3]

As the result of time exposure, the genre of portraiture is funerary in nature. It functions as a monument, whether of an alive or a dead person. A portrait acts as a reminder of the past, 'it sets up landmarks of the past'. Whereas the snapshot refers to the fluidity of time without conveying it, the time of exposure petrifies the time of the referent and denotes the latter as departed.[4] These different temporalities are best conveyed by two different aesthetic ideals. The instantaneous photographs called snapshots or 'event-like' have sharpness as their ideal. The picture-like images exemplified by the funerary portrait have the opposite ideal; the aesthetics of time of exposure work best when slightly out of focus. The blurred effect acts as a metaphor for the fading of time. This fading goes in both directions: from presence to absence and from absence to

2   Ibid., p. 113.
3   Ibid., p. 114.
4   Ibid., p. 116.

5   Ibid., p. 121.
6   Ibid.
7   Ibid., p. 123.

presence. The blur, as a result of soft focus, 'loosens the fabric of time'.[5] The soft-focus blur also makes the photograph picture-like and in that respect comparable to painting. Soft focus is comparable to the painterly technique of chiaroscuro, which is not the background of a shape, but its temporality. The shape which forms the painting's centre recedes or comes forward. This implies not just a spatial division but also a temporal process. Chiaroscuro

> … allows the protruding shape to be alternately summoned and dismissed. The painterly illusionism of depth finds its photographic equivalent in the lateral unfurling of the photograph's resolution, not only its blurred margins, but also its overall grain.[6]

The kind of view that is installed by the blur or by the grain, or in digital photography by the pixel, has its own kind of temporality. These picture-like devices allow the viewer to focus on details of the image and to travel through the image. Some details will be amplified by looking at them, and then the viewer will part from them and go on. 'The kind of time involved by this *travail* is cyclic, consisting in the alternation of expansion and contraction, diastole and systole.'[7] But the soft focus of the time exposure is not only a signifier of time's duration, of the time of imprinting. As Mary Ann Doane argues, it also supports the leisure of contemplation.[8] The work of British photographer Julia Margaret Cameron demonstrates that effectively.

8   Doane, 'Real Time', p. 29.

Soft-focus Blur and Duration

The out-of-focus effect as aesthetic ideal of the time of exposure can be recognized in the nineteenth-century style of the photo-portrait. In these examples of portraiture, it is especially the surroundings of the portrayed figure that are blurred. The images of Julia Margaret Cameron (1815–1897) are clearly part of this practice, but are more extreme. In her photographic portraits, not only the surroundings are blurred, but also the figures are out of focus, or in soft focus. Cameron's photographs are out of focus not because of a technical limitation, but intentionally. In her *Annals of My Glass House*,[9] her unfinished autobiography written in 1874, she wrote:

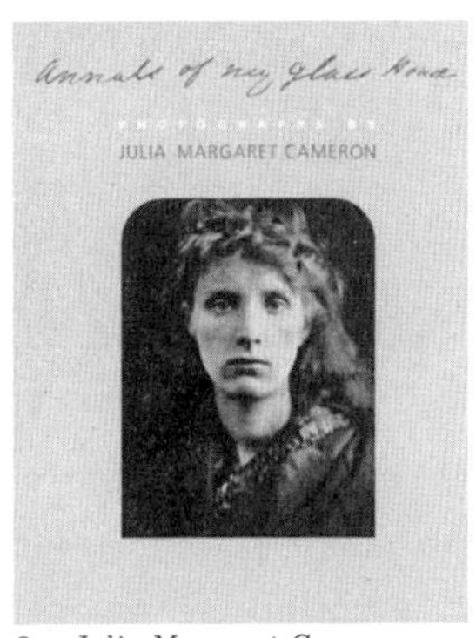

9   Julia Margaret Cameron, *Annals of my Glass House* (Seattle: University of Washington Press, 1997). Originally published 1874.

> I believe that what my youngest boy, Henry Herschel, who is now himself a very remarkable photographer, told me is quite true—that my first successes in my out-of-focus pictures were a fluke. That is to say, that when focussing and coming to something which, to my eye, was very beautiful, I stopped there instead of screwing on

123

10   Julia Margaret Cameron, *Annals of My Glass House: Photographs by Julia Margaret Cameron*, text Violet Hamilton (Claremont, CA: Ruth Chandler Williamson Gallery, 1996), p. 12.

11   Cameron, *Annals of My Glass House*, p. 15.

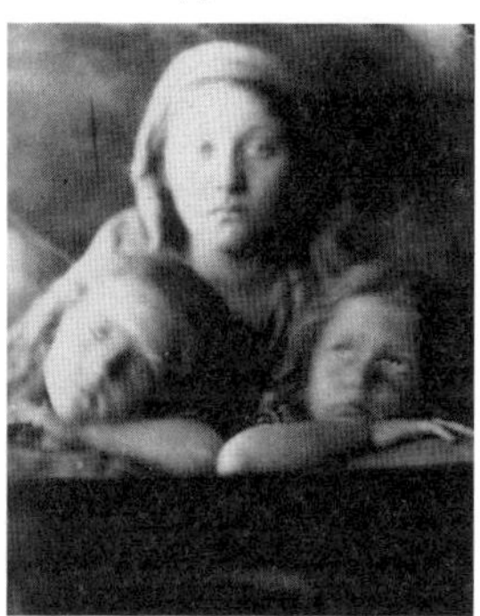

12a   Julia Margaret Cameron, *Mary Hillier and Two Children*, 1864.

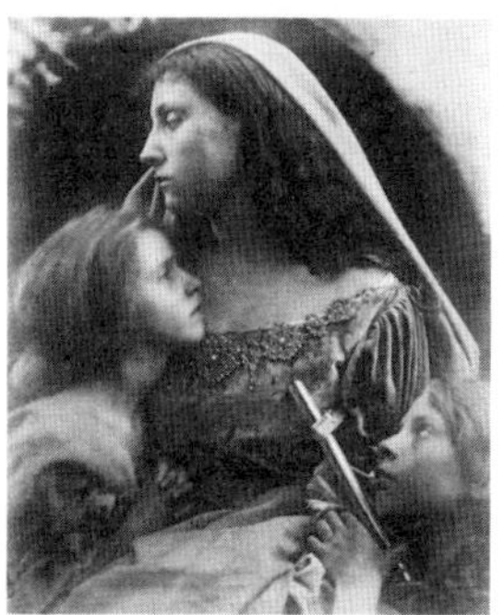

12b   Julia Margaret Cameron, *A Holy Family*, 1872.

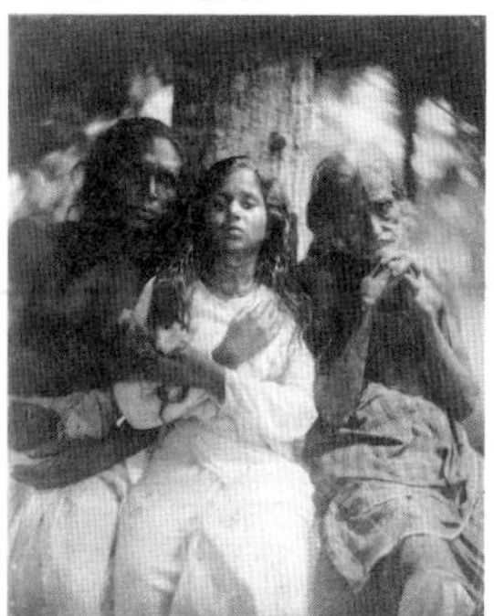

12c   Julia Margaret Cameron, *A Group of Kalutara Peasants*, 1878.

13   Ibid., p. 12.

the lens to the more definite focus which all other photographers insist upon.[10]

Although she also calls it the 'difficulty of focussing', Cameron does not want this difficulty to be solved by a sharp focus. Her discursive paradigm is not that of scientific photography, but that of art and aesthetics. When she receives a letter from a Miss Lydia Louisa Summerhouse Donkins asking to sit for her photograph, she ridicules this request because it shows a complete misunderstanding of Cameron's photographic practice. The letter writer wants 'to have her likeness taken'. 'I answered Miss Lydia Louisa Summerhouse Donkins that Mrs Cameron, not being a professional photographer, regretted she was not able to "take her likeness".'[11] Cameron's ironic answer expresses her intention to be an artist instead of a photographer; the last thing she wants is 'taking a likeness'.[12] She quotes from other responses to her work that emphasize the 'beauty' and 'her special style' instead of technical perfection. If there is anything she wanted to catch it is not likeness, but beauty: 'I longed to arrest all beauty that came before me, and at length the longing has been satisfied. Its difficulty enhanced the value of the pursuit.'[13] Not only in the *Annals* but also in her letters she relates her photographic pursuit with the concepts of 'beauty', 'the ideal', and 'high art'. In a letter from

1864 to the astronomer J.F.W. Herschel, whom she also portrayed in some of her photographs, she wrote: 'My aspirations are to ennoble Photography and to secure for it the character and uses of High Art by combining the real & Ideal & sacrificing nothing of Truth by all possible devotion to Poetry & beauty.'[14] Her use of capitals is telling about her artistic aspirations. She uses it also for 'Photography'. It is completely consistent with nineteenth-century conceptualizations of aesthetics.

Cameron was able to realize not only the painterly effect of chiaroscuro in her photographic images, but also that of *sfumato*. This painterly technique, introduced by Leonardo da Vinci, blurs outlines and modulates tones as if by smoke. This allows one form to merge into another. Cameron archived the effect of *sfumato* in her photographs by varying the focus, and, as a result, the depth of field. The two following images are good examples of Cameron's blurred, soft focus images and the mode of looking that they compel.[15]

Her images do not catch a single moment of the life of the portrayed figures. Although we see in the two juxtaposed images a young man (the Italian Angelo Colarossi) and an old man (the astronomer J.F.W. Herschel), the soft focus freezes, to use De Duve's words once more, 'the past tense of the photograph in a sort of infinitive'. The young phase of

14   Quoted in Violet Hamilton, 'Julia Margaret Cameron: The Art of Photography', in *Annals of My Glass House: Photographs by Julia Margaret Cameron*, text Violet Hamilton (Claremont CA: Ruth Chandler Williamson Gallery, 1996), p. 29.

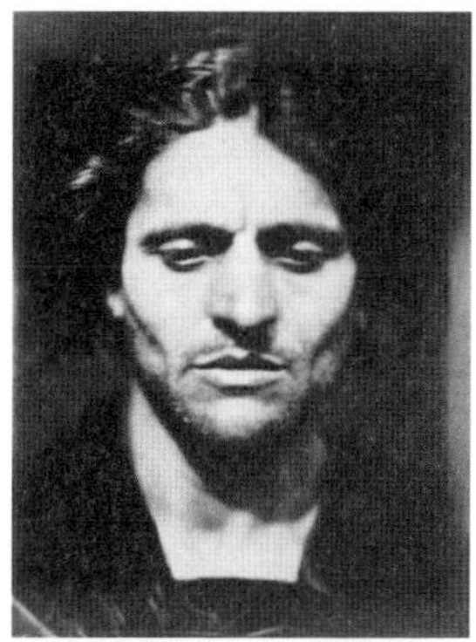

15a   Julia Margaret Cameron, *Iago, Study from an Italian*, 1867.

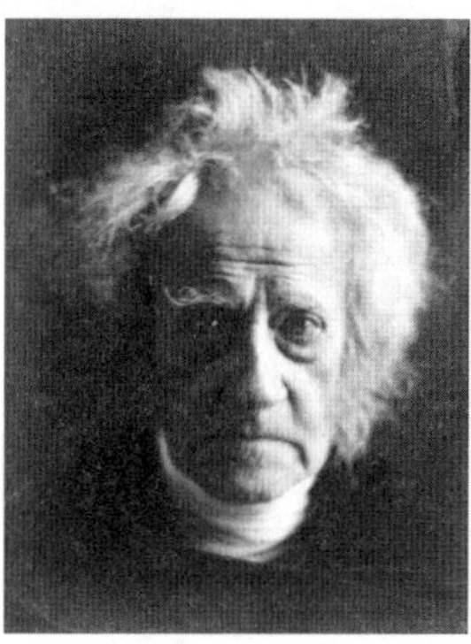

15b   Julia Margaret Cameron, *J.F.W. Herschel*, 1867.

life and the old phase of life are not presented as 'moments' in a lifetime, but as the embodiment of the duration of time condensing the whole lifetime of these two figures each in one single image. In that sense, there is no real difference between the photograph of the young man and the one of the old man. Both their lives and characters can be contemplated on the basis of the durational quality of both images.

Although the two images have in common that they both condense the whole lifetime of these figures in their portraits, there are also striking differences between them. The young man is a lower-class Italian man; the old man is an upper-class English scientist. The first is nameless; the second has the name of an individual. The nameless man has downcast eyes; the man with the name looks in the camera. The way Cameron indexed the image of the Italian man is indicative of its temporality and of the kind of contemplation the image enables. She refers to the image as 'Iago study from an Italian'. Iago is a character from Shakespeare's play *Othello*. His character is consumed with hatred and jealousy. He is deeply unpleasant and represents evil and cruelty for its own sake. Although I am not sure if I can read all this from this image, it is significant that Cameron intended to condense this whole evil life in the portrait of an Italian man of the lower class. In addition to the fact that his eyes are downcast as if in guilt, it is due to the blur caused by the soft-focus technique that she is able to entice the contemplation necessary for such a reading of the image. She describes the mode of looking evoked by her work as a 'startling of the eye with wonder & delight'. She does this in a letter to the same Herschel. She does not present her images as the result of catching like-ness, but as revelations:

> I have been *engaged* in doing that which Mr Watts has long been urging me to do—a series of Life sized heads—They are not only *From* the Life but *to* the Life and startle the eye with won-der & delight I hope that they will astound the Public & *reveal* more of the mystery of this heaven & our art.[16]

The duration of time implied by her soft-focus images characterizes not only her portrayed subjects, but also the mode of looking that her images enable.

The soft-focus blurs of Cameron are the result of an intended imperfect focusing of the lens. Blurs can, however, be the effect of a variety of causes. They can also be the result of movement: a move-ment of the camera or of the photographed subject. According to De Duve, the kind of images in which such movements result is, although blurred, not pic-ture-like, but event-like, even though the intention to catch a moving event does not manifest itself

127

16   The capitals and italics are part of the original letter. The letter is quoted in Hamil-ton, 'Famous Men & Fair Women', p. 31.

17   Christian Metz, *Film Language: A Semiotics of the Cinema* (Oxford: Oxford University Press, 1974), p. 9.

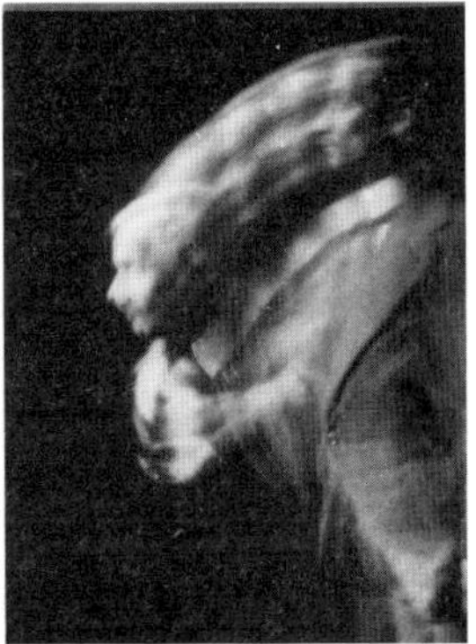

18a   Anton Giulio Bragaglia, *The Bow*, 1914

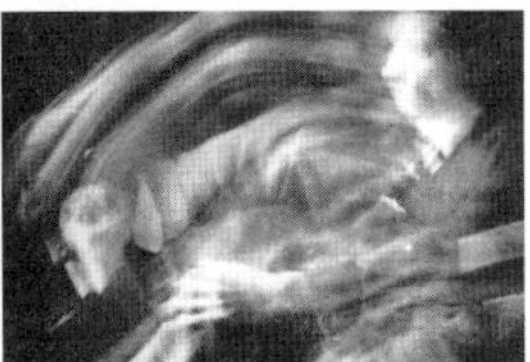

18b   Anton Giulio Bragaglia, *Change of Position*, 1911.

through sharpness, but through blurring. This kind of blurs points to the limit of snapshot photography. Movement can only be represented by actual movement, such as the movement of film. When motion creates a blur in photographs, it represents movement negatively, in the photograph's failure to capture it. In the words of film theorist Christian Metz:

> Because movement is never material but is *always* visual, to reproduce its appearance is to duplicate its reality. In truth, one cannot even 'reproduce' a movement; one can only re-produce it in a second production belonging to the same order of reality, for the spectator, as the first. It is not sufficient to say that film is more 'living,' more animated than still photography, or even that filmed objects are more 'materialized'. In the cinema the impression of reality is also the reality of impression, the real presence of motion.[17]

Anton Giulio Bragaglia's experimental applications of futurism to photography, what he calls photo dynamism, are good examples of images of which the blur is caused by movement of the subject in front of the camera.[18] If photography can only represent movement negatively, in its failure, this also indicates the relativity of De Duve's distinction between event-like images and picture-like images. This distinction loses its edge because when the captured moving event creates a blur in the image instead of sharpness, what we first of all see is an image instead of a moving subject. The real movement of the human figures in Bragaglia's images is absent; motion has been translated into the materiality of the blur.

Spooked Images

Other examples of blurs created by movement can be found in the work of Francesca Woodman. The temporality of her blurred figures is, however, not at all event-like. The blurs in her images look like spectres and spectres are usually read as the haunting of a different temporal dimension. The figures in Woodman's photographs are often described as angels, which seems to confirm the idea that a different temporality is at stake.[19] After all, angels belong to a different temporal ontology as they are supposed to be living in heaven. In the case of Woodman's blurs it is, however, not clear if she evokes another temporal dimension or a spatial one. In all of her images, Woodman explores different conditions of her body, dressed or naked, contracted or expanded, imprisoned in a small space or emerging in the space that surrounds her. Rather, the blurred figures in her images, usually Woodman herself, indicate a

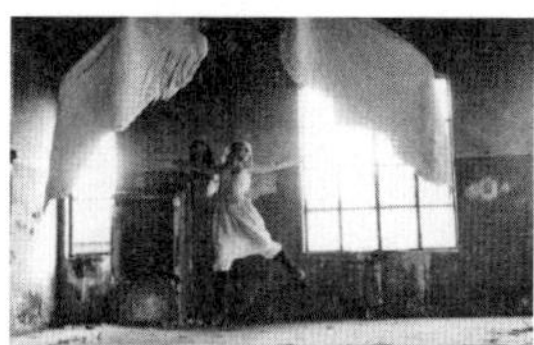

19a   Francesca Woodman, *Untitled*, from Angels series, 1977.

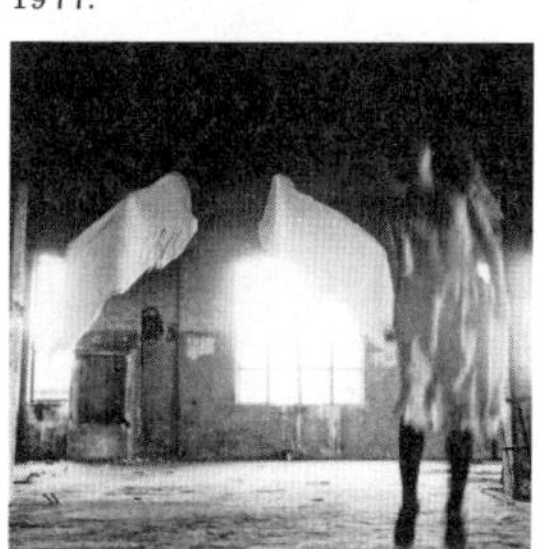

19b   Francesca Woodman, *Untitled*, from Angels series, 1977.

129

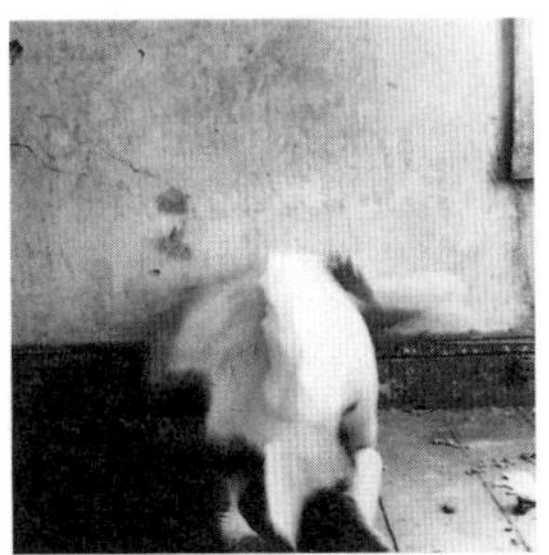

20a Francesca Woodman, *House, Providence, Rhode Island,* 1975–1976.

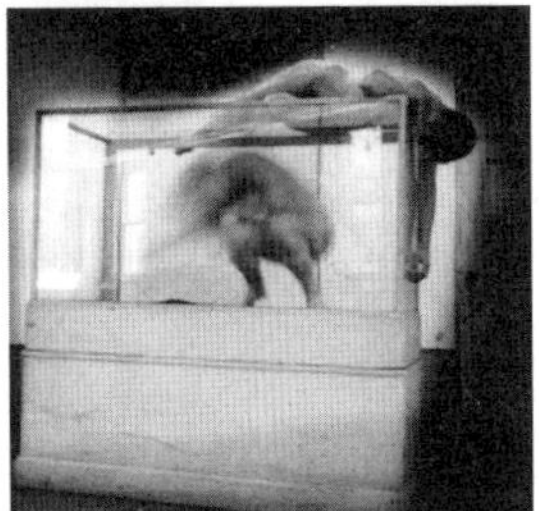

20b Francesca Woodman, *Space, Rhode Island,* 1976.

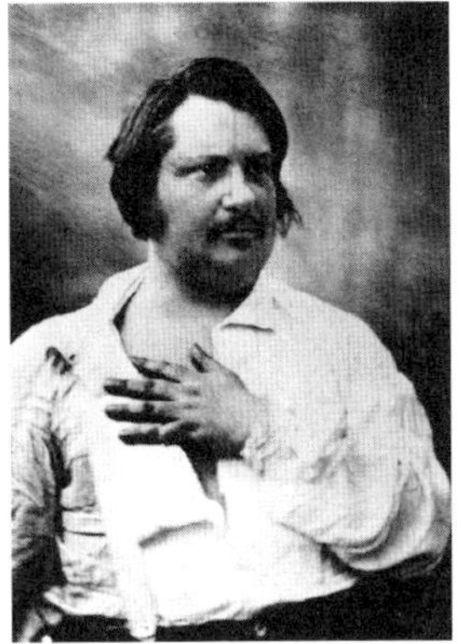

21 Félix Nadar, *Honoré de Balzac,* 1856.

22 Nadar, 'My Life as a Photographer', *October* 5 (1978), p. 9.

condition of not being fully embodied by the body she inhabits. Woodman represents herself as being out-of-sync with the body she lives in. The blur is one of her devices to demonstrate that idea.[20]

In the rest of this section I will, however, especially explore the spectre as a manifestation of a different temporal dimension and of the spectral nature of photography as such. The nineteenth-century French writer Honoré de Balzac,[21] for instance, understood photography as spectral. He was known for his superstitious reaction to photography. According to French photographer Nadar, not only 'the uneducated and ignorant' held such beliefs; 'The lowliest to the most high', trembled before the daguerreotype, and the brilliant intellect of Balzac was one of them. Balzac was said to believe that 'all physical objects are made up entirely of layers of ghostlike images, an infinite number of leaf-like skins laid one on top of the other'. Balzac concluded that 'every time someone had his photograph taken, one of the spectral layers was removed from the body and transferred to the photograph. Repeated exposures entailed the unavoidable loss of subsequent ghostly layers, that is, the very essence of life'.[22] Nadar suggests that for Balzac, photography perhaps did not only peel off spectral layers from the body, but the damage caused by this transferral was 'repaired through some more or less instantaneous process of rebirth'. In that case the photographically portrayed subject would be compensated for his loss in and by the portrait. The subject is reborn in the portrait, but only as a spectre. When the subject returns as a spectre, it implies that the photographic image is not just the harbinger of death, but more actively its cause. The photograph peels off spectral layers from the body and appropriates them in order to create an illusion of that body as image.

Balzac's account of photography suggests that the photographic image is haunted, and, indeed, the most famous and influential reflections on photography suggest precisely that. In his 'Little History of Photography', Walter Benjamin calls the phenomenon one encounters with photography 'new and strange'.[23] The haunting quality of photography seems for him to be a haunting by the referent of the image. Writing about a mid-nineteenth-century portrait by Hill and Adamson he writes: 'In that fishwife from New Haven, who casts her eyes down with such casual seductive shame', there is something

> that does not merely testify to the art of Hill the photographer, but something that cannot be silenced, that impudently demands the name of the person who lived at the time and who, remaining real even now, will never yield herself up entirely into art.[24]

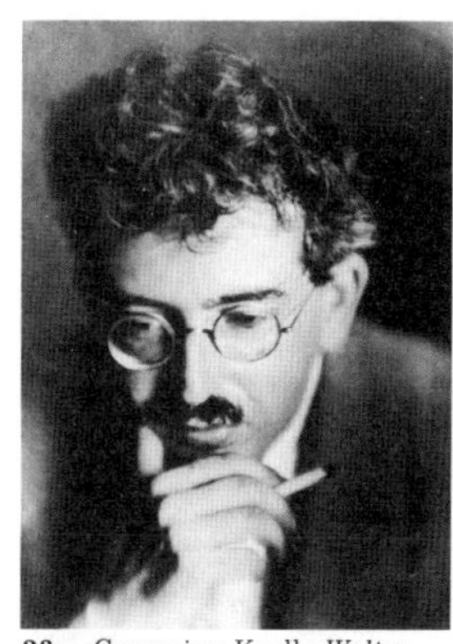

23 Germaine Krull, *Walter Benjamin*, 1926.

24 Walter Benjamin, 'Little History of Photography', p. 163.

131

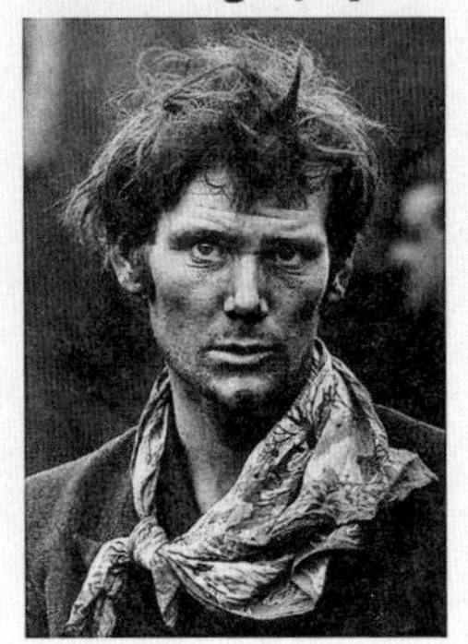

25 Susan Sontag, *On Photography* (New York: Farrar, Straus and Giroux [1973] 1978), p. 120.

It is not farfetched to see this impudent calling for attention that cannot be silenced as photography's haunting quality. In the case of Benjamin, the ghost that haunts the photographic image is the referent.

Susan Sontag, in her well-known book *On Photography* from 1977, also uses qualifications for photography that imply the haunting nature of the photographic images. Like Benjamin, she can only understand photography by contrasting the photographic image to painting. Photography is not only an image, as painting is, an interpretation of the real, it is 'also a trace, something directly stencilled off the real, like a footprint or a death mask'. In her account, the photographic image is not an ordinary ghost, it is more like a vampire, who is 'able to usurp reality' and feed on the referent.[25] But although it feeds on the referent, photography is not completely able to digest it. It can never entirely transcend its subject as a painting can. Like ghosts, the ontological dimension of photography is hovering. It is in between life and afterlife (death), or between representation and reality.

In what is probably the most canonical text on photography, *Camera Lucida*, Roland Barthes evokes the spectral nature of photography in yet another way. Like Sontag, he describes the photographic image as a failed transcendence: 'the event is never transcended for the sake of something'. As someone who dies but is not able to enter the afterlife is destined to become a ghost, just so a photograph's fate is an unsure ontological state: between representation and reality. But when he describes the contingency on which photography is based, the ghostlike nature of photography is not only ontologically explained, but also materially and visually. A photograph is 'wholly ballasted by the contingency of which it is the weightless, transparent envelope'.[26] Being weightless and transparent, albeit visible, the spectral nature of photography is undeniable. It brings also to mind the 'spectral layers' of which a photograph consists according to Balzac.

These different accounts of the spectral nature of photography seem to waver between different options.[27] Whereas the spectre in the photographs of Francesca Woodman and in the remarks by Honoré de Balzac and Susan Sontag seem to evoke and describe a spatial spectrality, Walter Benjamin and Roland Barthes foreground a temporal notion of spectrality. In the prevalent writings on photography it is especially the temporal spectre that is highlighted endlessly. In the following section I will further assess this temporal spectre.

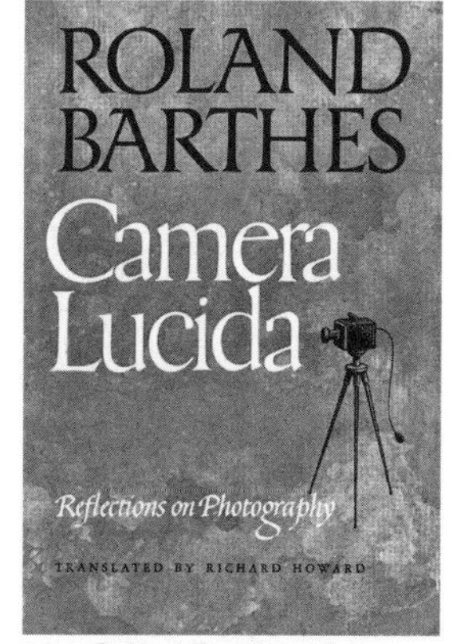

26   Roland Barthes, *Camera Lucida* (New York: Hill and Wang, 1981), p. 5.

27   For a brilliant overview and analysis of recent notions of spectrality, see 'The Spectral Turn' by Maria del Pilar Blanco and Esther Peeren in *The Spectralities Reader*, edited by the same authors.

Spirit Photography and the Untimely

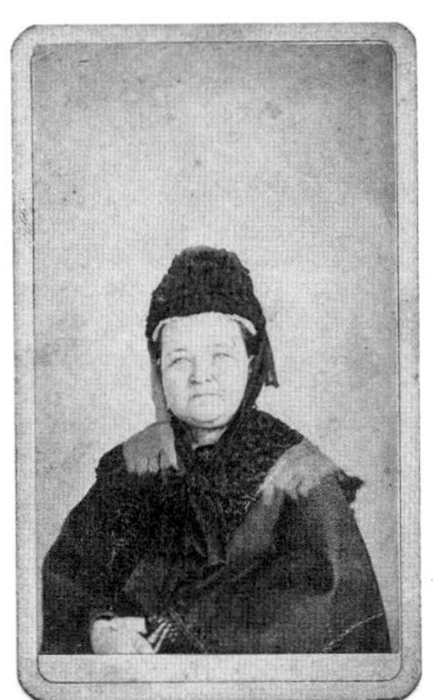

28a William H. Mumler, Mary Todd Lincoln, with the ghost of her husband Abraham Lincoln, 1872.

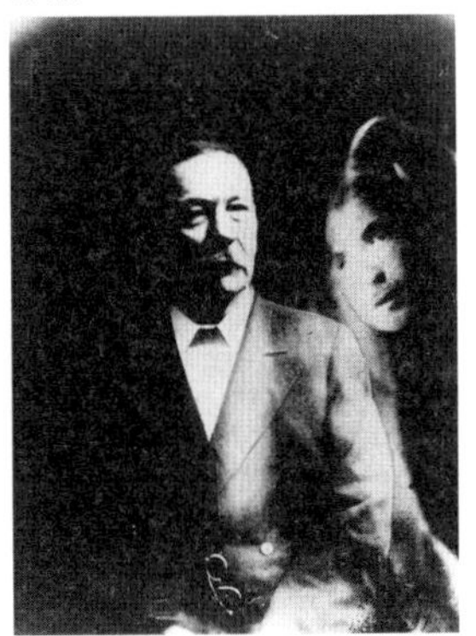

28b A Spirit Photograph that Sir Arthur posed for that purports to have the spirit of his son, Kingsley, who was killed in the Great War, 1919.

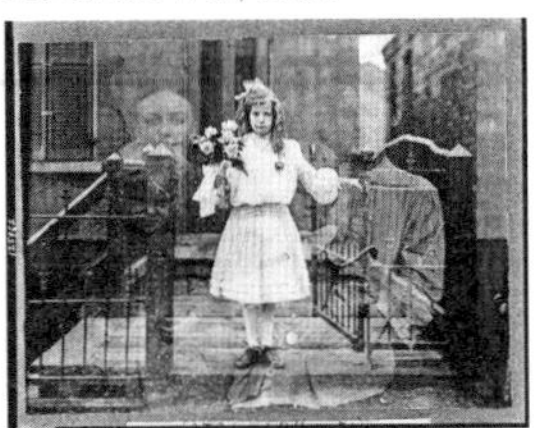

28c Frederik A. Hudson, *Ghost Image*, c. 1950.

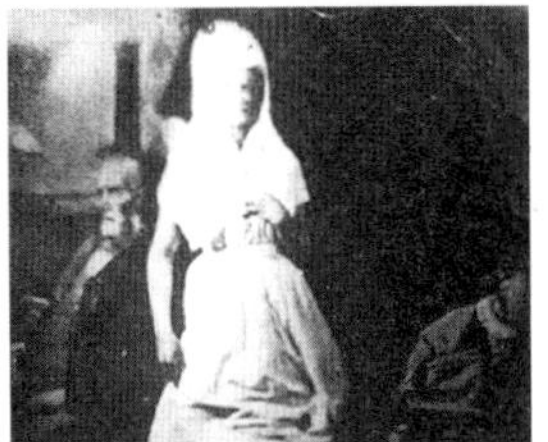

28d William Crookes, Photograph of the spirit of Katie King in the process of materialization, c. 1874.

In order to better understand blurred images from the perspective of the spectral nature of photography I would like to dwell for a moment on a photographic practice that literally shows phantom-like presences. The practice of spirit photography will serve as an emblem for all photography as a generator of ghosts. The spectral nature of photography is not reflected in a layering of the photographs (Balzac), but in the presence (or construction) of ghosts in the image. The temporal paradox of photography seems to take a slightly different turn in spirit photography. This kind of photography started in the 1860s, and is based on double exposure or other ways of doctoring and manipulating negatives. The images usually consist of a portrait of a living person to whom his or her loved one is being added in a ghostlike, blurred format. The first practitioner of this photographic genre was William H. Mumler. Other proponents are Fred A. Hudson, William Crookes and the notable writer Sir Arthur Conan Doyle.[28]

The discourse of spirit photography belongs to the fantasmatic and has a specific temporality that, according to some scholars, does not just define this peculiar genre, but is a constitutive feature of photography as such. Film scholar Tom Gunning

134

understands the temporality of the ghostliness of spirit photography as 'untimeliness'.[29] This noun refers to an inappropriate timing. The present captured in the image is haunted by a different temporal dimension. For the believers in spirit photography, this miraculous phenomenon bears witness to a 'leap out of time'. This makes the image timeless. For spiritualists consider spirit photography as visual proofs of immortality and of the afterlife of which the temporality has dissolved into eternity.[30] Eternity is, in fact, timeless.

These images are fascinating not because of what they indicate about a belief in ghosts, but because of what they reveal of our beliefs in photography, especially of the specific temporality of photography. These images are fantasmatic because they waver between 'visibility and invisibility, presence and absence, materiality and immateriality, often using transparency or some other manipulation of visual appearance to express this paradoxical ontological status'.[31] Whatever device is used for manipulating the negatives, the effect is usually a blur indicating the ghost's presence. A ghost-like presence in the image puts vision in crisis.

In these images, we no longer see *through* the photograph but become aware of the uncanny nature of the process of capturing an image itself.

135

29 Tom Gunning, 'To Scan a Ghost: The Ontology of Mediated Vision', *Grey Room* 26 (Winter 2007), p. 117.

30 Louis Kaplan, 'Spooked Time: The Temporal Dimensions of Spirit Photography', in *Time and Photography*, ed. Jan Baetens, Alexander Streitberger and Hilde Van Gelder (Leuven: Leuven University Press, 2010), p. 28.

31 Gunning, 'Spooked Time', p. 99.

32 Ibid., p. 112.
33 Ibid., p. 117.

Our gaze is caught, suspended, stuck within the transparent film itself.[32]

Vision recognizes a presence, but this presence wavers between the transparency of immateriality and materiality. For people interested in ghosts, this wavering indicates a metaphysical certainty: the existence of ghosts. For people interested in photographic images, this wavering indicates a visual and phenomenological uncertainty. We do not know what the status is of what we see. It embodies an ontological wavering.

The wavering presence of the ghost-like forms in the image suggests a temporal dimension. This temporality of ghosts is frequently understood as 'revenant', the return of things past. The revenant is a ghostly return, a return after forgetting or even after death. According to Gunning, this is why the ghostly represents a fundamental untimeliness, 'a return of the past not in the form of memory or history but in a contradictory experience of presence'.[33] Because of the impossibility to understand the paradoxical temporal dimension of the revenant, being present and absent at the same time, Gunning understands the ghostly as 'untimely', as being present at the wrong moment. Kaplan has pointed out how this 'spooked time' has a lot in common with what Derrida has called the 'ineluctable originality of the spectre'.[34] Derrida introduces the 'logic of haunting'—also called hauntology—in *Spectres of Marx*, amid a discussion of the spectres of Hamlet haunting Marx and Engels' *The Communist Manifesto*.[35] Derrida suggests that spectres or ghosts do not came 'after' (from the afterlife), but paradoxically that they are at the origin. It is this notion of spectres and ghosts as being at the origin that makes it relevant to understand the untimely nature of ghosts also as an untimely effect of photography. For the (haunted) photographic image challenges the distinction between what is present and what is not, between what is living and what is not.

In cinema, the ghostly is most effectively evoked by the still image. When still images occur in moving images they tend to emerge as harbingers of death and the ghostly.[36] I contend that in photography it is the blurred image that has a similar function of being the indication of the ghostly; because one of the effects of blurred photography is that it transgresses the distinction between hallucination and perception. In the words of Derrida:

> Everything is concentrated in the German
> expression *es spukt,* which translations are
> obliged to circumvent. One would have to say: it
> haunts, it ghosts, it spectres, there is some phan-
> tom there, it has the feel of living-dead. The

137

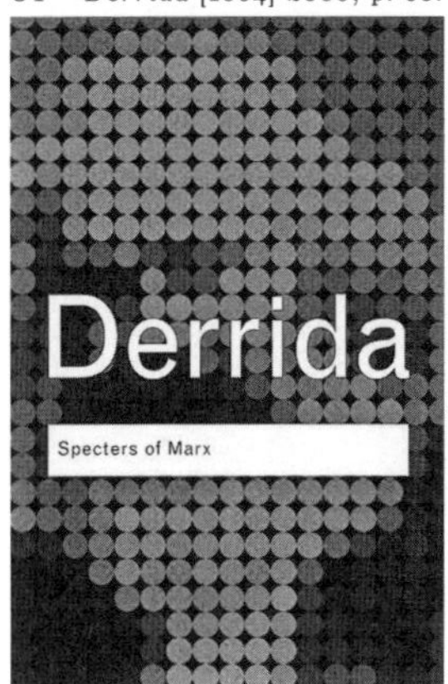

34   Derrida [1994] 2005, p. 53.

35   Jacques Derrida, *Specters of Marx* (London: Routledge, 2006). Originally published as *Spectres de Marx: l'état de la dette, le travail du deuil et la nouvelle Internationale*, 1993.

36   This has been argued by Garrett Stewart, in his *Between Film and Screen: Photosynthesis* (Chicago: University of Chicago Press, 1999).

37   Jacques Derrida, *Spectres of Marx: The State of Debt, the Work of Mourning, and the New International* (New York and London: Routledge, 2005 [1994]), p. 135–136.

38   For a rich commentary on spectrality in popular imagery in view of a social-political argument, see Esther Peeren, *The Spectral Metaphor: Living Ghosts and the Agency of Invisibility* (London: Palgrave, 2014).

subject that haunts is not identifiable, one cannot see. Localize, fix any form, one cannot decide between hallucination and perception.[37]

Derrida's theoretical account of the spectre is at the same time an apt description of the perception of blurred photography. For blurred images seem to be the result of a kind of spectral layering, which provides the image with its in-between condition, ontologically, phenomenologically, and temporally. The untimely returning ghost of photography is most acutely and intensely experienced in the blur.[38]

The untimely revenant differs temporally from the durational portrait images of Cameron. It concerns a different awareness of time. Duration is in opposition with the instantaneous; duration is slow and time-taking. In this respect, duration differs from the eternal, because the eternal does not imply awareness of time; it is the absence of time. Untimeliness can be understood as being temporally out-of-sync. Two moments in time, or two distinct temporal dimensions, overlap or intersect. Spirit photography shows such an intersection of temporal dimensions that do not easily fit. The figure of the spirit belongs to the timeless eternal, whereas its partner is caught in a durational portrait. When we consider spirit photography as exemplary for the temporal paradox of photography, it concerns, however, another intersection. Photography may intersect or overlap with the past—in the awareness that the moment present in the image belongs to the past—or with the present, presenting that moment perfectly life-like in the present in which we look at that image of the past.

Spooky Space: the Architecture Series of Hiroshi Sugimoto

In the cases discussed so far, the wavering presence of ghost-like forms in the image evoked unexpected temporalities. But as I already argued in the case of Francesca Woodman's images, the spatial dimension can also have spectral qualities. The architecture series of Japanese/American photographer Hiroshi Sugimoto seems to evoke the spatial presence of architecture in ghostly form. In this series Sugimoto exclusively shows iconic masterpieces of modernist architecture: Erich Mendelsohn's Einstein Tower, Le Corbusier's Villa Savoye, Ludwig Mies van der Rohe's Seagram Building, Frank Lloyd Wright's Guggenheim Museum, Frank Gehry's Guggenheim Bilbao, and many others.[39] However, these land-marks of modernism appear blurred. As iconic mas-terpieces, we remember these buildings sharply; they are fixated on our retinas. But Sugimoto's images

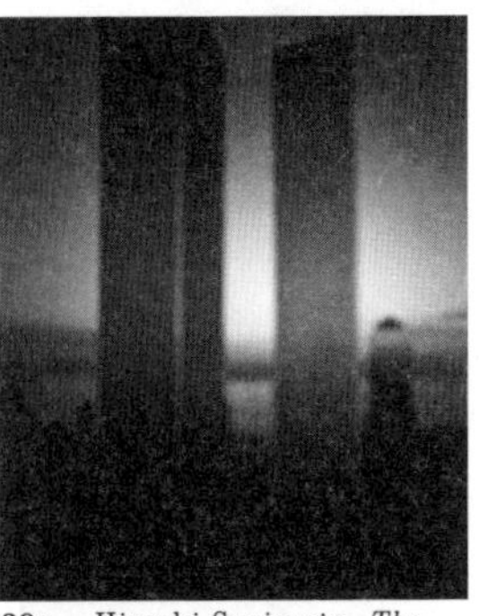

39a   Hiroshi Sugimoto, *The World Trade Center*, 1997.

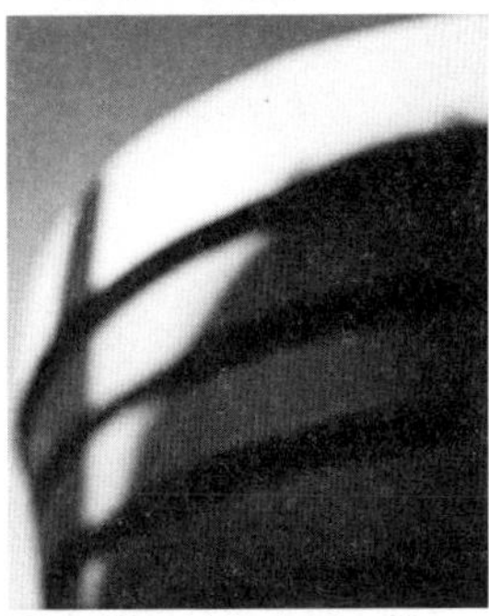

39b   Hiroshi Sugimoto, *The Guggenheim Museum*, 1997.

139

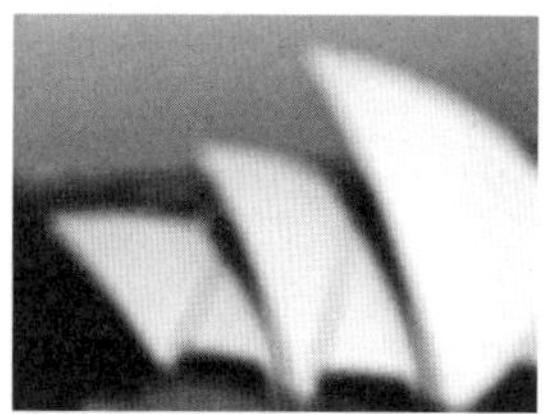

40a Hiroshi Sugimoto, *Sydney Opera House*, 1998.

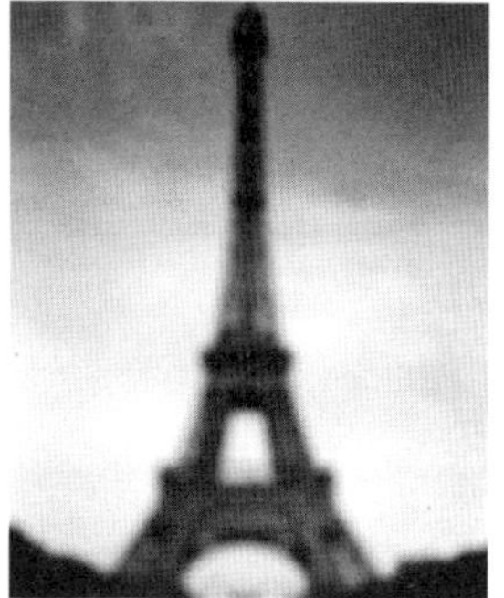

40b Hiroshi Sugimoto, *Eiffel Tower*, 1998.

41 Hiroshi Sugimoto quoted in Armin Zweite, *Hiroshi Sugimoto: Revolution* (Ostfildern: Hatje Cantz Verlag, 2013), p. 13.

show them as diffuse and intangible; it is as if they dissolve into formlessness. Nevertheless, they can still be identified. Even after having been transformed into a blurred image they maintain their identity.[40]

Sugimoto did not photograph any old, historical architecture: he selected only modernist examples, which can be relatively old, but look contemporary, even timeless. The temporal dimensions have been neutralized, at least by his choice of photographed objects. This is even the case in the image of the World Trade Center of 1997. Although this building is now utterly historical after it was destroyed by the terrorist attack of 9/11, architecturally and photographically in this image it is nevertheless present as a spatial construction. Strangely enough the blurred image of the World Trade Center does not differ visually—in its effect—from the other blurred images of modernist architecture.

In Sugimoto's image the World Trade Center has withstood a double attack, not only the one of terrorism but also the one of the blur. According to the artist, these modernist constructions are able to withstand 'the onslaught of blurred photography'. The blur is a kind of erosion of the image.[41] The qualities they originally have dissolve or disappear. And of course, the quality photography is famous for, i.e. its sharpness, is under siege in blurred photography. Despite their eroded visuality, the modernist buildings remain standing and we can still recognize them.

Not only in painting but also in photography, effective representation of architectural constructions depends heavily on the illusion of three-dimensionality. One of the highly reduced qualities in the blurred architectural images is the illusion of three-dimensionality. The illusion of depth is transformed into an almost flat image. In so far as these images create this illusion, it is projected onto them by our memories of the architectural constructions of which they were taken. This provides evidence for French philosopher Henri Bergson's point that perception is never limited to the present, but always entangled with memory.[42] The spatial constructions we see in the images are only spectres of the real buildings. They have lost their sharp contours, as a result of which we cannot definitively locate them in three-dimensional space. The illusion of three-dimensionality turns out to be dependent on the relationship among forms: in relation and in interaction with each other they create that illusion. When blurredness dissolves clear forms, the relations between forms weaken, and three-dimensionality dissolves. The buildings now mainly exist as spectral forms on the flat photographic image.

In Sugimoto's architectural series the way the

42 Henri Bergson, *Matter and Memory* (1896) (New York: Zone Books, 1991), p. 60; for an elaborate discussion of Bergson's ideas about perception and memory, see Mieke Bal, *Thinking in Film: The Politics of Video Installation According to Eija-Liisa Ahtila* (New York: Bloomsbury Academic, 2013), esp. pp. 15–17.

modernist masterpieces appear in the blurred images is 'out of sync' with the visual memories we have of them. This seems to complicate my assessment that the spectral effect of his images should be understood as spatial. However, the 'erosion' and 'melting down' of these architectural images by means of blurring them affected first of all the visuality of spatial forms, and as result, the illusion of three-dimensionality. The introduction of temporality does not take place in or by the blurred images, but in the process of looking at them. In the act of looking the viewer entangles the visual, spatial dimensions of the image with his or her memories. But this happens always, in all acts of looking; not only in front of Sugimoto's blurred images of modernist architectural masterpieces. Like many of his other series, this one can be understood as an allegory of a crucial photographic element. In this case it concerns the production of the illusion of three-dimensional depth. Negatively, by means of failed, blurred images, he makes us see what this effect depends on and how it is produced.

The Blur as Patina

American artist Cy Twombly became known first of all as a painter, secondly as a sculptor. Throughout his artistic career he also made photographs, which he only began to show by the end of his career. These photographs are mostly blurred. His blurs are the result of a very specific modern practice, called electrophotography. This practice involves the manipulation of prints through the process of scanning them on a photocopy machine. He often made multiple scans and enlargements of his original Polaroid prints, accentuating the grainy texture. The resulting prints dilute the crisp lines and shapes of the traditional photograph, and they enrich the colours and surface textures of details. The dilution of lines and shapes, and the enlargement of surface texture, especially create the effect of blurring.[43]

Twombly started to make his blurred images by means of electrophotography in the 1980s, when these photocopy machines became more easily available. The resulting images have much in common with the painterly images of pictorialist photographers such as Anne Brigman (1869–1950) and Robert Demachy (1959–1936).[44] The pictorialists did everything to elevate the medium of photography into the realm of art. Although he was first of all a painter, I do not think that this was Twombly's concern. More likely he was pursuing ways in which the blur of his images could create a special temporality: a wavering between duration and the untimeliness of spectral images.

143

43   See Arpad Kovacs, 'A Painter's Focus', *Apollo* December 2012, pp. 74–79, for a description of Twombly's way of making his blurred images.

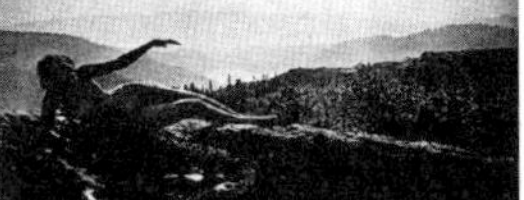

44a   Anne Brigman, *Dawn*, 1912.

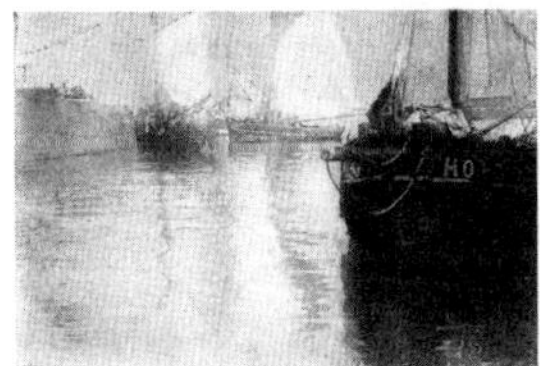

44b   Robert Demachy, *Honfleur*, 1905.

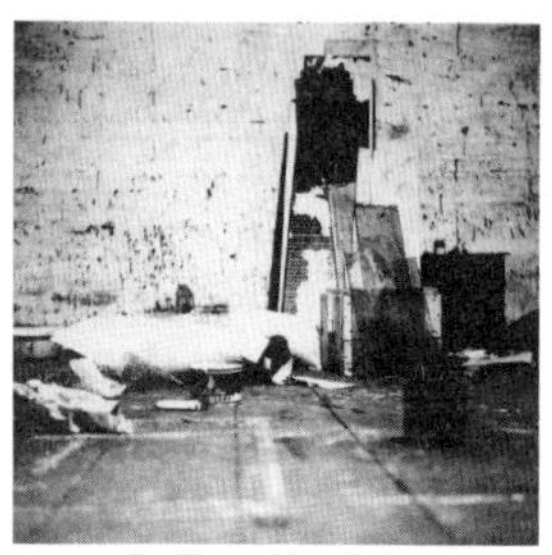

45a   Cy Twombly, *Robert Rauschenberg Combine Material Fulton St. Studio*, 1954.

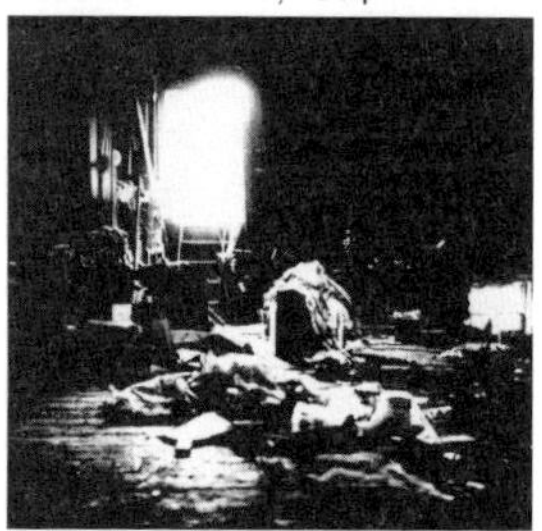

45b   Cy Twombly, *Robert Rauschenberg Combine Material Fulton St. Studio*, 1954.

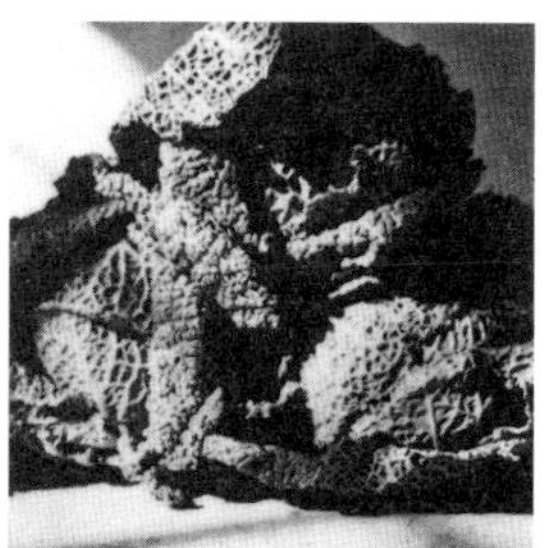

46a   Cy Twombly, *Cabbages, Gaeta*, 1998.

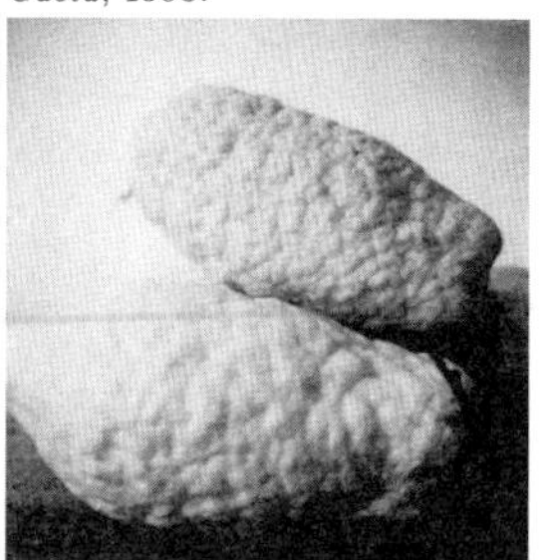

46b   Cy Twombly, *Lemons, Gaeta*, 2005.

Twombly's blurred photographs are not always the result of electrophotography. Already in the 1950s, he made photographs of the studio of Robert Rauschenberg. He placed the camera at a very low position, almost on the floor. As a result, the floorboards in the foreground are out of focus, whereas the wall of the studio further away from the camera is in focus.[45] Other devices he used to create a blurred effect are moving the camera slightly to blur the subject in front of the camera. Once we recognize the diversity of techniques Twombly used to create completely or partly blurred images, it is clear that he sought to avoid the aesthetic of sharpness in whatever way he could.

His electrophotographs of three cabbages and of two lemons are good examples of the blurred quality he pursues in his images.[46] The thick, fleshy texture of the cabbages, as well as of the lemons, is intensified by the seemingly craggy surfaces of the images. In both compositions, chiaroscuro contributes to the painterly effect. Parts of the cabbages are almost too bright, whereas other parts disappear in darkness. The same can be said about the two lemons. The surface on which they rest is not clearly distinguished from the lower side of the lemons because it is too dark there. Like almost all of his photographs both are still lifes. Hence, their temporality is not historically specific. They do not catch a particular

144

moment, as snapshots do. The cabbages are fully grown and the lemons are ripe. They are both on the verge of decaying. Although we do not see this decay in the image representing them, the slight blur through which we look at them announces that decay. The suggested temporality is neither event-like nor linear, but cyclical.

Quite a number of the electrophotographs have, however, a much more intense blur, such as those he made of images of flowers and tulips.[47] In those cases, the suggestion of decay can no longer be attributed to the represented flowers, but only to the images themselves. The blurred layer dissolves the visibility of the photograph. The blur is not really 'in' the image, like the revenants in spirit photography, but is *done to* the image.

Although from a formal point of view Twombly's photographs are hard to compare with his paintings, the temporality which is implied in both seems very similar. His blurs are then comparable to the violent markings of graffiti that is characteristic of most of his painting.[48] Krauss has argued that his graffiti-like markings are performative:

> Twombly took up graffiti as a way of interpreting the meaning of Action Painting's mark, and most particularly that of Pollock's radically innovative dripped line. For graffiti is a medium of marking

145

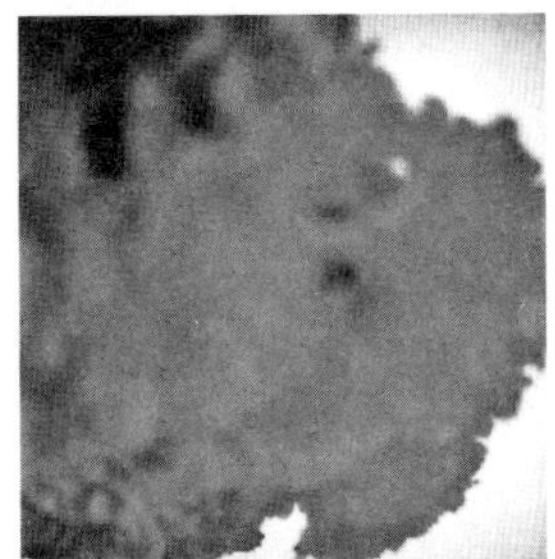

47a　Cy Twombly, *Flowers II, Gaeta*, 2005.

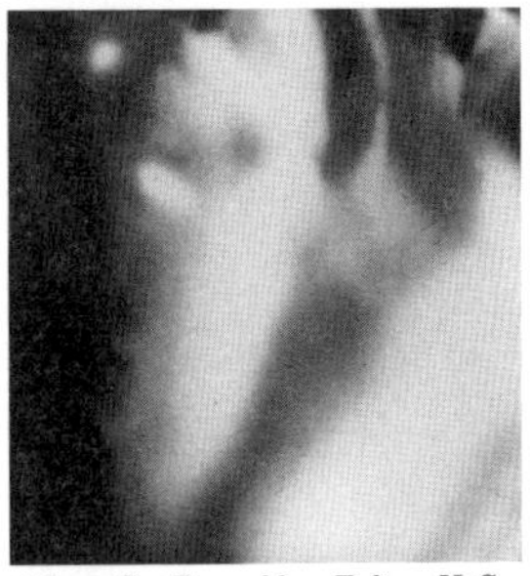

47b　Cy Twombly, *Tulips II C*, 1992.

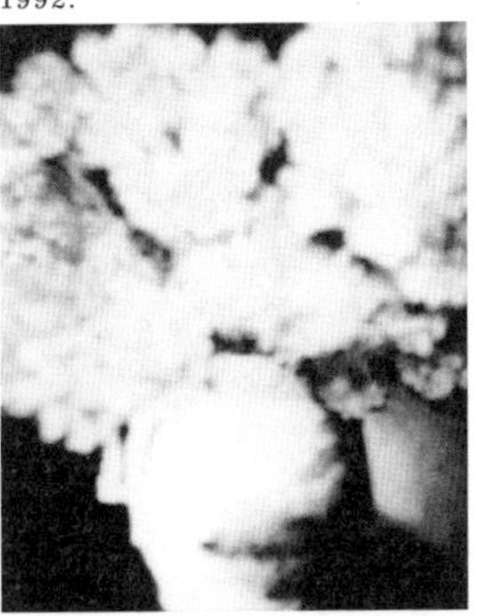

47c　Cy Twombly, *Flowers, Bassano in Teverina*, 1980.

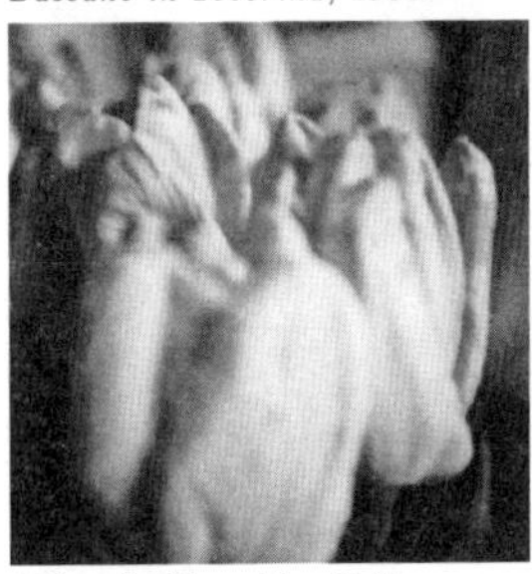

47d　Cy Twombly, *Tulips, Rome*, 1985.

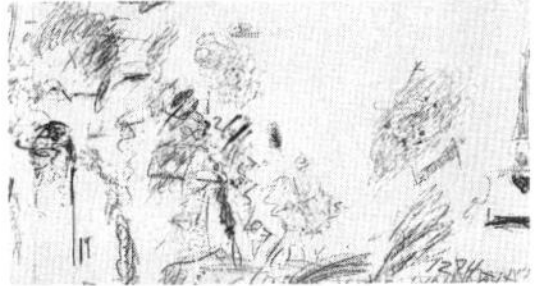

48　Cy Twombly, *Second Voyage to Italy (Second Version)*, (1962).

49 Rosalind Krauss, 'Cy Was Here; Cy's Up', *Artforum* 33, no. 1 (September 1994), p. 70.

that has precise, and unmistakable, characteristics. First, it is performative, suspending representation in favor of action: I mark you, I cancel you, I dirty you. Second it is violent: always an invasion of a space that is not the marker's own, it takes illegitimate advantage of the surface of inscription, violating it, mauling it, scarring it. Third, it converts the present tense of the performative into the past of the index: it is the trace of an event, torn away from the presence of the marker. 'Kilroy was here', it reads.[49]

The temporal dimension of graffiti converts the present tense of the performative into the past tense of the index, Krauss writes. At first, this understanding of graffiti applies also to the photographic image in general. The indexical nature of photography, its reference to a moment that now belongs to the past, has become common sense in the wake of Roland Barthes' *Camera Lucida*. Barthes underscores the image's indexicality, and as a consequence, its pastness. He does not take the illusion of the present tense of photography into consideration. However, this is, rather, the result of its iconicity: the viewer is confronted with a moment in time that looks as lifelike as the present we live in. The presence offered by the photographic image is not only spatial, but also that of the temporal present. But especially with older images, it is the indexical past that overrules the iconic present and the viewer is hit by the awareness that this-has-been. As I will argue later in the chapter on archival images, Barthes' phenomenological account of photography in terms of the shock specific images can bring about, goes against the grain of what Kracauer has to say about the difference between recent and old photographs. The latter argues that over time the photographic image becomes severed from its referent. It is only in recent images that the referential, indexical function of the medium of photography can be assessed.[50] But Barthes' indexicality of old images concerns the temporality of the photograph, whereas Kracauer's indexicality of recent images concerns the spatial, referential dimension.

Because of the photograph's iconicity and life-likeness, the present tense of the performative is not the same as the illusion of presence. It is the result of an act performed in the present. In the case of graffiti, it is the result of the violent marking and dirtying of the surface on which the marking is done. Twombly's blurs also seem to have been 'done to' the images they cover, befouling them, dissolving their transparency, but also making them look old as if a patina now covers the once pristine, transparent images. Twombly's belabouring of the original Polaroid images by means of colour photocopy

147

50 See Siegfried Kracauer, 'Photography', in *The Mass Ornament: The Weimar Essays*, trans. and ed. by Thomas Y. Levin (Cambridge, MA and London: Cambridge University Press, [1963] 1995), pp. 47–64, p. 54.

51   Bill Maurer 2006, quoted by Shannon Lee Dawdy, *Patina: A Profane Archaeology* (Chicago: University of Chicago Press, 2016), p. 154.

machines are literally acts performed onto the original Polaroids. But even without being aware of the process of producing these blurred images, they look as if a layer of time is covering the image. This layering of time translates into a seemingly age-old patina. His images do not catch one single moment in time; the present tense of his reworking of the original images is converted into the past of time that has passed. The patina that seems to cover his images is the visualization of time passed and passing.

This visualization of time by means of patina is brilliantly explained by anthropologist Shannon Lee Dandy in her book *Patina: A Profane Archeology*. She understands patina as the capturing of social forces and social relations and making these forces, these abstractions, temporarily concrete. But temporarily concrete does not mean temporarily familiar. Again, the temporal dimension takes the shape of a spectre. Using Derrida's reading of the spectre in the work of Marx, she understands the relationship between objects and subjects, or matter and thought, as a spectre that moves in and out of both. She quotes Bill Maurer to elaborate this: 'A shadow from another time, whose time has gone, but yet manifests itself in *this* time… is *out of sync* with the rest of today's time-space… not quite fully in or out of it.'[51]

In the case of the work of Marx the spectre represents the history of human relationships that

haunts every object. In the case of Twombly, however, we are not looking at haunted objects but
at haunted images. His images are also out-of-sync;
and this out-of-syncness creates the illusion of patina. The patina that covers his photographs is best
understood in terms of Susan Stewart's reading of
sepia-toned photographs. 'The acute sensation of the
objects—its perception by hand taking precedence
over its perception by eye—promises, and yet does
not keep the promise of, *reunion*.'[52] In line with this
view, I contend that the perception of Twombly's
photographs activates senses that are much more vis-
ceral than the distanced eye. The photograph's representation does not promise a 'reunion' that is
only virtual, as any representation does, but one that
is bodily, at least almost. They create a sensation of
'a shadow from another time', which is cyclical rather
than linear or event-like.

Thomas Ruff's Blurred Portraits

German photographer Thomas Ruff never mistakes
a photographic image for the world it shows. He systematically explores different photographic genres
such as portrait photography, architectural photography, landscape photography, and nude photography;
different uses of the medium in scientific photo-

149

52   Susan Stewart, *On Longing
of the Miniature, the Gigantic,
the Souvenir, the Collection*
(Durham: Duke University
Press, 1993), p. 139; quoted by
Dawdy, *Patina*, p. 155.

53   Matthias Winzer, 'A Credible Invention of Reality: Thomas Ruff's precise Reproductions of our Fantasies of Reality.' In *Thomas Ruff: 1979 to the Present*, ed. Ute Eskildsen and Matthias Winzen, Cologne: Walther König, 2001, p. 138.

54   See the interview with Thomas Ruff in *BiNational: German Art of the late 1980's* (Cologne: Walther König, 1988), p. 262.

graphy and press photography; the distribution of photographic images in various media; and last but not least the different conditions of the medium in analogue as well as digital form, as negatives, or as photograms (camera-less photography). His interest in photography performs in the most serious way the kind of attention for the 'translations' and 'transformations' the photographic image is based upon according to Kracauer and Flusser. It is almost as if he has taken the message of these two media theorists to heart in his explorations of the different manifestations of the photographic image. For instance, in an interview he makes the following remark, which is rather significant for a photographer: 'What has always interested me is the picture language, the information contained in a picture—without reference to the context where the picture appears.'[53]

His remarks about his series of portraits deconstruct the sentimental, humanist ideology projected onto this genre by common sense. He declares that the picture he takes of a person has nothing to do with the person anymore. The portrait has its own reality, its own autonomous existence. The portrait becomes independent of the person it represents.[54] His making of series of portraits instead of individual portraits also contributes to the deconstruction of the genre. In his own words:

When a single person is depicted, then the photograph is apparently about that single person.
The fact that I work in series, however, is an
indication that I am not the only person in the
world, that there are millions of other people
who are just as important as the individual portrayed. I didn't want to exalt the individual person in the portrait.[55]

55 Thomas Ruff, quoted in Winzer, 'A Credible Invention of Reality', p. 142.

Ruff has made several series of portraits. From 1981
until 2001, he made small format portraits of 24 × 18
cm. They seem to be modelled on the photographic
images of bureaucratic, archival institutions, like the
passport photograph. The models are positioned in a
strictly formal pose; they are looking at the camera,
and most of them are only presented as busts. What
we get to see are rather expressionless, but self-confi-
dent faces, faces of people who face bureaucratic
authorities. The models are placed against different
coloured backgrounds. This shortens the depth of
the image. It looks as if the spatial dimension in
which the subjects are placed is reduced to nothing.
We see faces without interiority and without any
spatial context.

Ruff radicalized these principles for a series of
Large Portraits, which he started in 1988, stopped in
1991, but took up again in 1998. From now on, the
models are always placed before the same light-grey

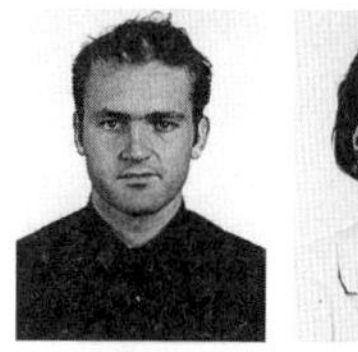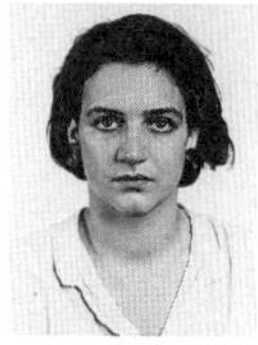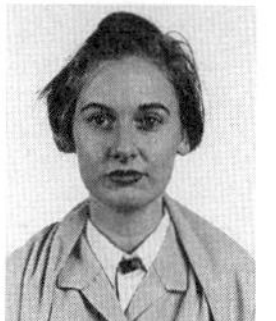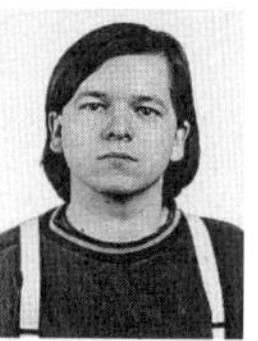

56 'Large Portraits', in *Thomas Ruff: Oberflächen, Tiefen* (Vienna: Kunsthalle Wien, 2009), p. 168.

57 Thomas Ruff, *Blue Eyes M.V./B.E; Blue Eyes M.B./B.E.; Blue Eyes L.C./B.E.; Blue Eyes C.F./B.E.*, 1991.

background without any shading. This increases the uniformity. They are always shown as busts, and the photographs were enlarged to about five times their original seizes. The sharpness of the images remained the same. Although the subjects already have no spatial context because of the light-grey background before which they are placed, due to the large format they are even more emphatically detached from the real world. What remains of them is a flat image. There is no eye contact with the viewer anymore because they rise above and gaze beyond their viewers. Physical details become picture points and abstractions, with little reality effect. 'The portrait emancipates itself from its referent and changes from a likeness to a free image, an independent iconic unit that celebrates its flatness as essence.'[56]

In 1991, he made a series entitled *Blue Eyes* for which he used images of the earlier portrait series. The prints are slightly larger than the other series, 39.5×29.5 cm.[57] This series foregrounds the picture's own reality even more explicitly than the passport-like images He used digital technology to replace the irises of the eyes in twelve of his portraits with the bright blue eyes of another model, whose colour was intensified in the print. In 1995, he made the series *Retouched*. These can be compared to the *Blue Eyes* series because they have also been explicitly transformed, or retouched. The format is very small, 14.7 × 10 cm. He used a method of transformative representation that is as old as photography itself: the colouring of photographs. Ruff applied eye shadow, rouge, and lipstick on the portraits with a pigment-free retouching paint.[58]

Between 1994 and 1995 he made a series titled *Other Portraits*. These portraits were made in two formats, both much larger than the other portraits so far: 200 × 150 cm and 73.5 × 55 cm. The thrust of all of Ruff's portrait series is that photographs of faces are not depictions of people, but images that have a reality of their own. In the *Other Portraits* this idea is even more emphatically conveyed. The best way to describe the images is by explaining how Ruff produced them. Experimenting with composite faces, Ruff came across a picture-generating machine used by the police in Germany in the 1970s to generate phantom pictures. Through a combination of mirrors, four portraits are combined in the machine and transformed into one composite picture. Throughout the history of photography, images have been manipulated by a variety of techniques such as retouching, double exposures, various darkroom procedures, and nowadays, digital processing. Ruff did not use any of these techniques but borrowed the picture-generating machine from the historical collection of police equipment in Berlin. With the machine he combined

58   See Thomas Ruff, *Thomas Ruff: 1979 to the Present*, ed. Ute Eskildsen and Matthias Winzen (Cologne: Walther König 2001), p. 234.

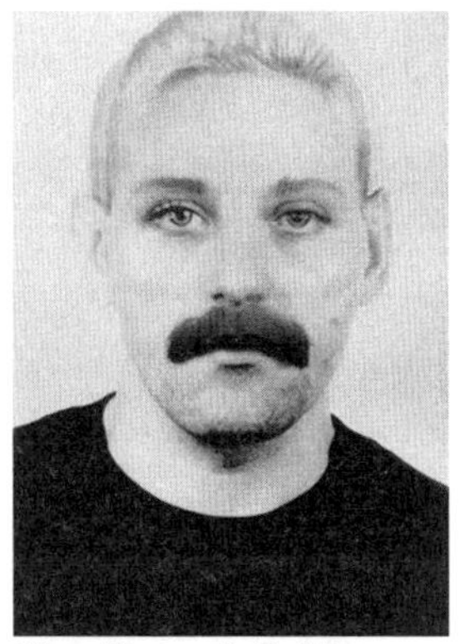

59a   Thomas Ruff, *Other Portrait no. 122/138*, 1994–1995.

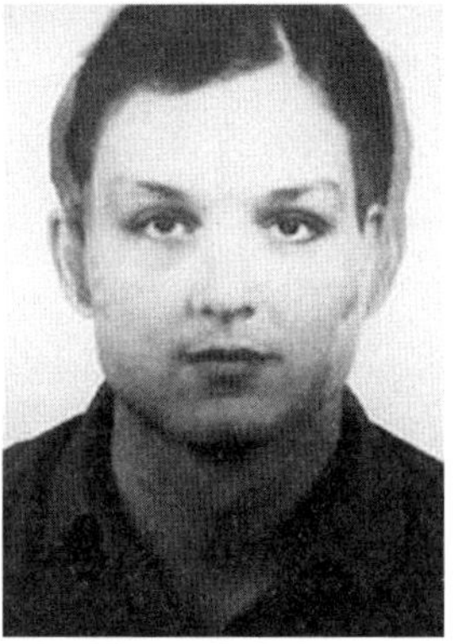

59b   Thomas Ruff, *Other Portrait no. 102/13*, 1995.

60   Winzer, 'A Credible Invention of Reality', p. 144.

two of his portraits into one and printed the new picture as a silkscreen on paper.[59]

Although Ruff shows the faces only frontally, the images remind us of Andy Warhol's series of 'Most Wanted Men'. Warhol used police photographs of most wanted criminals, showing these criminals in frontal and profile views. Ruff's composite images have a slight blur, some more than others. The combining of the images is visible, because they tend to not completely overlap. The slightly blurry effect makes emphatically clear that these faces are constructs without interiority. The faces rather look like masks, as 'something external stripped of all inwardness, a social interface to which the police have access, at an imaginary level at least'.[60] Although these blurry images show constructed masks without inwardness, identity, or referent, this kind of image of faces functions as social interfaces of which the police and other archival bureaucratic institutions make use.

With his *Other Portraits*, Ruff publicizes something that is as commonplace and unnoticed as it is invasive: the photograph's dispossession of the depicted person, something that happens covertly in every photograph. I know of no one who is happy with his/her photograph, no matter how much everyone else—family, school,

154

employer, state, other states—may require such a photograph.[61]

The blur in Ruff's *Other Portraits* can be seen as a resistance against this dispossession of the depicted person. The other's gaze at the portrayed person, mechanically bundled in the photographic eye, is not fully able to dispossess the person's visual identity. This gaze does not succeed completely in intruding in the sitter's self-image. Access to his inwardness is blocked due to the blur, revealing the image as constructed.

Poor Images and Exhibitionism

Ruff has not only taken on the genre of photographic portraiture, but also that of nude photography. The stakes of this generic exploration, or visual research, of a specific photographic practice are quite different. He was not interested in 'contemporary nude photography of the kind currently carried on by fashion photographers, who take supposedly interesting photographs of pretty models in some pleasant ambiance'.[62] Implicitly, Ruff seems to take distance from highly successful photographers like Helmut Newton. Instead, he did some research on the Internet and found there a whole market of

61 Ibid.

62 Susanne Leeb, 'Such-maschinen: Ein Interview von Susanne Leeb', *Texte zur Kunst* 36 (December 1999), p. 73.

63   Hito Steyerl, 'In Defense of the Poor Image' (2009), in *The Wretched of the Screen* (Berlin: Sternberg Press, 2012), pp. 31–45.

64   Ibid., p. 32.

pornographic images that interested him much more. He was especially interested in exploring the conditions under which that imagery is perceived.

The pornographic images that can be found on Internet are, to use the words of Hito Steyerl, 'poor images'.[63] She defines the poor image as follows:

> The poor image is a copy in motion. Its quality is bad, its resolution substandard. As it accelerates, it deteriorates. It is a ghost of an image, a preview, a thumbnail, an errant idea, an itinerant image distributed for free, squeezed through slow digital connections. Compressed, reproduced, ripped, remixed, as well as copied and pasted into other channels of distribution.[64]

Steyerl's description is not only a precise description of pornographic images on the internet, but also of Ruff's enlargements of them. Both are ghosts of images and poor in all respects. Ruff emphasized the poorness of the images by enlarging them to very large formats of sometimes 200 × 130 cm. The visible pixels create an overall blurred image. He explains why he produced these blurred images the way he did as follows:

> The screen resolution is 72 dpi, i.e., quite poor. If you enlarge such an image to the current size, a pixel would be 2 cm large. I had to think of

something … I started moving the pixels around. If you do that, the processor makes 36 wonderful smaller pixels out of one 2cm pixel, and I used this technique to get the images in this quality. I chose blurredness because the material is so ugly. It has to be reworked.[65]

The blurred condition of his images seems to have been required by the 'ugly' nature of pornography; however, it installs a specific mode of looking that is highly self-reflective. The description of the blurred effect of Monet's paintings of water lilies by Gottfried Boehm applies as well to the blurs in Thomas Ruff's pornographic images:

> The things we recognize cannot be separated from the fact of blurredness. The angle is 'dual' not because we perceive both 'things' and blurred pictorial elements. It is dual to the extent that everything that appears does so on the condition that it is blurred … The subject does not disappear, but its figuration is subject to delayed translation. [This] reflects the fact that the gaze has forfeited its naïve confidence in real facts … The fact of seeing cannot be subtracted from what is seen.[66]

Conventional pornography in photography and film relies always on two crucial components. First of all,

65   Brigitte Werneburg, 'An interview with Thomas Ruff', quoted in Winzer, 'A Credible Invention of Reality', pp. 149–150.

66   Gottfried Boehm, 'Strom ohne Ufer', quoted in Winzer, 'A Credible Invention of Reality', p. 150.

67 For a fundamental analysis of the function and effects of the screen, see Kaja Silverman's *The Threshold of the Visible World* (1996), especially the chapter 'The Screen' (pp. 195–227), about Cindy Sherman's photographs entitled *Film Stills*.

its reality effect. This explains why pornography is always realistic; sexual stimulation by means of modernist or postmodernist texts or images seems to be unconceivable. The other crucial element is the voyeuristic gaze it enables. The viewer is outside the scene that he looks at, belonging to another world. This voyeuristic positioning provides power and pleasure to the viewer. Both defining elements of pornography seem to be missing in the poor images of internet pornography, and even more so in the enhanced poor images of Thomas Ruff. The poor images function not like windows through which the viewer voyeuristically gazes at sexual action. They are rather opaque screens onto which the viewer can project his fantasy to be part of the scene he watches.[67] The poorness of the image is, I contend, an important precondition for this transformation of window into screen. I will argue this by the detour of another new medium: not photography, but the webcam. Although mostly producing moving instead of still images, the webcam excels in producing poor images. Only recent practices in the old 'new' medium of photography can be qualified as poor. Internet pornographic still images are a prime example.

The visual medium of the webcam is a small camera, which sends images to a computer connected to the internet. After this medium was introduced in the mid-1990s, it has become a standard apparatus in many studios, households, and bedrooms. I do not want to suggest that this medium has any essential function or specificity. Its medium specificity is only partly defined by its technical features and possibilities. It is also determined by how it is used by historical and cultural practices.[68] New media uses and practices tend to cause changes in the media landscape at large. A new medial practice can cause shifts in the functions and practices of other media. For example, the introduction of photography into the media landscape of the mid-nineteenth century has deprived painting of, or perhaps we should say liberated from, some of its functions. The same can be said of the webcam. The webcam has fulfilled some ideals which were earlier pursued by the video camera and longer ago by the film camera. The dream concerning one medium is realized in another, more recent medium. For many webcam users the ambition of a comprehensive representation of the world, spatially as well as temporally is finally fulfilled: 'The webcam makes possible the endless, unedited film, the eternal film.'[69]

The dream or ideal materialized by the webcam is not new at all. There are films and videos in which a similar practice is demonstrated. Andy Warhol's films *Sleep* (1963) and *Empire* (1964), and more recently, Bruce Nauman's video-installation

68 See for a discussion of medium specificity, Krauss, 'A Voyage on the North Sea', mentioned before.

69 The ways and contexts in which webcams are being used are many. Its first use is extremely simple as well as exemplary for most of its later uses. The very first webcam was used in 1993 in the department of computer science at the University of Cambridge for surveilling a coffeepot. In order not to walk in vain to the room where one could get coffee, the so-called 'Trojan room', and find there an empty pot, students installed this new apparatus to the pot and connected it to their computers so that they could check from their desk if there was any coffee left. Two years later they connected these images to the World Wide Web and the information was shared with millions of people. The fact that so many people watched these images was not motivated by what the images showed, but what they promised: a comprehensive representation of the world. Soon after, in 1996, Jennifer Ringley, a student from Pennsylvania, materialized part of the promise by showing on the Web images of her life at home in real time that were taken by a camera connected to her computer. Internet users could see everything she was doing: playing with her animals, sleeping, combing her hair, making love with her boyfriend, and so on. The stream of images was life, was unedited, and it was in real time. The webcam is used as lifecam. See Bianca Stigter, 'Staren naar een stuk kaas', *NRC Handelsblad*, 2 May 2008.

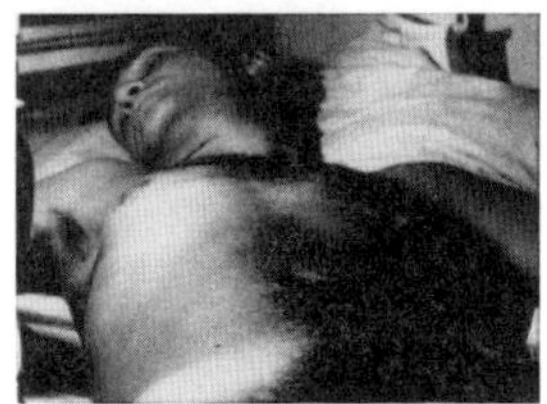

70a   Andy Warhol, *Sleep*, 1963, film still.

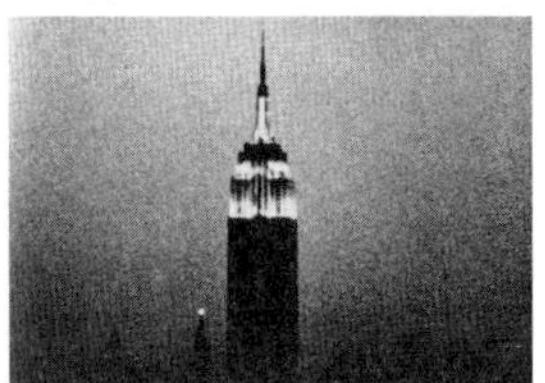

70b   Andy Warhol, *Empire State Building*, 1964, film still.

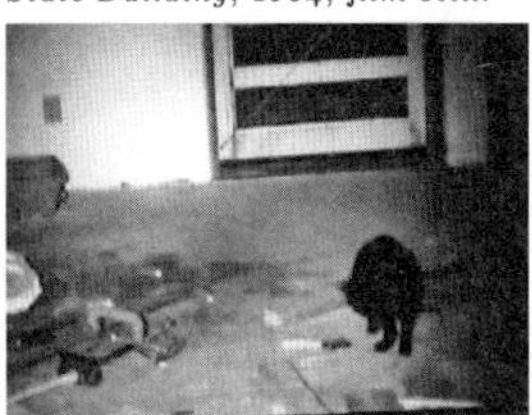

70c   Bruce Nauman, *Mapping the Studio—All Action Edit (Fat Chance John Cage)*, 2002, film still.

Mapping the Studio—All Action Edit (Fat Chance John Cage) (2002) are probably the most famous examples.[70] *Sleep* shows the poet John Giorno, Warhol's lover in those days, sleeping. He is filmed from a number of different angles and some shots are repeated. Although this film is not really, or not completely in real time, it creates the impression it is. In that respect, *Empire* is more radical. It consists of eight hours and six minutes of continuous real time black and white film of the Empire State Building, from early evening until nearly 3 AM the next day. In his video-installation, *Mapping the Studio*, Bruce Nauman records the nocturnal activity in the artist's studio of his cat and an infestation of mice during the summer of 2000. With seven projections and multiple audio tracks of ambient sound, Nauman used this traffic as a way of mapping the leftover parts and work areas of the last several years of other completed, unfinished, or discarded projects.

The webcam has given rise to a great variety of practical uses. Webcams are now focused on mountains so that you can see if there is enough snow on the ski run; on young children, so that the parents can see if they are still asleep; on roads, so that drivers know if there are traffic jams; on the person sitting at a computer, so that the person they are chatting with knows what they look like. The latter example demonstrates a fundamental change in visual technologies. The possibility of showing your interlocutor at the chat box what you look like is first of all used by friends and family members in order to enhance the connection and its intimacy. The speaking or writing of words is completed by showing the face that speaks them. This possibility is fully exploited in the sex industry. Thanks to the webcam, the client cannot just chat with the persons who are supposed to fulfil their sexual desires, but these persons also show themselves, or rather their face and body while talking with the client. This use of the webcam is so extraordinary because voyeurism, a crucial aspect of more traditional visual technologies, is now overshadowed by its complementary other: exhibitionism. This exhibitionism is not only exploited in the sex industry. Most webcam images shown on internet are utterly boring. Showing these images seems to be more important than seeing them. The transformation caused by the webcam is that for the first time there are now more people who want to be looked at than people who want to watch.

This change is not only exploited by the sex industry; it also seems to be its demise. There is less and less interest in professionally made porn films with professional porn actors. People who watch porn movies now prefer to watch amateur porn films shown on websites exclusively devoted to these webcam films. The fact that these films are clumsily

71   For a critical reading of pornography, see Linda Williams, *Hard Core: Power, Pleasure and the 'Frenzy of the Visible'* (Berkeley and Los Angeles: University of California Press, 1989).

made and that they usually do not show particularly attractive bodies appears not to be experienced as negative. The point is not *what* viewers are *seeing*, but *that* amateur actors are *showing*. It is the identification with these amateurs showing themselves, which makes watching them into an erotic experience, an experience which is more exciting than voyeuristically watching attractive bodies performing sexual acts. The boredom caused by so many webcam images shown on the Web, pornographic or not, also reveals the boring nature of pornographic film as such. It is only in the fulfilment of the dream of pornography in webcam images that we become aware of how boring pornographic images have always been. Its excitement is not to be located in what can be seen in these images, but in the fact that they are shown.[71] This difference is fundamental, because it displaces the nature of our relationship to these images from voyeuristic to exhibitionistic.

The attraction of pornographic and other webcam images is foremost produced by its strong reality effect. Their reality effect is, however, stronger and of a different nature than that produced by conventional film and photographic images (not poor but rich images) because, paradoxically, they are unedited and clumsily made. The fact that we are aware of the fact that these images were made, and by whom, and where, from which position, only makes the reality effect stronger, for the production of these images stems from real life, instead of from professional studios, where the production process can be made invisible.

In pre-new-media times, intimacy with people you did not know could only be experienced in art and in literature. In other words, we needed art and literature in order to be intimate with strangers. And when I use the term 'intimacy' I am not necessarily referring to sexual intimacy. I am using it to indicate a kind of relationship or contact in which we become aware of the most personal desires and anxieties of other people. By identifying with characters and situations in literature or art, we could share desires or anxieties of people we did not know. But this possibility offered by literature and art is conditioned by its fictionality. The webcam has taken over this possibility so far exclusively realized by art and literature. However, the way the webcam enables intimacy with people we do not know differs ontologically from the way art and literature do. As strong as the reality effects of art and literature can be, they are ultimately framed by their fictionality. The intimacy we can have with strangers via webcams is not with fictional persons. They are real even if they are role playing. They exist, although we do not know them. This increases the reality effect of the intimate 'encounters' with them.[72]

163

72 For an analysis of how webcams affect the relationship between private and public, self and other, see José van Dijck, *Mediated Memories: Personal Cultural Memory in the Digital Age* (Stanford University Press, 2007).

As I argued before, with the webcam there are, for the first time, more people who want to be looked at than people who want to look. Not only amateur pornography, but also the postings on Facebook of images of the dinner people are eating are another example of this strange phenomenon that is in fact a major cultural transformation. Viewers are not interested in seeing this, but the people who are posting it want to show it. When using the terms voyeurism and exhibitionism I am no longer applying it in the more limited erotic or pornographic sense as I did in my example of amateur pornography. I use it in a more general sense indicating a distinction between a passive consumerist attitude and a more active positioning. This can be erotic, but not necessarily so.

The viewer of these images is not looking for their meaning, but gets access to them by means of identification with the exhibitionistic impulse behind them. Watching them is less a matter of signifying transactions than of an event that one experiences directly or bodily. In the case of webcam images the affective process of identification leads to feelings of excitement, arousal or anxiety. This counters the affect of boredom produced on the level of significa-tion. The fact that many people continue to look at webcam images (besides in very practical situations of surveillance) should be understood in terms of the affects they produce and enable, not in terms of the shadows of meaning that they nevertheless offer. The poor images of pornography function not as windows through which the viewer voyeuristically gazes at sexual action. As in the case of Ruff they are rather literally opaque screens. The viewer can project his fantasy to be part of the scene he watches onto these screens. The poverty of the image is an important precondition for this transformation of window into screen.[73]

Thomas Ruff's series of pornographic images foreground the poorness of contemporary new media images, but, although found on the internet, they are not necessarily based on amateur pornography. Even if his images are taken from professional photographic images, they do not install a voyeuristic look, but an exhibitionist one. That is due to the poverty of the images, I contend. The poverty of Ruff's blurred images has the same effect as the clumsily made and unedited images of amateur pornography. As already argued, this increases the reality effect. It makes it stronger, for the production of these images stems from real life, instead of from professional studios. In the same way, the poverty of Ruff's images does not counter a reality effect, but contributes to it.

Viewers of his pornographic images see images and do not have the temporary illusion to see, and be present at, the intimacy of people having sex. But the

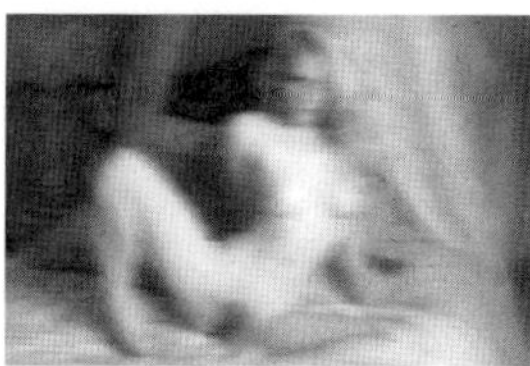

73a   Thomas Ruff, *Nudes cs02,* 2011.

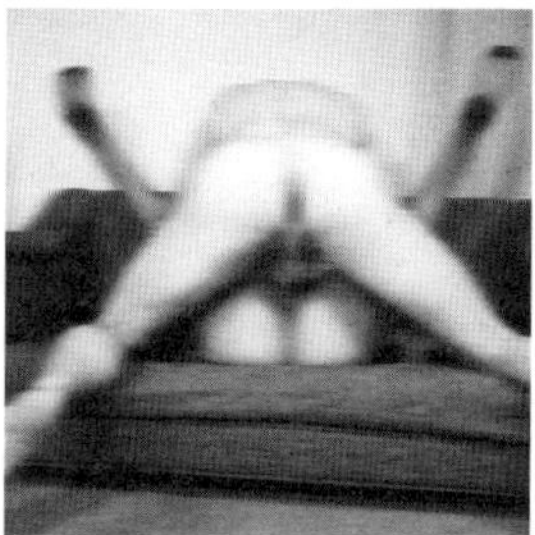

73b   Thomas Ruff, *Nudes vg02,* 2000.

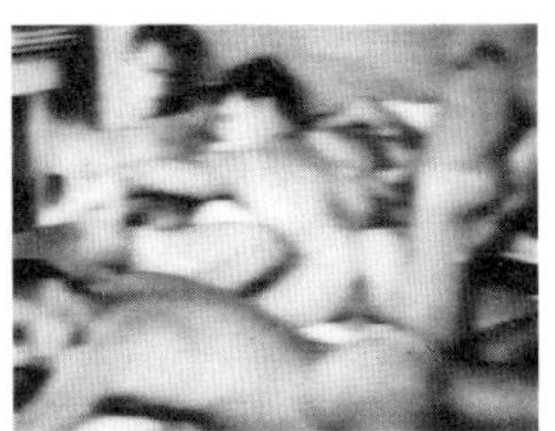

74a Thomas Ruff, *Nudes eb05*, 2003.

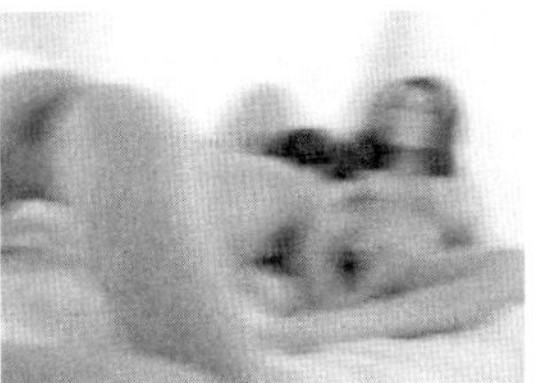

74b Thomas Ruff, *Nudes alo04*, 2001.

fact that they are looking at images does not undermine their pornographic effect. The pornographic effect of these images relies, however, on a different positioning of the viewer than conventional pornography, played by professional actors and resulting in 'rich' rather than poor images.

My reading seems to be confirmed by the very positive responses Ruff got to his new series. When his *Nudes* were shown for the first time in New York and Berlin in 2000 the responses were extremely enthusiastic, much more so than when he showed other series of photographs for the first time. He had never thought that people would be so positive about images presenting pornography as art. He was not sure what had spurred that enthusiasm. I contend, however, that the pornography affect of arousal was not at all decreased by the poverty of the images. Thanks to their poverty the viewers could identify with the exhibitionist subject position usually identified with the ugly poverty of amateur pornography. Under the guise of having an aesthetic experience, the viewers could now express their excitement openly and shamelessly.[74]

The blurred and poor nature of Ruff's nude photographs has in common with all the other blurred images discussed in this chapter that it refers to a condition of the photographic image and not of the referent. The specific, material condition of his nude

images enable and activate a specific mode of looking, an exhibitionistic one that is. But more generally, what a blurred condition of photographs brings
with it is very divers. It can activate a specific look,
but it can also evoke a specific temporality, namely a
temporality that is spectral. A spectral temporality of
the images can imply duration, as in the images by
Cameron, but it can also imply timelessness, as in
spirit photography. Whatever the temporality of a
blurred image is, it is always in opposition with the
temporality of the instantaneous. The spectrality of
blurred images can also have spatial ramifications, as
was the case in Francesca Woodman's images. The
figures in her images are not fully embodied by the
bodies they inhabit, which is expressed by ghostly
blurs. But whatever the condition of the image manifesting as blur does or means, blurred photographs
seem to be the result of a kind of spectral layering,
which provides its in-between condition, ontologically, phenomenologically, or temporally.

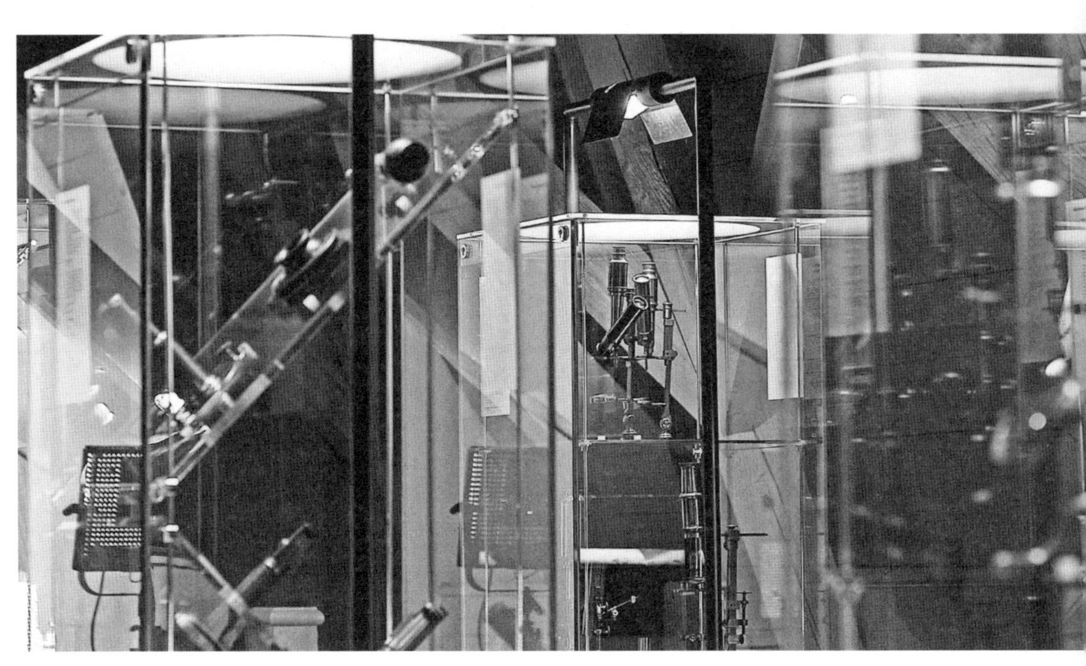

Roos Theuws, *Kitab al Manazir*
(Book of Optics), 2013–2014.

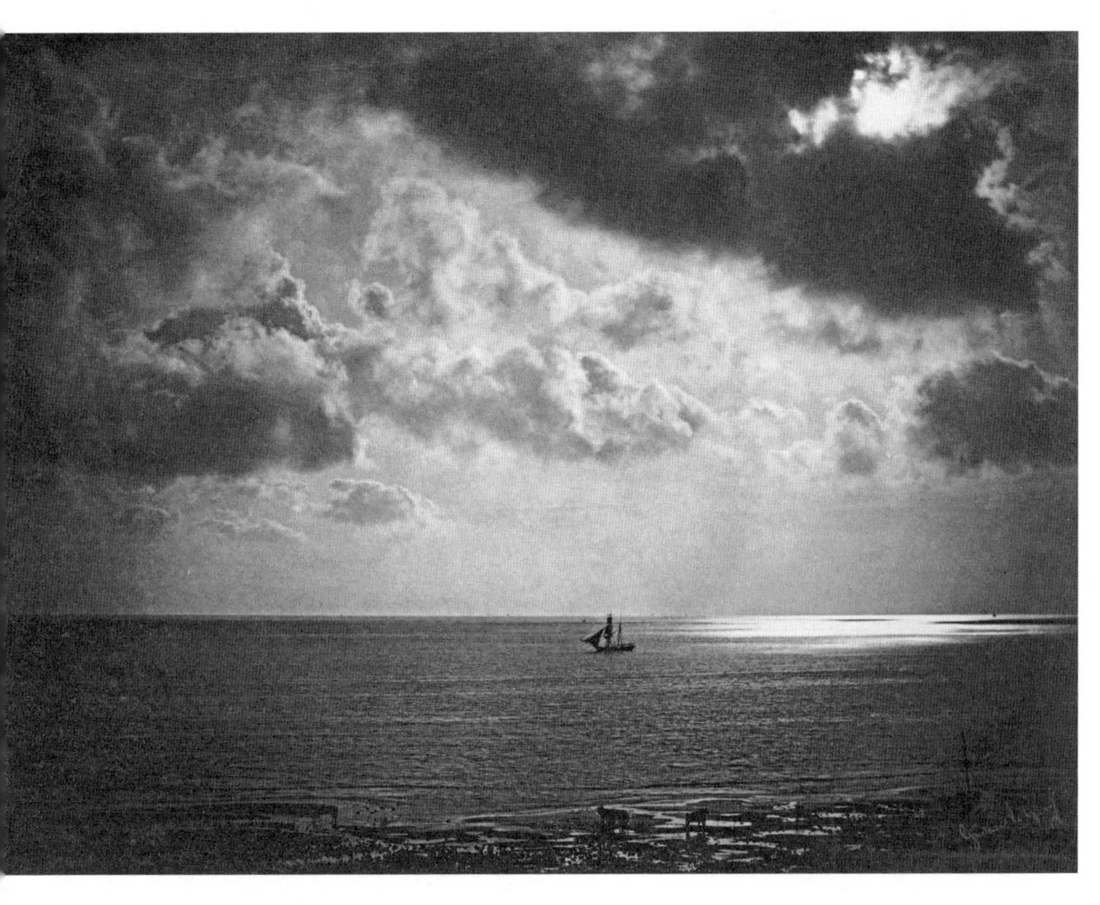

Gustave Le Gray, *The Brig on
the Water*, 1856.

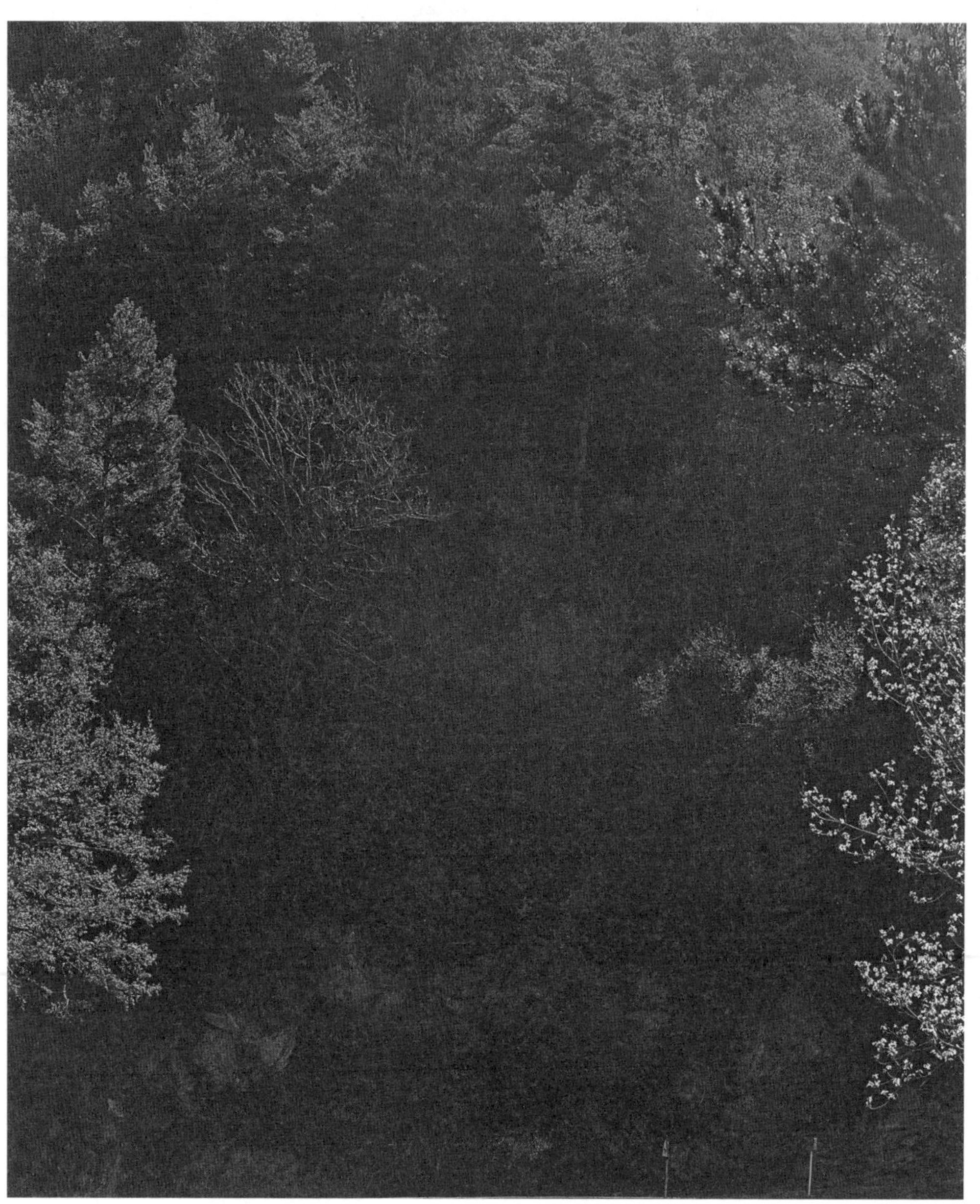

Awoiska van der Molen, *#274-5*,
2013.

Under- and
Over-exposed Images

When God created the heavens and the earth, the first distinction he made was the one between light and darkness. That's how the story goes according to Genesis 1. Only after God made this distinction the other distinctions could come about, such as the one between water and air (heaven), and sea and land. This is the order of events, because only after the differentiation between light and darkness has been made can the other distinctions become visible and, in their visibility, become real. When there is too much light, visibility suddenly dissolves into blindness. When there is not enough light, visibility returns to darkness, in other words, to invisibility.

Not only the creation of the world but also that of the photographic image depends on light and on the differentiation of light and darkness for its existence. Exposure to light is the precondition for the

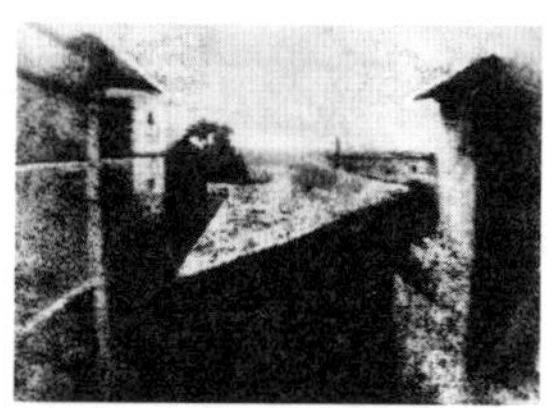

1   Joseph Nicéphore Niépce, *View from the Window at Le Gras*, c. 1826.

2   Joseph Nicéphore Niépce, 'Memoire on the Heliograph', in *Classic Essays on Photography*, ed. Alan Trachtenberg (New Haven: Leete's Island Books, 1980), p. 5.

photographic image to come about. Over- and under-exposure puts the photographic image at risk. Being exposed to too much or too little light exposes the image *qua* image. It makes us see what the constitutive element of the image is and that its substance is light. Light is not only photography's substance, however; it is also the agent at work in the process that photography is, and which results in the photographic image. In the cases of over- and under-exposure, the agency of light can result in blindness or darkness. But rays of light can also be reflected or deflected, not showing a scene or an object; just light as such. Then, light does not just enable the image, but becomes the image: in such cases, light shows itself 'self-reflexively' as the substance of photography.

In his 'Memoire on the Heliograph', Joseph Nicéphore Niépce, by many regarded as the inventor of photography (in spite of the claims of Hippolyte Bayard, who staged his own suicide out of misrecognition), clearly held the action of light responsible for the automatic creation of images:[1]

The invention which I made and to which I gave the name 'heliography' consists in the automatic reproduction, by the action of light, with their graduations of tones from black to white, of the images obtained in the camera obscura.[2]

Significantly, he derives the name for his technique from the sun (*helios* in Greek). The resulting image is described as an 'automatic reproduction' not because there is no agency involved, but because human intentionality and agency are reduced to an absolute minimum. The agency at work is the action of light. He describes this agency in great detail as bringing about an interaction with the chemicals exposed to it:

> Light in the state of combination or decomposition reacts chemically on various substances. It is absorbed by them, combines with them, and imparts to them new properties. It augments the natural density of some substances, it even solidifies them and renders them more or less insoluble, according to the duration or intensity of its action.[3]

The action of light is not only described as the creator of the image. After it has done that, it continues its agency and ultimately destroys the image again. Its interaction with the chemicals should be fixated in order to prevent that destruction. Niépce's invention partly consists of a varnish he developed of 'a solution of bitumen of Judea in Dippel's animal oil'. Due to the animal oil, which dries rapidly, the image solidifies. After the plate has been coated with this varnish it can be exposed to light again.

3   Ibid., p. 5.

173

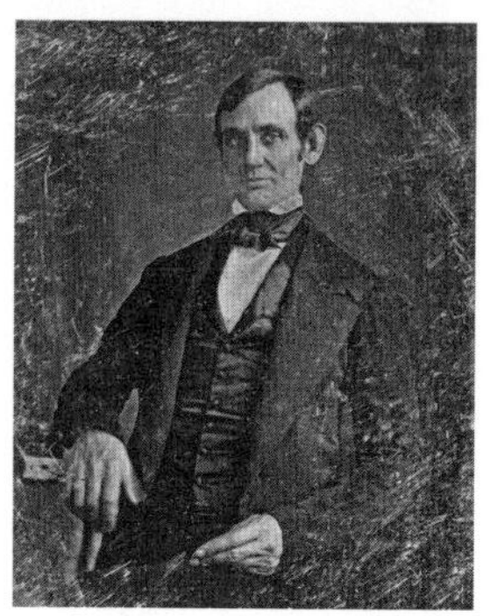

4   Nicholas Sheperd, *Daguer-rotype of Abraham Lincoln*, 1846.

5   Louis Jacques Mandé Daguerre, 'Daguerreotype', in *Classic Essays on Photography*, ed. Alan Trachtenberg (New Haven: Leete's Island Books, 1980), p. 12; emphasis in text.

Daguerre's improvement of Niépce's invention concerned the sharpness of the image, the graduation of tones and the perfection of details, but especially its rapidity, which entails that it requires a much shorter exposure to the action of light.[4] In the description of his invention, Daguerre claims that the difference in its sensitivity to light as compared with Niépce's process is as 1 to 70, and compared with chloride of silver, it is as 1 to 120. 'In order to obtain a perfect image of nature only *three to thirty minutes at the most* are necessary, according to the season in which one operates and the degree of intensity of the light.'[5] Daguerre's improvement of the photographic process demonstrates that the agency of light is difficult to manage. When the exposure to light's agency takes a long time, it reduces the sharpness of the image. In the case of portraits, sitters are not able to stay immobile for such a long time, as we have seen in chapter Two; in the case of landscape or architectural scenes shadows are not stable and will move when the position of the sun changes. According to Daguerre, the photographic process should ideally not take longer than three minutes, 'so that the shadows in nature should not have time to alter their position'. The agency of light is not only at work in interaction with the chemicals on the plate, but also in the world that the photographic plate tries to capture and fixate.

Daguerre's invention was successful in handling the action of light in three respects. First of all, the sensitivity of the substance of the daguerreotype plate was so high, that it even responded to the feeblest light rays. Second, also because of the plate's sensitivity, the whole process took less time than Niépce's process. In his report of the Commission of the Chamber of Deputies charged with the examination of a proposed bill granting Daguerre and Niépce's son an annual life pension for turning over their photographic process to the French state, Dominique Arago describes the advantages of the increased rapidity as follows:

> The rapidity of the method has probably astonished the public more than anything else. In fact, scarcely ten or twelve minutes are required for photographing a monument, a section of a town, or a scene, even in dull, winter weather. In summer sunlight the time of exposure can be reduced to half. In the southern climate two to three minutes will certainly be sufficient.[6]

The third respect in which Daguerre's invention improved photography concerned, however, the destructive agency of light. Thanks to the fixation of the image, the effect of sunlight on the finished pictures does not diminish, even after years, either 'their purity, their brilliancy, or their harmony'. 'Nature's

6   Dominique François Arago, 'Report', in *Classic Essays on Photography*, ed. Alan Trachtenberg (New Haven: Leete's Island Books, 1980), p. 19.

7   Ibid., p. 18.

8   Lady Elizabeth Eastlake, 'Photography', *London Quarterly Review* (1857), pp. 442–468; reprinted in *Classic Essays on Photography*, ed. Alan Trachtenberg (New Haven: Leete's Island Books, 1980), p. 57.

most subtle pencil, the light ray', seems to have been effectively disciplined by Daguerre's invention.[7] The creative as well as the destructive agency of light is channelled into directions that enable Nature to make images of itself without the help of human intentionality.

Already in a very early account of photography, from 1857, Lady Elizabeth Eastlake refers to the mythical story of the creation of the world in Genesis I as analogous to the agency of light in photography. She describes how rays of light create order and make the creation of images visible. But she also argues that the kind of image that the agency of light enables differs from how the human eye encounters the visible world:

> … our only purpose is to point out that the defects or irregularities of photography are as inherent in the laws of Nature as its existence being coincident with the first created all things. The prepared paper or plate which we put into the camera may be compared to a chaos, without form and void, on which the merest glance of the sun's rays calls up image after image till the fair creation stands revealed.[8]

Lady Eastlake explains at length the difficulties of managing the agency of light. Whereas the God of Genesis seemed to have had no problems in

176

mobilizing light in the creation of the earth, the deployment of light in the creation of photographic images is more difficult to handle.

The first problem of 'photographic action' arises in the interaction of rays of light with the paper and the chemicals in and on which the images are supposed to come about. The murky atmosphere of London with its temperate skies establishes very good conditions for this interaction. In general, cloudy days are better than sunny ones. 'Contrary, indeed, to all preconceived ideas, experience proves that the brighter the sky that shines above the camera the more tardy the action within it. Italy and Malta do their work slower than Paris.'[9] Eastlake explains that under the brilliant light of a Mexican sun, half an hour is required to produce effects which in England would occupy but a minute.

Another problem is caused by the fact that the whole spectrum of light rays does not have the same agency. Some light rays affect the sensitive plate or paper faster than others.

> It had long been known that this power, whatever it may be termed—energia—actinism— resided more strongly, or was perhaps less obstructed, in some of the coloured rays of the spectrum than in others—that solutions of silver and other sensitive surfaces were sooner

9 Ibid., p. 56.

10   Ibid.
11   Ibid., p. 57.
12   Ibid.

darkened in the violet and the blue than in the yellow and red portions of the prismatic spectrum.[10]

The varieties of light rays all have their own agency and this results in images in which the relations between the different graduations of black and grey are incongruous with the colour relations of the scenes or objects of which the image is taken. The relation of one colour to another is found changed and often reversed. She gives the example of the deepest blue being altered from a dark mass into a light one, and the one most golden-yellow from a light body into a dark one.[11]

Eastlake's account of photography provides a very accurate description of the paradoxical agency of light in photography. Light rays are described as the agents that bring the photographic image into existence. But the same light rays are also responsible for the 'failure' of photography in making 'correct copies'. 'It is obvious, therefore, that however successful photography may be in the closest imitation of light and shadow, it fails, and must fail, in the rendering of true chiaroscuro, or the true imitation of light and dark.'[12]

I am struck by the verb 'fail', as well as by the standard of chiaroscuro. Eastlake reminds her readers that Nature is not made up of lights and shadows. Nature consists of innumerable reflected lights and half-tones, which play around every object, softening the hardest edges. In the photographic image,

> [Nature's] strong shadows swallow up all timid lights within them, as her blazing lights obliterate all intrusive halftones across them; and thus strong contrasts are produced, which, so far from being true to Nature, it seems one of Nature's most beautiful provisions to prevent.[13]

Especially skies are difficult to photograph in early photography. Clouds in the sky dissolve in the photographic image and they form one monochromatic unity, as if the sky was a sheer blue or monotonous grey. Depending on the photographic process clouds become monochromatic dark or light. One solution was to combine different negatives for one single print. French photographer Gustave Le Gray (1820–1884), well known for his seascapes with dramatic skies, is reputed to have photographed the sky and the sea independent from each other, and then combining the two negatives. The resulting print does not show traces of the different exposure times needed for sea and sky.[14]

From the start, then, photography struggled with the agency of light. The visibility in which light resulted was not self-evident; the effects of light in

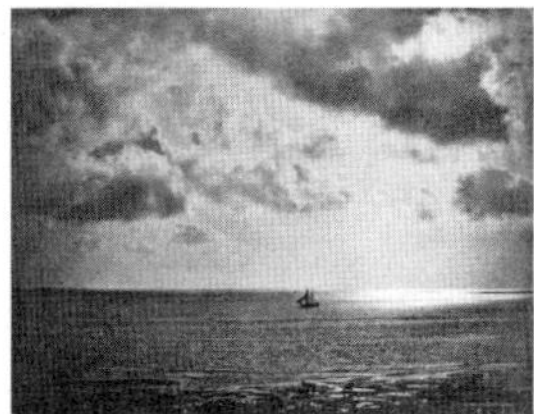

14   Gustave Le Gray, *Brig on the Water*, 1856.

179

the photographic image could be different from how light rays worked in the real world. Although photographic technologies developed rapidly and Daguerre's invention seemed to have improved it in important ways, the management of light rays continued to be one of the major problems of the medium.

Painting with Light

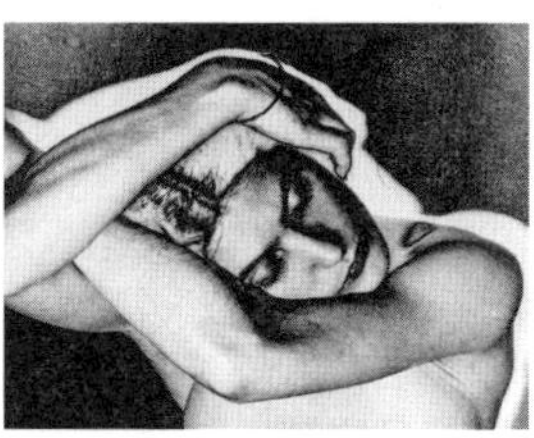

15a Man Ray, *Solarisation,* 1931.

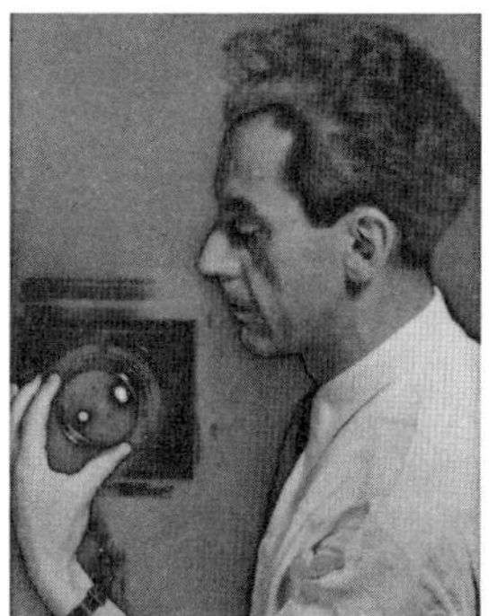

15b Man Ray, *Solarised Self-Portrait with Camera,* 1932.

As the term already suggests, overexposure to light is usually seen as negative. But a surrealist artist like the American Man Ray was able to control overexposure in the form of solarisation in such a way that he created artistic, painterly effects with it. Solarisation is a kind of overexposure that goes back to the first half of the nineteenth century. The term was first used by John William Draper in 1840 to denote the chemical change that partially transforms a negative into a positive image when the negative is subjected to a short exposure to light during development. A different term for the same process was introduced forty years later in France by the scientist Armand Sabatier; there it is called the Sabatier effect. Man Ray saw the first solarised image in the United States before he moved to Paris around 1919, when his mentor Stieglitz had discarded a photograph which he considered to be ruined by overexposure.[15]

In 1928 an accident happened to Man Ray's lover of that moment, photographer Lee Miller, which resulted in Man Ray's further exploration of the process and effect of solarisation. I will quote a long passage on how Miller recalled this accidental discovery, because it provides an adequate account of the effects of overexposure and the necessity to control light in order to transform its destructive potential into something positive:

> Something crawled across my foot in the darkroom and I let out a yell and turned on the light. I never did find out what it was, a mouse or what. Then I quickly realized that the film was totally exposed: there in the development tanks, ready to be taken out, were a dozen practically fully developed negatives of a nude against a black background. Man Ray grabbed them, put them in the hypo and looked at them, the unexposed parts of the negative, which had been the black background, had been exposed by his sharp light that had been turned on and they had developed and came right up to the edge of the white, nude body. … It was all very well my making that one accidental discovery, but then Man had to set about how to control it and make it come exactly the way he wanted to each time.[16]

16 Lee Miller, 'My Man Ray', *Art in America* May–June 1975, pp. 56–57.

17 Man Ray, quoted in Arturo Schwarz, 'Man Ray: The Wizard of Light', in exh. cat. *Man Ray: Photographs and Objects* (Birmingham AL: Birmingham Museum of Art 1980), p. 10.

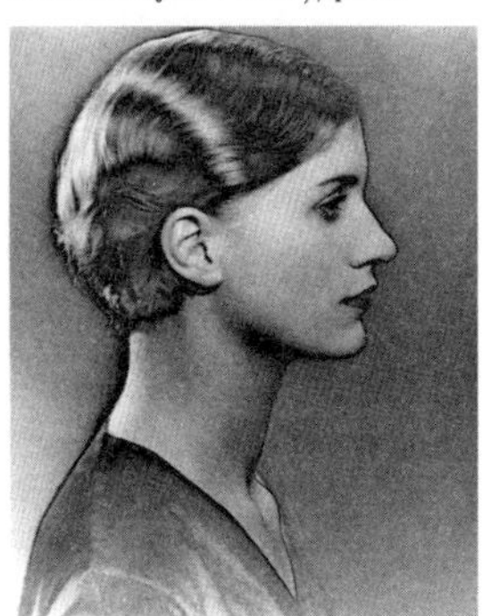

18a Man Ray, *Solarised Portrait Lee Miller*, 1929.

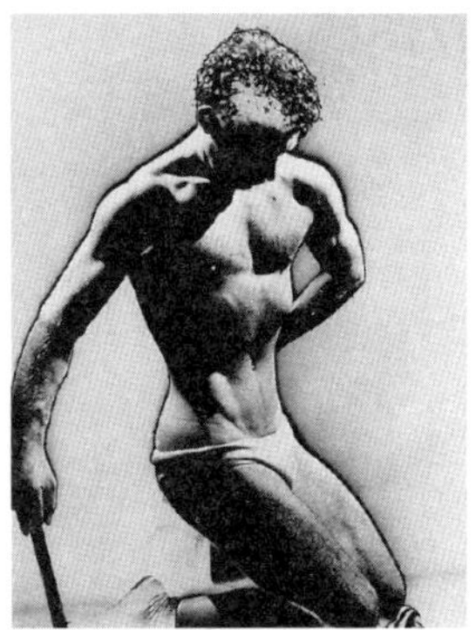

18b Man Ray, *Solarised Male Body*, 1933.

This accident was a crucial moment in Ray's development as photographer. He deployed the overexposure of solarisation to make images that were not showing the world but showed the image as image. Countering the transparency of the photographic image he transformed that image into the equivalent of painting or drawing. Ray remarked about his motivation to control solarisation as follows:

> I was trying to master, to dominate, the technical side of photography to explore new areas. The technique in itself was not important to me, I was interested only in the result; the technique enabled me to get away from photography, to get away from banality, what I seek above all is to escape from banality, and here was a chance to produce a photograph that would not look like a photograph.[17]

Ray made solarised portraits of Miller (1929), Breton (1928–1929), Duchamp (1930), Braque (1930) and himself (1930). The portraits look as if an electromagnetic field surrounds the heads and bodies.[18] The contours are accentuated by a black line as in drawing. The solarised images of nudes, especially female nudes, but also some male nudes have light effects that are even more dramatic. One can notice a partial reversal of values on these photographs, accompanied by a remarkable edging. Not only are

182

the contours of the bodies accentuated by black
lines, but due to solarisation, the contrast between
light and dark areas is intensified. According to Ray,
solarisation gave him the opportunity to use light as
a painter uses his pigments. As a result, critics assign
to his solarised portraits and nudes qualities that are
usually exclusively seen as inherent in painting or
the artistic, and not in photography. Ray is considered as not only achieving a physical portrait of his
subjects, but also a psychological one.[19] Although
this kind of distinction between art and photography
is highly problematic and conventional, it is useful in
this case because it demonstrates how the overexposure of solarisation enables us to see the visibility of
the image instead of the visibility of the world it
shows.

Ray's success as a surrealist artist was also established by his deployment of double exposure. This
technique is the overlaying of two negatives, usually
in the enlarger but in some cases in the camera at the
moment of the shot. This technique makes it possible to add movement or relief to the image, but also
the illusion of another dimension. Ray used double
exposure very often. His most famous double
exposed image is probably *Marquise Casati* from
1922.[20] The image shows a woman staring straight
into the camera with doubled eyes. The double-
exposure results in a blurred, dreamy double-vision

183

19   See Schwarz, *Man Ray:
Photographs and Objects*, p. 11.

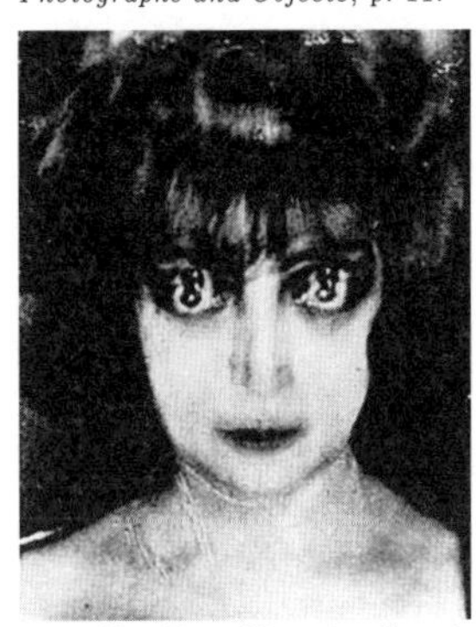

20   Man Ray, *Marquise Casati*,
1922.

of the woman. This reflects back on the viewer, whose desire for the woman can be recognized in the image also serving as mirror. The image is like a jarring two-way mirror in which both desired subject and desiring viewer reflect each other.

Ray deployed light in yet a completely different way in what he called, probably punning on 'rays (of light)' and his own name, 'rayographs'. These photographic images were made without a camera. He described the process of rayography as the 'direct impression of luminous rays that create pure inventions, a technique of a precision that painting cannot attain'. At first, he placed objects directly on sheets of photo paper. A reverse image was obtained after the paper was developed in the normal way. But then he began to vary both the distance of the object from the sensitive material and the distance and position of the light sources.

In fact, Ray's rayographs are examples of photograms. As explained earlier, a photogram is a photographic image made without a camera by placing objects directly onto the surface of a light-sensitive material such as photographic paper and then exposing it to light. This results in a negative shadow image showing variations in tone depending upon the transparency of the objects used. The parts of the paper that have received no light appear white and those exposed through transparent or semi-transparent objects appear grey. Some of the first photographic images made were photograms. William Henry Fox Talbot called them 'photogenic drawings'. His images of lace in *The Pencil of Nature* are examples of this. He made them by placing leaves and objects on sensitized paper.[21] But because the sensitivity was still poor at that time, he had to put the paper outdoors on a sunny day for exposure. But also the well-known 'cyanotypes' by English photographer Anna Atkins are photograms. She made use of Sir John Herschel's cyanotype process, yielding blue images. In 1843 she published cyanotypes of botanical specimens in the first book to be illustrated with photographs, titled *British Algae: Cyanotype Impressions*.[22]

What makes Ray's rayographs different from other photograms is the effects he created by varying the distance from the objects to the paper and varying the distance of the light source to the objects.[23] Also his unusual juxtapositions of identifiable objects, such as film rolls, spoons, combs, hands, or pearl necklaces, create striking images of a world of objects. For the surrealists Ray's rayographs were not recordings but transmutations of the object world. The images are unexpected creations instead of representations. In 1923, the poet Robert Desnos wrote the following about Ray's rayographs:

185

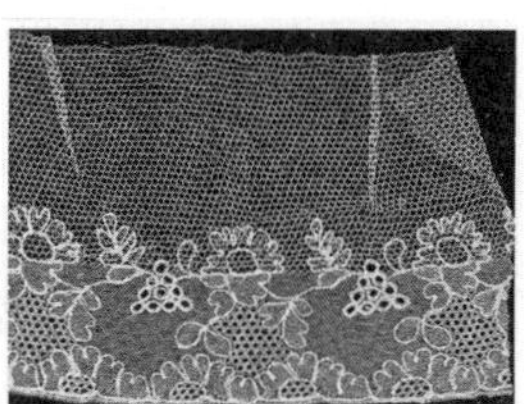

21a   William Henry Fox Talbot, *The Pencil of Nature*, 1844, Plate XX, 'Lace'.

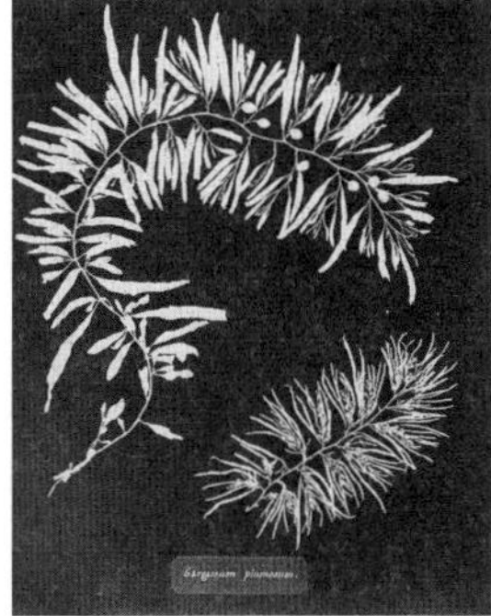

21b   Anna Atkins, page from *British Algae: Cyanotype Impressions*, 1843.

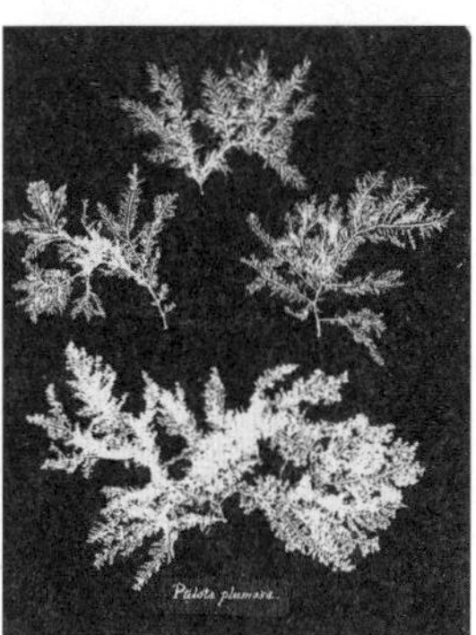

22a   Anna Atkins, *Ptilota Plumosa*, 1843.

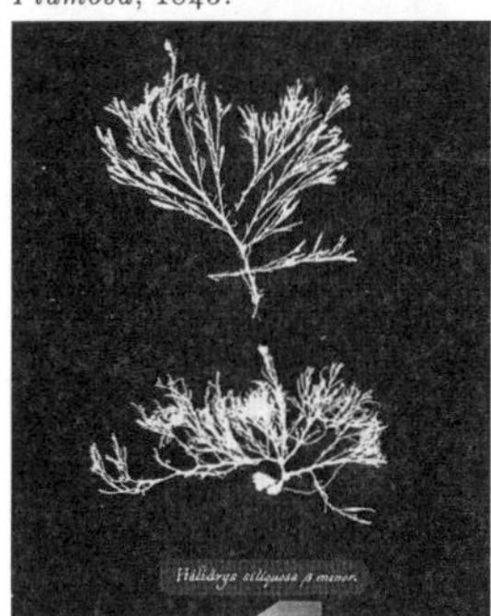

22b   Anna Atkins, *Halydrys Siliquosa*, 1843–44. Plate 19 from Volume 1 of *Photographs of British Algae, Cyanotype Impression*, n.d.

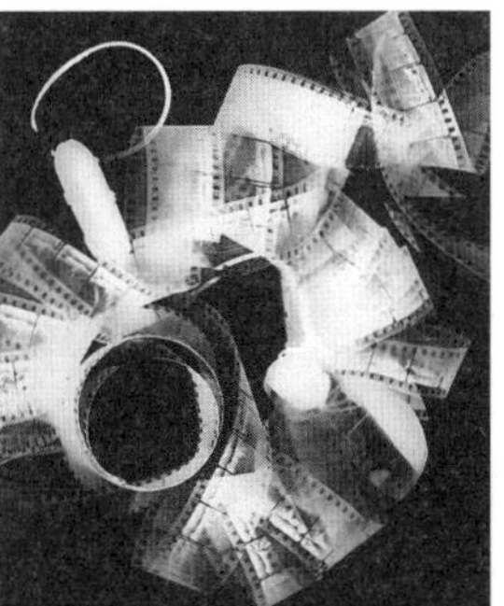

23b   Man Ray, *Rayograph*, 1923.

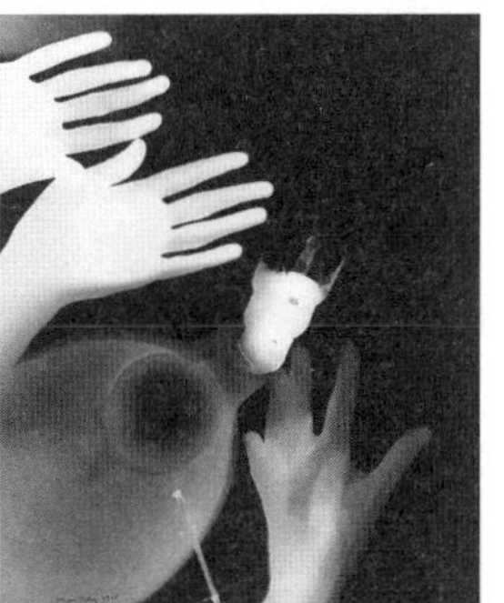

23a   Man Ray, *Rayograph*, 1925.

24   Robert Desnos, 'The Work of Man Ray', *Transition* 15 (February 1929), p. 265.

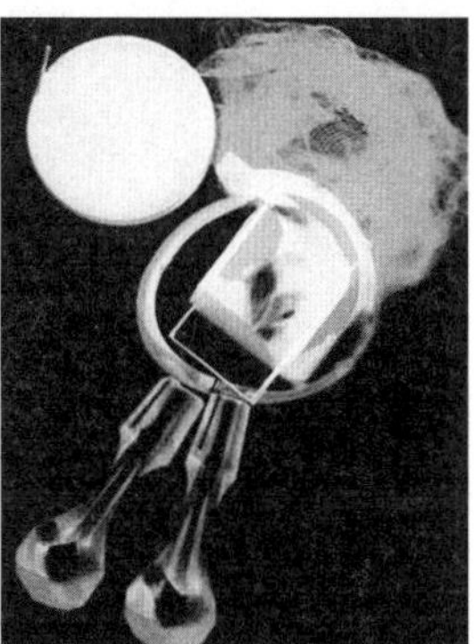

25a   Man Ray, *Rayograph*, 1922.

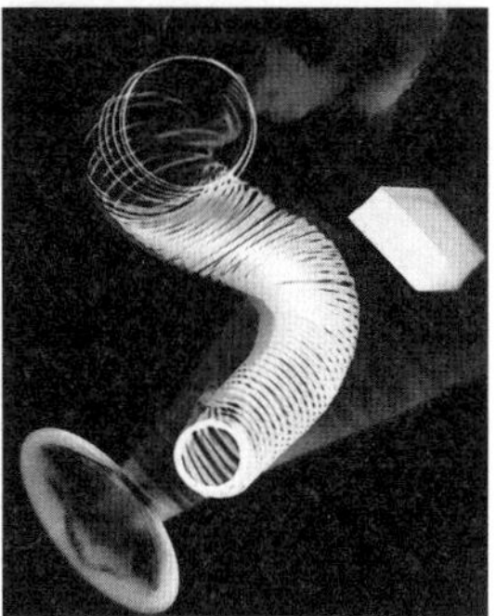

25b   Man Ray, *Untitled Rayograph*, 1922.

There does not yet exist a word to designate Man Ray's invention, these abstract photographs in which he makes the sun's specter take part in adventurous constructions. As children we used to silhouette our hands on citrate paper exposed to the sun. From this simple process he has proceeded to create landscapes foreign to our planet, revealing a chaos more astonishing than any envisaged by a Bible: here the miracle lets itself be captured without resistance, and something else besides leaves its anguishing mark on the revelatory paper.[24]

In Desnos' comment of Ray's images, the agency of light takes the form of the sun's spectre, which is presented as the agent of creation.[25] The creation of light is more astonishing than the creation in Genesis 1, because light is not the pre-condition of the photographic image, but its creator. The paradox of the 'awesome miracle' allowing to be captured and the qualifier 'anguishing' suggest an eerie mix of admiration and hesitation.

At the same time when Man Ray was making his rayographs, the Hungarian artist László Moholy-Nagy was making photograms, which at first sight are very similar. He made many of these photograms with the assistance of his wife Lucia Moholy-Nagy, who was a professional photographer. An important difference, however, is that in the rayographs of Ray light is used to highlight clearly defined objects. Moholy-Nagy makes abstract spatial impressions by means of objectless light forms. We see light as light on a black ground; the light forms objectless spatial forms. These spatial forms seem to float. The fact that we do not see objects illuminated by light but abstract light forms, purifies light from its material support in the service of representation. As a consequence, we see light directly as light instead of indirectly through what it illuminates.[26]

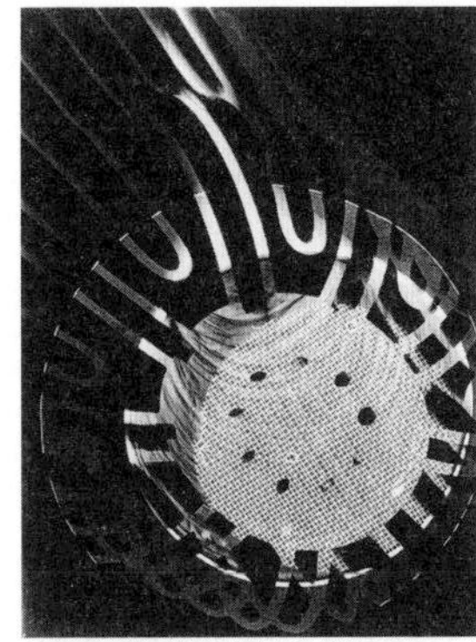

26a   László Moholy-Nagy, *Photogram*, 1923.

Moholy-Nagy photograms are the results of the formation of light and shadow, produced solely by a process of lighting. The lighting consists of placing objects and light-absorbing materials under fluid light rays. The result is a differentiated blackening of the light-sensitive paper. Whereas Ray usually worked with only one light source, Moholy-Nagy at times used several moving light sources so that shadows continuously passed over the paper. Several stages of lighting were involved in the making of a single image. He described his deployment of light as follows:

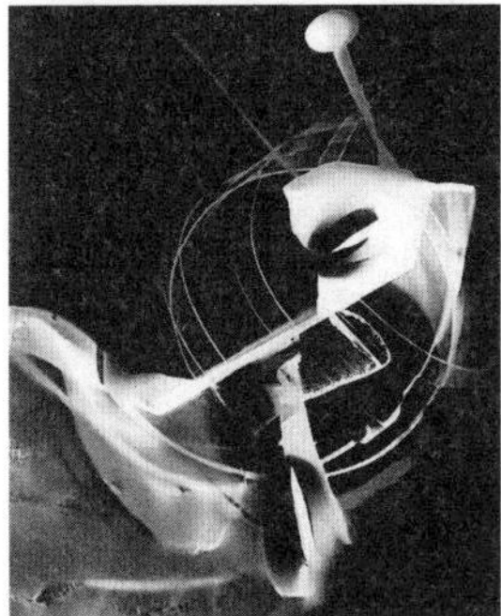

26b   László Moholy-Nagy, *Photogram*, 1940.

> A small quantity of white is capable of keeping in balance by its activity large areas of the deepest black, and it is less a question of form than one of the quantity, direction, and the positional

27   Moholy-Nagy, quoted by Andreas Haus, 'The Manipulation of Light and the "New Vision"', in *Moholy-Nagy: Photographs and Photograms* (New York: Pantheon Books, 1980), p. 17.

relationships of particular manifestations of light. … The light-sensitive layer—plate or paper— is a tabula rasa, a blank page on which one may make notes with light just as the painter working on his canvas uses, in a sovereign manner, his tools, brush and pigment.[27]

In contrast with photography on the basis of negatives, in photograms the light exposure results in blackness. The more light, the deeper the blackness. Only where overlaid material absorbs the light will light forms become visible. The spatial 'nothingness' or emptiness in Moholy-Nagy's photograms are the (over-)exposed areas, where the agency of light has been at work.

Spotting Light

In several respects the photographs of contemporary Belgian artist Dirk Braeckman look amateurish or even failed. The reasons why they look failed all concern formal procedures. Many of his images are muffled with a dull grey haziness. They contain a slight blur that covers the whole image. This muffled quality is not ghostly, but rather suggesting the quality of poor images. Furthermore, they tend to be very frontal. Whereas, due to its inherent embodiment of linear perspective, the photographic image usually contains a perfect illusion of depth, this quality is not at all turned to good use here. Their frontality does not allow the viewers to enter the spaces to which they are invited. Or better, these images are not really inviting, also because of the kind of depressing spaces they show but grant no access to.[28] They look like the rooms in run-down hotels in which one wants to spend as little time as possible. These rooms were once chic, but now they are examples of bad taste and look cheap. The rooms remind one of the kind of hotels in European cities near railway stations, where prostitutes meet their clients. Braeckman's images with female figures or parts of their bodies also suggest situations of prostitution. The women look extremely vulnerable, unhealthy and cheap.[29]

A third formal element causing unease in the viewer is the way Braeckman frames his images. According to philosopher and critic Frank Vande Veire, in Braeckman's images framing appears 'to be mainly a negative gesture. He cuts away rather than focuses'. The cut-off framing gives the impression of being arbitrary, 'because there is nothing about the selected view that can claim any particular attention or fascination, not even for its banality or tasteless-ness, which never tends to the bizarre'.[30] Insignificant objects, such as curtains, carpets, chairs are

189

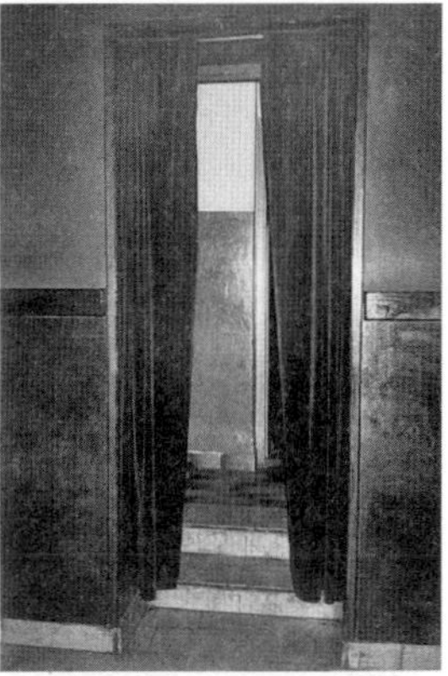

28a   Dirk Braeckman, *B.O.-D.U.00*, 2004.

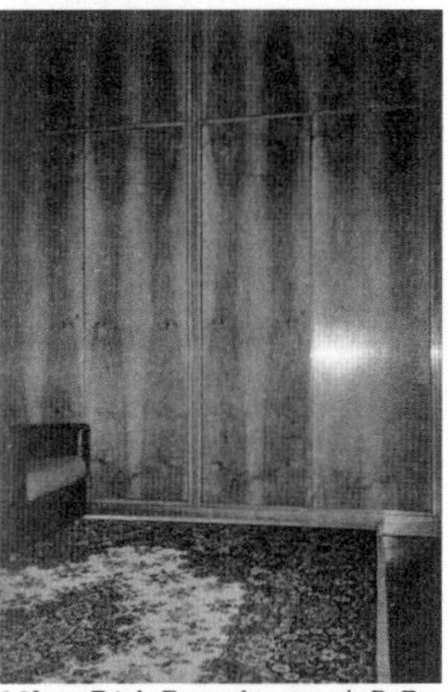

28b   Dirk Braeckman, *A.D.F.-S.B.2-03*, 2003.

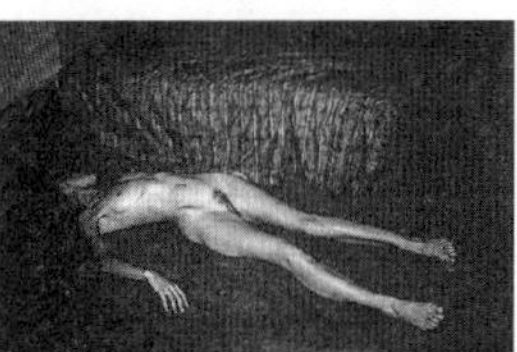

29a   Dirk Braeckman, *Vladivostok. Model#7-07*, 2007.

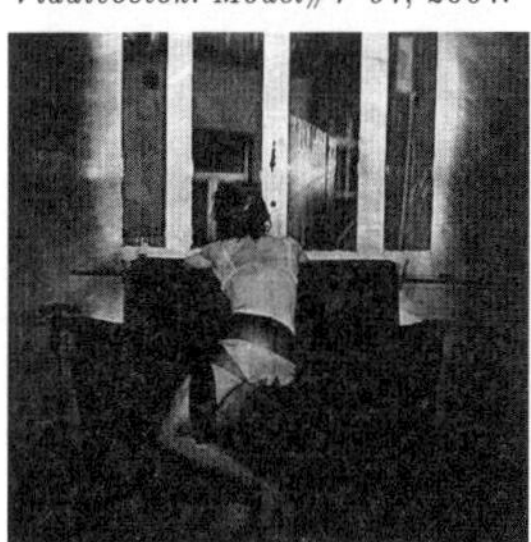

29b   Dirk Braeckman, *Angèle-Bxlles Nord*, 1988.

30   Frank Vande Veire, 'Blind Auto-Reflexivity: Dirk Braeckman's Light on Photography', *A-Prior* Spring/Summer 2002, p. 47.

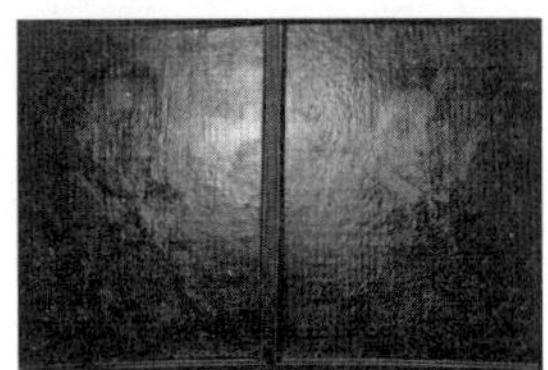

31a   Dirk Braeckman, *S.B.–G.E.–97*, 1997.

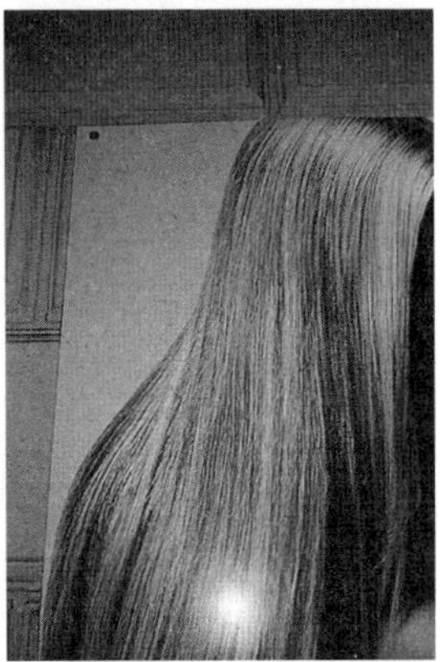

31b   Dirk Braeckman, *K.L.–D.K.–12*, 2012.

not framed as still lives closed in on themselves. The framing does not make these insignificant objects significant. It makes it difficult to understand where the attraction of Braeckman's images comes from.

Braeckman's images also contain many so-called 'doublings'. He takes images of photographs, of paintings, or even of a photograph of a painting. These doublings are also very frontal, having almost no depth at all. And like most of his other images they are awkwardly framed. All the formal elements that make his images seem failed come together in these doublings. Of course, taking an image of another image appears to be a self-reflexive gesture. But what are these images reflecting on? Like his other images, Braeckman's doublings contain reflections of light. In the double image below, what is striking is that the two paintings are photographed by one single light source. What binds them is less the portrait format than the large, overwhelming stain of light that makes them near-invisible.[31]

He takes his photographs with flashlight. In the spots of light visible on furniture, curtains, wood panelling, coverlet, hair, bodies, but also on the photographed images, the photographic act exposes itself. We see this act in the reflected flash. The flash is supposed to illuminate the photographed space, object or figure. But it fails to do this when it reflects back on itself. In the image of the double portrait this is the case in the most radical way. The two portrayed figures are almost invisible. The reflected flash light shows the photographic act instead of the figures this act was supposed to show. Symmetrically, the other photograph of a single photograph, of a woman's head with long hair shows the failed illumination twice, and in a subtler way. The photographed image shows a soft reflection of light on the hair of the female figure. But in addition, Braeckman's photograph of this photograph has a strong spot of light, explicitly unmasking the photographic act catching it in the act instead of the world it was supposed to catch. In the words of Vande Veire:

> The glints of the flash on a sofa, a table leg, the painting of a mountain and a frosted glass window are all stuck there motionless, like a sick spot in the image, a spot where the image displays a kind of burn hole where it wishes to realize itself with its greatest intensity. The light at this spot is doing exactly the opposite of what it should do: making itself invisible, spreading itself unseen over the surface of the objects and gently pushing through. The light implodes. It drops dead against the subject as if against a wall and just lies there like a squashed eye, something

dead glistening, enclosed in the rigidity of the photograph.[32]

The spots of light that drop dead against the surface of objects, of skin, of hair, are the blind spots of the photographic medium where the agency of light reflects itself instead of the world. There is the sense that all lighting, illumination and enlightenment is ultimately in vain, a failure, because not able to break out of its own narcissistic desire to expose itself. Braeckman spots light in the form of spots of light, in those moments when light exposes itself, and in its failure to illuminate. It is in this failure that photography as a medium can no longer pretend to be transparent.

The spotting of light happens when the flash is reflected and deflected on surfaces. In the photograph of the photograph of the woman's hair both alleged accidents happen. It is then that the photographic act becomes visible as a self-reflexive act. When this act exposes itself, it shows who or what the agent of photography is. For, 'the photographic act' is an ambiguous term. We tend to see the photographer who presses the button of the camera as the agent performing the photographic act. And when it is not the photographer who is seen as the agent, it is the camera as technological agent. But Braeckman's self-reflections do not expose the photographer, nor the camera; instead, they expose light as the performing agent. It is the agency of light that becomes visible in the form of the flash's reflection.

Light Exposed/Time Exposed

Hiroshi Sugimoto, whose work was already discussed in an earlier chapter for his allegorical series of dioramas and wax museums, and for the series of photographs of modernist architecture, became first known by his series of Theatres. Although yet another series, the one of his seascapes, is known under the title *Time Exposed,* his *Theatres* can be seen as allegories of photographic exposure to light in time, and as a result of visibility, with invisibility as a result. The series consists of frontal images of old movie theatres with the screen in the middle of the stage. The screens attract our attention as the proverbial windows on the world. But all screens are blinding white. The screens are empty; nothing is visible on them or through them. The light that radiates from the screens illuminates the baroque frames around the screens and the theatre spaces in which they are situated.

Nothing is visible on the screens because they are overexposed. They have been exposed to

193

33   Hans Belting, *Looking through Duchamp's Door: Art and Perspective in the Work of Duchamp, Sugimoto, Jeff Wall* (Cologne: Walther König, 2009), p. 92.

moving images during the entire length of a feature film's projection. The exposure time of Sugimoto's camera was as long as the length of the film. Whereas normally the screen as such is not visible because covered with the projection of moving images, it is now filled up with accumulated light present in the film's storyline of about one and a half hour. The accumulated light reflects on the surrounding space. The visible room emerges from the light of an invisible film. The agency of light is shown in its duality. The screen is blank and blinding because of overexposure. But due to that overexposure and the resulting white screen, the surrounding space becomes visible. In a situation of regular exposure to light that space would remain invisible.

Although the film inside the camera was exposed to light for a long time, it was not able to register the moving images that were constituted by that light. The moving images were emptied and a blinding white light emanating from the photographed screen is the result. Film has given birth to a photograph. In the words of Belting: 'The camera's rigid mechanics annul all of the images that have been run through before our eyes during the length of the film and produce only a "photograph" in its etymological sense: an image of pure light.'[33] Watching a film, but also looking at a photograph, we do not see the light itself, but images enabled by light. Sugimoto's photographs of theatres reveal what we cannot see: the light that enables images, moving images or photographic images. The time of exposure is placed in the light. His *Theatres* are in that respect exhibitions of time, as well as exhibitions of light.[34]

In his introduction to Sugimoto's book *Theatres*, Hans Belting wonders if the time unit of a film has become invisible in the photograph of it or whether it has adopted a transformation of its visibility:

> The time event, as is the movie, dissolves into a space where many sediments of time remembered are buried in a simultaneous view. A photograph of the usual kind arrests time or cuts out a time fraction never to happen again. Sugimoto seems to have done something similar, which yet secretly indicates a stern opposition to any photographers' confidence in grasping time.[35]

The simple idea of grasping time, as in snapshot photography, is complicated by a situation in which not a single moment but the entire length of a film is caught. Although this is a long time, it is not the same as unspecified duration; it still concerns time as event, even though linearly stretched out. But by stretching the event out over a long period of time, it becomes clear that time cannot be grasped: the spatial screen shows nothing and is instead blinding. The dimensions of time and space have dissolved

195

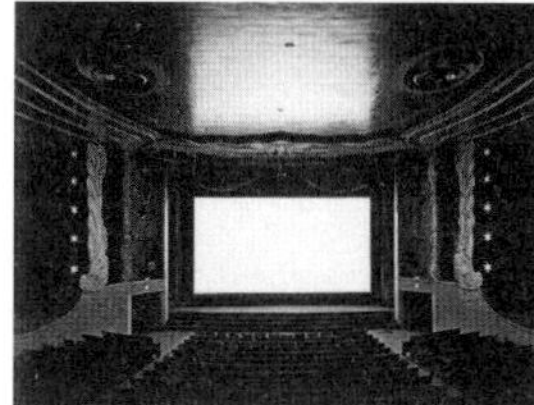

34a   Hiroshi Sugimoto, *Orinda Theater, Orinda*, 1992.

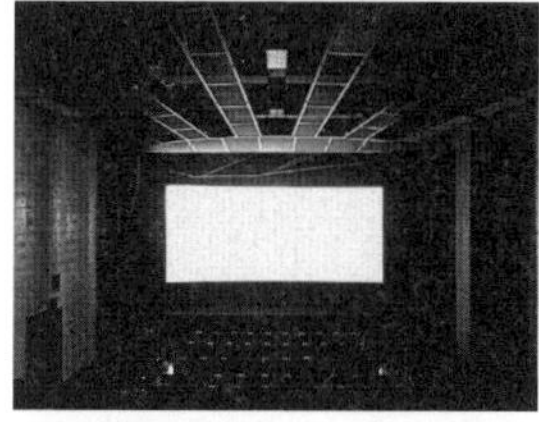

34b   Hiroshi Sugimoto, *Cinema Rise, Tokyo*, 1996.

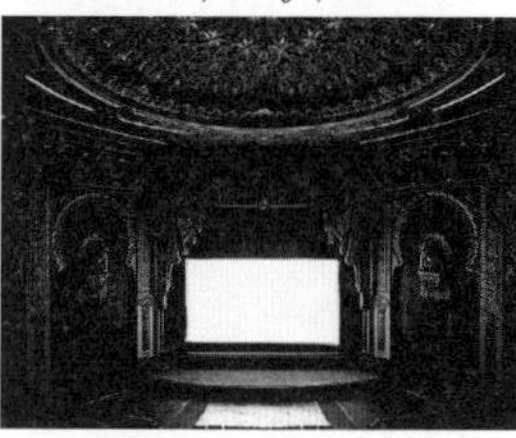

34c   Hiroshi Sugimoto, *Alhambra, San Francisco*, 1992.

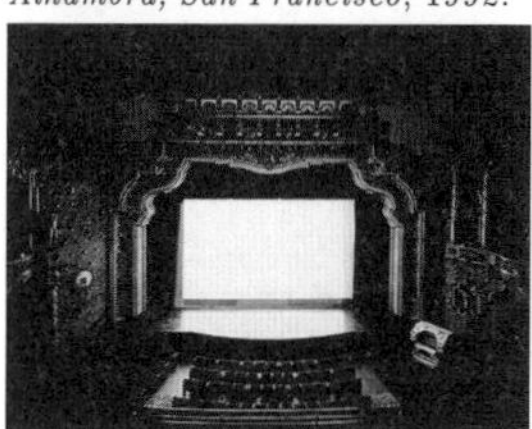

34d   Hiroshi Sugimoto, *Carpenter Center, Richmond*, 1993.

35   Hans Belting, 'The Theater of Illusion', in *Theaters: Hiroshi Sugimoto* (New York: Sonnabend, 2000), p. 10.

into each other. Due to this dissolution of time into space, Sugimoto's *Theatres* can be seen as depictions of time.

The agency of light is conditioned by the length of exposure time. But time is not only light's condition; conversely, light also works as the condition of time. The different temporalities of photography and film demonstrate the agency of light in time. This is so because the temporality associated with the photographic image differs from the temporality experienced while watching moving images. The time that is embodied by the photographic image is past time, the moment that is no longer; the theatres are old and obsolete. The spatial illusion we are confronted with in the image is at the same time a confrontation with the past tense. The time illusion of film, however, is present time. What we see on the screen seems to be happening at the moment we are looking at it; they are living images or images seen in real time. But both temporalities, the one of past time and the one of present time, merge and dissolve in the white screen.

The empty screens in Sugimoto's *Theatres* also function as allegories of 'all possible images whose illusion is wanted and needed'.[36] In that respect, the dark theatres resemble our minds, which continually produce and replace images of vision, of memory and of the imagination. Our minds are the theatres of

196

moving images, which, in their virtuality are full and empty at the same time. When we read Sugimoto's *Theatres* as allegories of exposure, it is exposure to light, to time, but also to the activity of the mind and the imagination.[37]

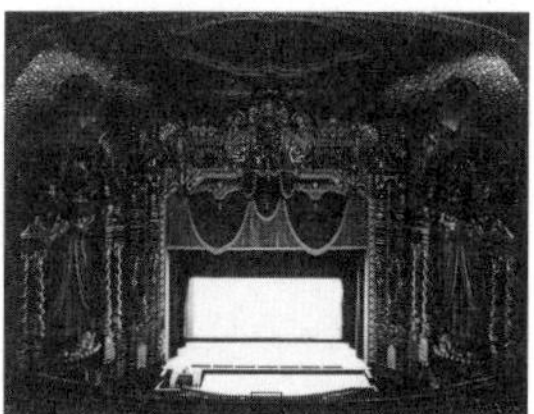

37a   Hiroshi Sugimoto, *Canton Palace, Ohio*, 1980.

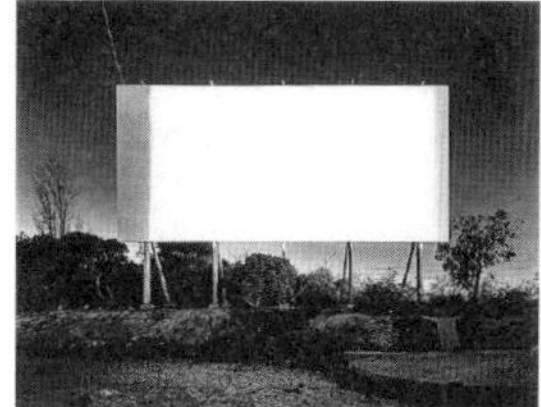

37b   Hiroshi Sugimoto, *Drive-In*, 1993.

Chiaroscuro Revisited

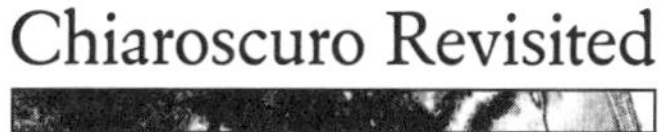

We have seen the peculiar use of the term chiaroscuro in Lady Eastlake's text. In black-and-white photography, strong tonal contrast between light and dark is also called chiaroscuro. This is a mainstay that determines how the viewer gets access to the presented illusionistic space. Chiaroscuro models and shapes forms so that they make a three-dimensional impression, because three-dimensional volume of form is best achieved by light falling against it. Chiaroscuro uses light to model forms by means of a value graduation of white to grey and black and a division of light and shadow shapes. Images in which chiaroscuro is at play usually show gradual transitions between light and dark. It is the distribution of light and darkness that makes forms and shapes come forward or recede backwards. The most common use of this kind of distribution of light is the contrast between a well-lit object or figure and a very dark background. In painting and drawing

197

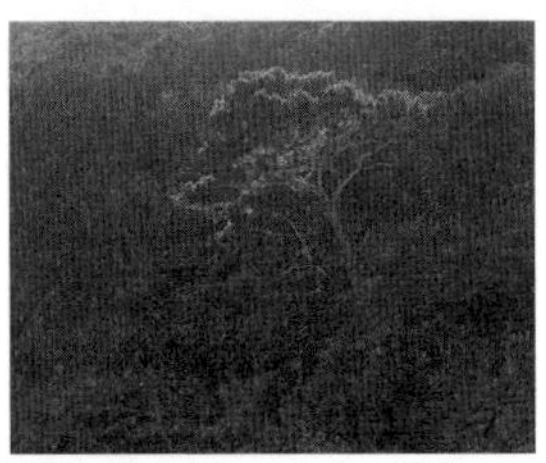

38a Awoiska van der Molen,
#367–7, 2013.

38b Awoiska van der Molen,
#312–11, 2011.

chiaroscuro is a specific technique deployed to create dramatic effects. In photography, one may use it as an artificial technique comparable to its deployment in painting and drawing. The photographer then uses lamps to illuminate and to create shadows. Yet, because of the fact that in photography light is not an added effect but its agent and medium, one can also say that chiaroscuro is a basic potential characteristic of photography that is either embraced or not.

In the images of Dutch photographer Awoiska van der Molen, the distribution of light by chiaroscuro is used in puzzling, unconventional ways. Her work consists of landscapes in which no trace of human habitation or activity is visible. We see again and again landscapes with mountains, trees, leaves, or stones. The landscapes, sometimes taken during the night or early morning, are made with slow shutter speeds of almost fifteen minutes. What all of her photographs have in common is their fundamental uneventfulness. Her images are in that respect the radical opposite of snapshot photography, which has built its reputation by the catching of an event or situation. The lack of events and specific moments seems to be combined with the spaces she selects for her photographs: landscapes. The presented landscapes are never the background or context for an event or narrative. Even the cyclical temporality of the seasons is not evoked by her landscapes.[38]

The term landscape refers to a space in the external world as well as to a representation of it. In the latter meaning landscape is a genre within figurative art. In the former meaning landscape is a material reality designed by and for humans. This ambiguity is not a coincidence but utterly significant. In the words of Mieke Bal:

> The term landscape indicates a humanized relationship to nature, whether this relationship is one of dominion, of self-affirmation through the conquest of nature, or, on the contrary, a desire to transcend and efface the self in the face of nature, as what we call since Kant 'the sublime'. Both attitudes spring from a fundamental discontentment with the limitations of human embodied existence. Attempts to separate the two appearances of landscape—as outside and as representation—are themselves imbricated in such conceptions, in either the attitude just mentioned or in the paradox of their coexistence.[39]

The translation of space by photographic technology seems at first sight a mechanical translation of nature into culture. The ordering that takes place through the optical lens is by definition that of linear perspective. The landscapes made by Van der Molen by means of her camera seem to be consistently immune for this mechanical translation, however. The

39 Mieke Bal, 'Timely Remains', in exh. cat. *Jussi Niva: Timely Remains* (Helsinki: Parvs Publishing, 2010), p. 89.

199

familiar ordering according to the principles of linear perspective has no grip on it. There are no trees or figures in the foreground via which the viewer can enter the image, no clear lines that lead the viewer into the depth of the image. Like the term landscape, which does not allow a clear distinction between nature and culture, Van der Molen's landscapes seem to annul this distinction. In the case of her so-called 'landscapes' we seem to be confronted with real, pure nature, at least at first sight. For no human or technological ordering of it has taken place.

Western culture knows two traditional *topoi* that locate nature outside culture. Both are evoked by Van der Molen's landscapes. The first one is that of the biblical paradise, the Garden of Eden, the place of pure nature because guilt does not yet exist. The second one is the Kantian idea of the sublime as experience that is post-cultural.[40] When man is located with his back to civilization eye to eye with wild oceans or steep mountains, he has an experience that is supposed to be outside the familiar possibilities of representation. We call such an experience sublime.

The landscapes of Van der Molen are a combination of these two extremes of allegedly pure nature. They are like paradise but also like the sublime, because they look most like how we imagine nature must have looked right after the creation. The creation of the heavens and earth, invoked at the beginning of this chapter as described in Genesis 1, took several days. God made distinctions between light and darkness, between sea and land. It is clear that it was a heavy job for God to make these distinctions. Again and again, there were moments of rest and contemplation at which he looked back at what he had just created. The famous words: 'And God saw that it was good' return like a refrain as a closure of busy days on which a lot of work has been done. In all of her images, Van der Molen's landscapes seem to represent this moment of rest after a process of creation. The uneventfulness of her images and the rather undefined temporal dimension, between day and night, contribute to this effect. It always concerns a transition, a moment of rest within an overwhelming process. What we then see, or what we look back at is like paradise because it is untouched. The term 'Garden of Eden' is, however, not really appropriate, because her landscapes do not know the ordering that gardens have. Paradise only becomes a Garden of Eden on the sixth day, the day on which God created man and woman. Van der Molen shows paradise only in its sublime state, which means during the first five days of creation.[41]

The distinction between light and darkness that God made is an absolute distinction. It distinguishes

41a Awoiska van der Molen, #274-5, 2011.

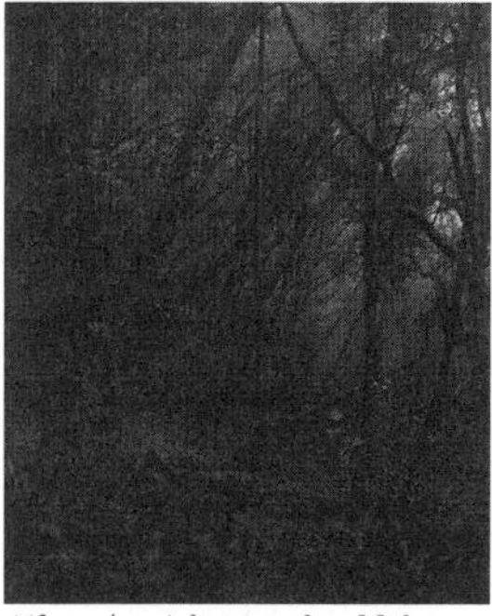

41b Awoiska van der Molen, #343-18, 2013.

day from night. His distinction does not acknowledge any gradual differentiation of light and darkness, no real gradual transition or distribution of light and darkness, no shimmering twilight, dim or semi-darkness. In short, no chiaroscuro. Most of Van der Molen's landscapes are the result of long exposure times: they are taken during the night or early morning with long exposure times of sometimes fifteen minutes. In spite of this, they are mostly very dark. There are spots of light in them, but these areas of light do not distribute light around them. In the image of a forested valley, the valley itself is veiled in deep darkness. All we see are individual leaves enlightened by the scant sunlight. But these rays of sunlight on the leaves do not reflect. They do not illuminate the surrounding space. In this respect, Van Der Molen's images differ in a fundamental way from Sugimoto's Theatres, in which the light that radiates from the screens illuminates the frames around the screens and the theatre spaces in which they are situated. Another image of a dense forest only shows some traces of light behind and in-between the branches and trunks. This visibility of the image depends completely on the contrast of light and darkness without any value modulation of light.

Although belonging to very different genres, the landscape images of Van der Molen have in common with the interiors of Braeckman that they are not inviting. With Braeckman's photographs one is faced with spaces without being admitted to them. Van der Molen's landscapes do not enclose; they keep the spectator at a distance. Like Braeckman's interiors, Van der Molen's landscapes are usually not presented from a special, oblique angle; they are presented frontally. This frontal view on most of the landscapes blocks access to them. As argued earlier à propos of Braeckman, linear perspective is not effectively utilized in these landscapes either, which explains the fact that the viewer is not invited into her worlds of creation. As a result of not taking advantage of linear perspective, the spaces of these landscapes cannot be itemized or measured. They remain distant and in a certain way they become almost abstract.

The images show worlds as if they have recently been created, worlds we can only look at from a distance. This is a statement about nature and the world, but also about photography. By reducing chiaroscuro to its most basic principle, namely the contrasting of light and darkness, photography too is deconstructed into its most elementary constituents. Even in those images that are relatively light compared to most of her images, the light does not reflect or illuminate. Instead, light absorbs light.[42] Light is not shown as the agent and enabler of an illuminated world. This was the case in the early accounts of

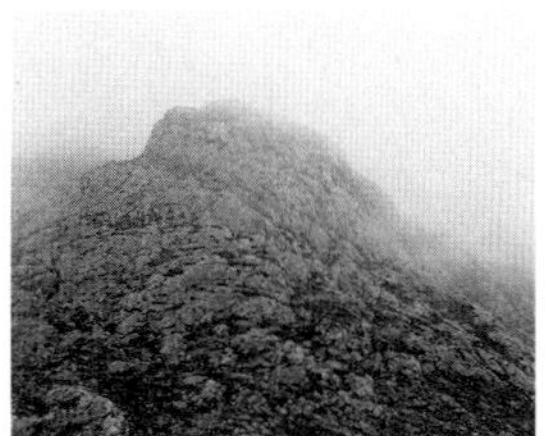

42a   Awoiska van der Molen, *311–16*, 2011.

42b   Awoiska van der Molen, *336–12*, 2012.

photography, discussed at the beginning of this chapter. It is shown in its sheer materiality, as the stuff out of which photography and the world are made. Light, then, is no longer just the agent of photography. In Van der Molen's images light absorbs light, feeds cannibalistically on itself. The Janus-head of light is shown in her work: not only agency, but at the same time the matter out if which the image is created.

Slow Seeing and Reflecting Images

43   Dubois, 'Photography Mise-en-Film', p. 20.

In the introduction, I quoted Philippe Dubois who argued that an oblique perspective on a medium, meaning seeing it in light of another medium, is the most effective way of understanding the specificity of a medium. Let me quote him again:

> I think we have never been in a better position to approach a given visual medium by imagining it in light of another, through another, in another, by another, or like another. Such an oblique, off-center vision can frequently offer a better opening onto what lies at the heart of the system. … We might begin with this simple idea: that the best lens on photography will be found outside photography.[43]

Although I fully agree with Dubois, I decided at that point not to follow his advice and not to focus outside the medium of photography for reflections on photography, but to focus on the other within: on alternative photographic practices not acknowledged by the dominant approach, or by the snapshot. However, to conclude this chapter I will bring in an outside perspective from another medium: I will discuss the video installation *Kitab al Manazir* (2014) by Dutch artist Roos Theuws as a reflection on the photographic image and of the processes that enable that image.

In the range of sensory experiences pain occupies a unique position, because pain can be experienced without any referential object. We can feel pain without being aware of what it is that causes the pain. In this respect, the visual sense seems to be the opposite of pain. The experience of visuality only emerges in contact with a visual object. Without such an object, without something we see, we don't see anything. Elaine Scarry opposes the two senses as follows: 'Physical pain is an intentional state without an intentional object; imagining is an intentional object without an experienceable state.'[44] In the work of Roos Theuws, however, visual experience is challenged in such a way that it becomes itself a state or process that we can experience or look at. The vision we have seems to turn inwards and as a result we see

44 Elaine Scarry, *The Body in Pain: The Making and Unmaking of the World* (Oxford: Oxford University Press, 1985), p. 164.

45   The video installation *Kitab al Manazir* was exhibited in Gallery Slewe in Amsterdam from 19 April until 17 May 2014.

not only images but also the technical and bodily processes from which these images result. This vision-turned-inwards provides insights into the photographic image.

Her video installation *Kitab al Manazir* is a prime example of a dissection of the photographic image and of the processes that enable that image.[45] Its title *Kitab al Manazir* is Arabic, which stands for The Book of Optics. Although this text was originally written in Persian, in the video work it is recited in Arabic. This is a seven-volume treatise on optics written in the tenth century by the medieval Arab scholar Ibn al-Haytham, known in the West as Alhazen. The *Book of Optics* presented experimentally founded arguments against the then widely held 'extramission theory' of vision, as proposed by Euclid in his *Optica,* and in favour of an 'intromission theory'. This now accepted theory, also supported by Aristotle, argues that vision takes place by light entering the eye. Alhazen's work transformed the way in which light and vision were understood, earning him the title of the 'father of modern optics'.

The video installation consists of three monitor screens of the same size, but placed on different walls. The three screens present different positions within the same space: a room in the Science Museum Boerhaave in Leiden. All the objects displayed in this room are optical objects and instruments. As we can expect in a conventional science museum, the room is packed with those objects and instruments, and many of them are placed in vitrines. In each of the three different videos the camera moves slowly through this space along a straight line. The viewer is aware of the camera movement, although it is a very slow one.[46]

In each video one object especially draws our attention: a mirroring sphere, which reminds us of the well-known round mirror in Jan van Eyck's Portrait of Giovanni Arnolfini and his wife from 1434. In this painting the round mirror is placed centrally in the middle of the composition between Arnolfini and his wife on the most remote wall of the interior space of the painting. The composition of this painting is organized on the basis of the principles of linear perspective. Within this structure the round mirror functions as the vanishing point but also points back at us, as we see an image reflected in the mirror. In Roos Theuws' video images it is not immediately clear if the mirroring sphere also functions as a vanishing point. Although it attracts the attention of the viewer because our gaze is led into the direction of this object, it is not obvious that all the other optical objects are visually organized along lines that point to this mirroring sphere. The sphere is reflecting. Because of the reflections on the round surface the camera has difficulty focusing on it. It is

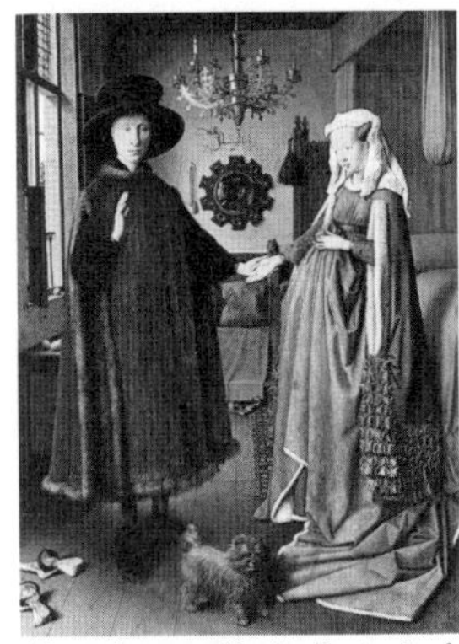

46a   Jan van Eyck, *Portrait of Giovanni (?) Arnolfini and his Wife*, 1434.

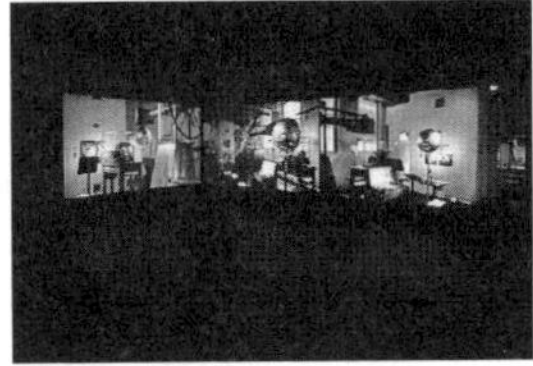

46b   Roos Theuws, *Kitab al Manazir*, 2013.

207

47   See Bergson, *Matter and Memory* ([1896] 1991).

not really able to assess the distance to it, and as a consequence cannot establish a vanishing point for the composition.

One of the effects of linear perspective is a clear and stable positioning of the viewer in front of the image. In Jan van Eyck's painting this effect occurs indeed. The viewer is positioned centrally, in the middle of the forefront of the painting. The three screens of Roos Theuws' installation do not effectuate such a stable positioning of the viewer. This instability is even increased by the fact that we are facing three instead of just one video. And because of the fact that the three screens are not placed on the same wall, we never have an overview that would allow us to see the three images at the same time. We have to look back and forth; our vision is necessarily supported by memory. This installation compels a revision of the common notion of how our senses work, especially the sense of sight. The visual experience is not only made up of a visual object world, but also of processes that are internal and intentional; in this case memory. *Kitab al Manazir* demonstrates Bergson's philosophy about perception and memory, to which I have referred already several times in this book.[47]

Although we recognize the same objects in the same space in the three videos, it is difficult, perhaps even impossible to understand where you as viewer are positioned in relation to this space, or where in relation to the objects in this space.[48] This is rather amazing because technologically generated images such as photography, film and video are supposed to do exactly that. The optical lens that is used by all three media translates the represented space automatically and mechanically into an organization of space that follows the rules of linear perspective. Especially architectural spaces and structures are susceptible to such a translation. The museum room in *Kitab al Manazir* is such an architectural space but the expected effect fails to occur. This space, cluttered with optical objects and instruments, remains immune to the organizing effects of linear perspective.

Because of the fact that the three video screenings represent the same space, one would expect that the principle of the stereoscope would apply; not literally, on our retinas, but figuratively, in our minds. Although consisting of not two but three images, the stereoscope scope effect would then lead to a merging of the three individual images into one while we were looking at them. However, this merging of different images into one never takes place. The visual field remains fragmented in all respects. When I say in all respects I mean the relations between the respective screens as well as the viewer's relation to it.

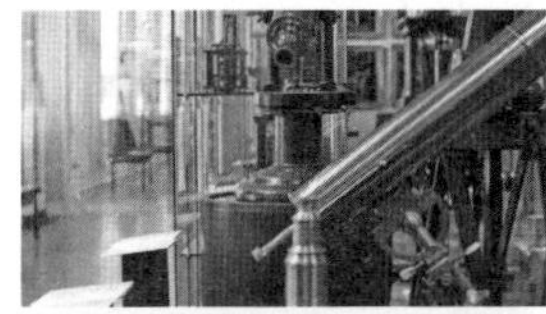
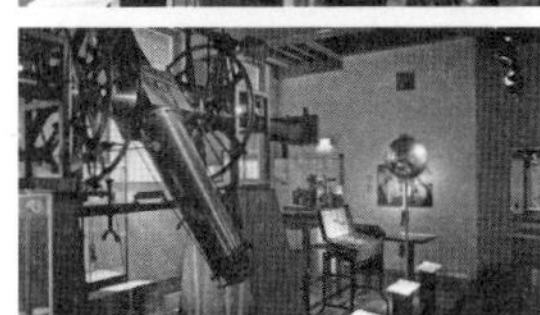
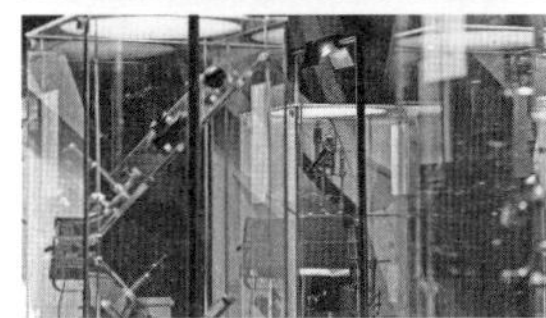

48   Roos Theuws, *Kitab al Manazir*, 2013, three video stills.

The many reflecting surfaces in the museum room result in a confusing distribution of light. It is that ill-distributed light that cancels out the effects of linear perspective, which results in a paradoxical visual situation. Looking at this fragmented visual field the viewer has no real points of reference. The viewer recognizes the kind of optical objects and instruments in the museum room, but is not able to recognize any visual organization of the objects in relation to each other. The effect of this paradox is like a montage of visual impressions that do not cohere. Again, we can make them cohere by means of our memory and postulate the knowledge that all objects are placed next to each other in the same museum room. But in our visual experience they remain fragmented and frustrate the coherence of a visual field that can be grasped.

After fifteen minutes, the mirroring sphere appears simultaneously on all three screens as the central object. Next, vitrines and reflections repeat themselves on all three screens. Whereas in the first part of the video images the reflections were concentrated on the mirroring sphere, in the second part the reflections return all over the space of the museum room. Intensified by lamps above the vitrines, mirroring reflections fragment the visual field even more, which makes it impossible to grasp the visual field of these moving images. It is first of all the

camera itself that is confronted with this impossibility: it gropes and scans the reflecting surfaces in
order to get control; its focus is groping the visual
field. But it is clearly out of control. As a consequence, the viewer too has difficulty establishing a
stable viewing position in front of the fragmented
visual fields on the three screens. This impediment
of viewing is in sharp contrast with the promise of
perfect looking raised by the optical instruments in
the reflecting vitrines.

The video installation *Kitab al Manazir* can be
seen as a deconstruction or more literally, dissection
of the technological image, including the photographic image, and of how our look tries to grasp
that image. The way Theuws deconstructs the image
is by hampering its constitutive elements and processes. Firstly, our look is deconstructed by the compelling conclusion that looking is not only constituted by what one sees, the visual object, but also by
memory, an internal and intentional process. The
only way to integrate the visual fields of the three
screens of *Kitab al Manazir* into one cohering field is
by means of memories of what we have seen before.
The visual field itself lacks any organization that
would make it coherent and graspable. What is dis-
abled in this video installation is the organizing effect
of linear perspective. Because of the abundance of
light reflected by glass vitrines and optical apparat-

uses, the optical lens used by a video camera fails to translate the represented space into an organization of space that follows the rules of linear perspective, whereas this translation should have happened mechanically. Due to the many mirroring reflections this space seems to be immune to it.

The video installation demonstrates also how deconstruction works. It is not by following the rules and adopting the principles of a certain process or medium that we can understand it in its constitutive elements. We can understand and dissect a medium, deconstruct it by hampering it. It is only then that the constitutive elements separate themselves and become visible, like the separation of oil and water. That is why the way Theuws operates in this installations reminds me of Hiroshi Sugimoto's *Theatres* series, discussed earlier in this chapter. Although Sugimoto's medium is still photography and Theuws' medium is in this case the moving video image, they both assess their respective mediums by demonstrating a moment at which their medium fails to work. As we have seen, Sugimoto's technique adopted for producing the *Theatres* series was as follows. His photographs record a film during the entire length of its projection on the screen. He succeeds in this by using the projection time of a feature film as the exposure time of his camera. But the motion of the film images creates emptiness in the photograph. The screen, on which the pictures appear and disappear, remains empty in the photograph. It cannot keep the number of images it attracts.[49]

But there is more to Theuws' way of grasping the technological image of video and as extension also of photography. The deconstruction of the technological image and the way we grasp that image can be pursued by video as well as photography. Theuws has conducted the same deconstructive project also by means of the photographic image. The mirroring sphere, which is the central object in the first part of the video installation *Kitab al Manazir* is also the central object in three large-format photographs. Originally, the photographs were stills, taken from the video films.

The sphere is an instrument for measuring the distance between galaxies. In each photograph, the sphere is placed on a stem and is photographed frontally in the centre of the image. The background of the museum room is absent. The difference between the three images is the reflection in the mirroring sphere and the darkness or lightness surrounding the sphere. There is no connection between the reflections in the sphere and the surrounding context of the sphere. That connection is broken as if the reflection had turned inwards. The inwardness of these reflections is even foregrounded in the second

49   For an excellent reading of Sugimoto's work, see Hans Belting, 'The Theatre of Illusion', in *Hiroshi Sugimoto: Theaters* (New York: Sonnabend Sundell Editions, 2000).

213

photograph *KaM002*, the one that is greyish compared to the other two that are either light or very dark. It is as if there were a veil between viewer and sphere, which makes the reflections almost impenetrable. The opposite effect is established in the very dark one, *KaM003*. The reflections in the dark sphere make the reflections look like an eye, confronting the viewer with its look. This association is also established by how the object is placed frontally on a stem. It has the superiority of an object that looks back at the viewer in front of the image. The viewer is confronted with the Gaze; he is facing it.

A smaller photograph consists of an excision of the visual field of the second part of the video installation. The excision shows lamps, parts of the vitrines, and of reflections that cannot always immediately be located, nor can we see where they come from. The excess of reflections makes it impossible to know what is foreground and what is background. Whereas in the moving video image the viewer could notice how the camera was not really able to focus because of the many reflections, in this still photograph the inability of the camera has been displaced onto the viewer. This photograph is, in a sense, an allegorical representation of the problem the camera struggles with in the video images. The next photograph is the same shot but from a greater distance. This provides spatial context to the vitrines and to the objects in the vitrines. Although there is still an abundance of reflections, they do not the image in the same way as the earlier photograph that zooms in on it. Taking distance from the scene enables the eye to regain control over it. But only more or less.

The issue of distance is explicitly at stake in another photograph, *KaM300*, which is a combination of two images, one on top of the other. The first one is in black and white, placed below the other one, and shows optical instruments that make it possible to see from a great distance. The image on top, which is in colour, is a close-up of silicon. The distance to it is minimized by means of close-up. Distance is clearly crucial in what we can see. When we come too close, we don't see anything. Taking distance makes it possible to see and to gain control over the visual field. But when the distance becomes too enormous we again fail to see anything.

The photographs as well as the video images of *Kitab al Manazir* were taken in the room of Museum Boerhaave in Leiden where optical instruments are displayed. All these instruments are meant to measure and manage the function of seeing in relation to distance. Microscopes enable extreme close-up seeing, whereas telescopes enable seeing from a great distance. One of these optical instruments, a kind of sundial, is the subject of another photograph. This measuring instrument is decorated with the twelve signs of the zodiac. But this zodiac seems to be more than just decoration. In order to indicate what this Enlightenment instrument is all about it needs another symbolic system. The symbolic system that manages distance by means of measurement can only explain what it pursues by means of symbolic signs. Through ironic downplaying it exposes its own limitations. It can measure but it cannot name.

Whereas all the optical apparatuses in Museum Boerhaave are meant to manage the function of seeing, Theuws' works concentrate this function on a specific object: the technological image. The optical lenses used to make these images are not able to focus on what they see when light is reflected, instead of absorbed. The reflections in and on the mirroring surfaces and objects result in over-exposure to light. This over-exposure does not allow the camera to order the space in view along the principles of linear perspective, nor cannot it take any decisions on what element to focus on because it cannot assess distance. It is precisely when the technological image of photography is hampered in the processes that bring it about, that we see and understand how the photographic image is constituted. I started out this chapter by the truism that the photographic image depends for its existence on light and on the differentiation of light and darkness. But now

we also understand why light is also responsible for
the undoing of the photographic image.

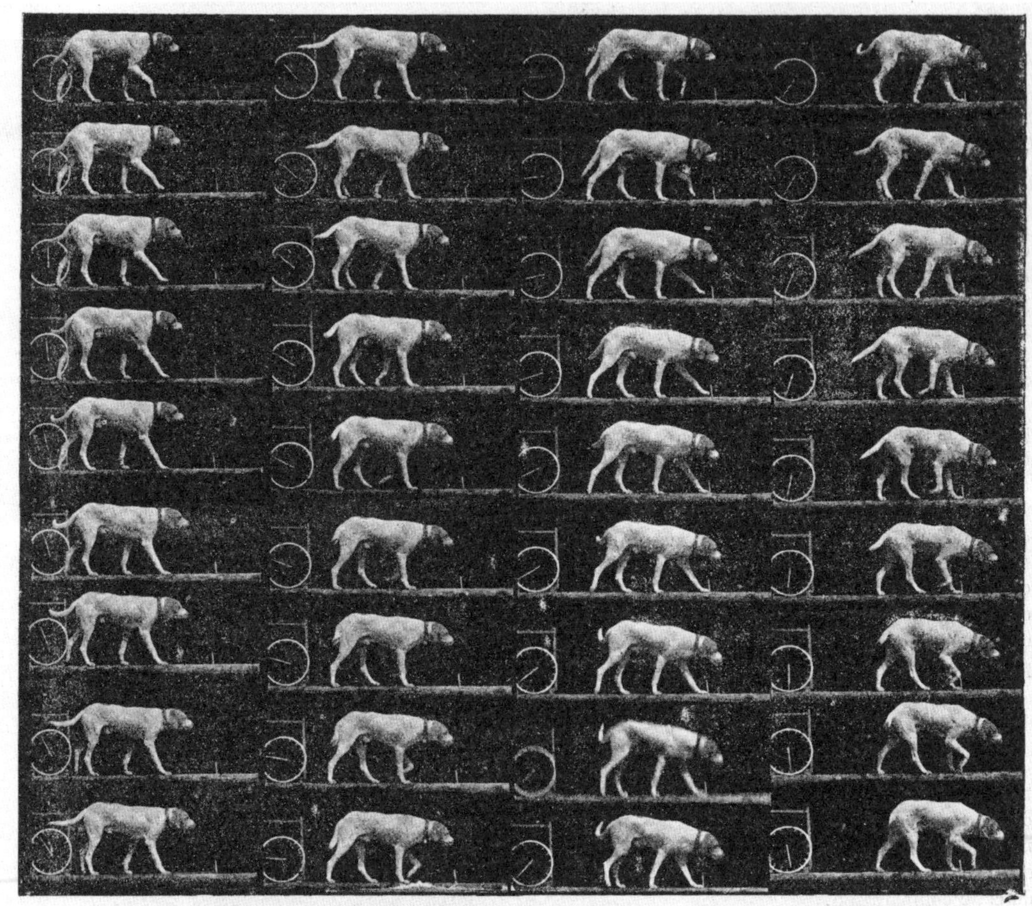

Fig. 4. — Chien march nt. 36 images pour la durée d'un pas; la première est en haut de la figure et à gauche, 1re colonne; la dernière à droite et en bas, 4e colonne. Durée totale du pas : 45/60 de seconde.

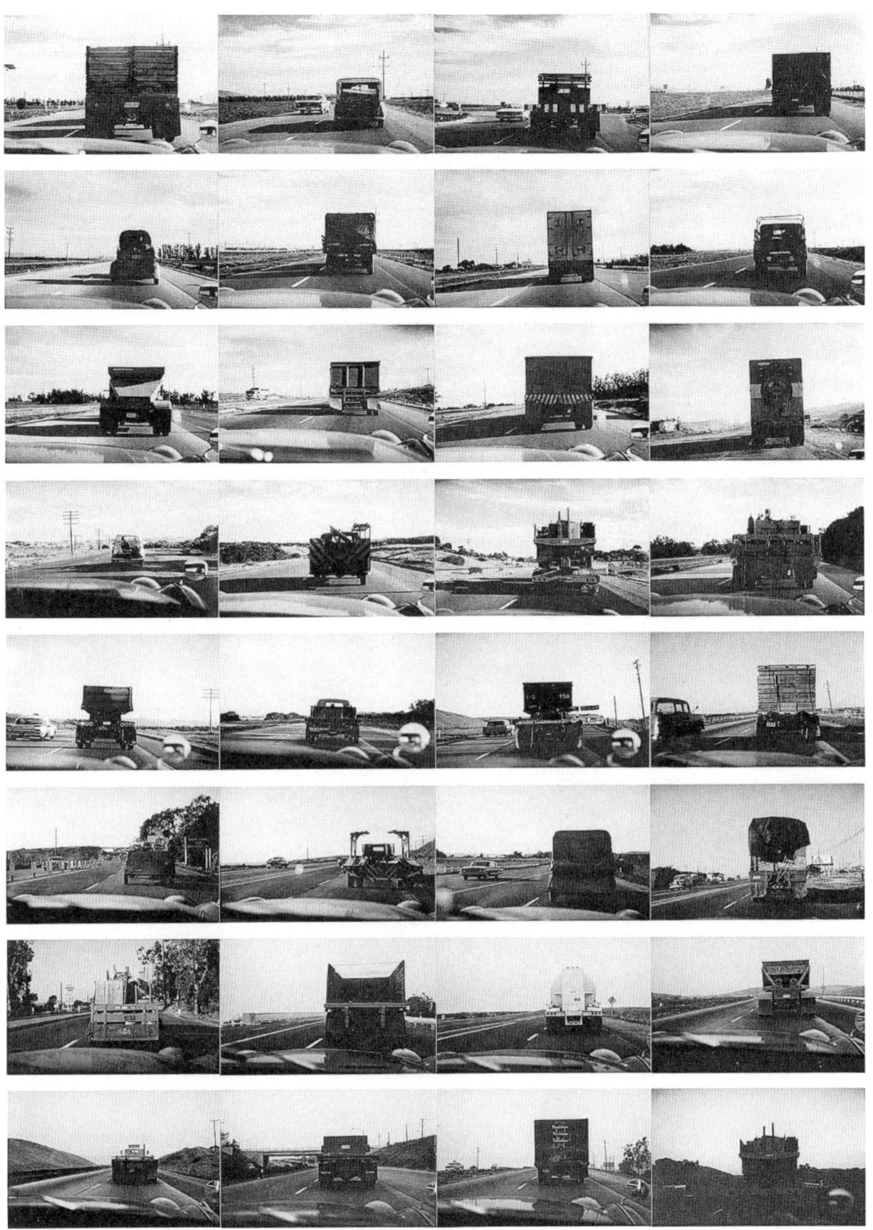

John Baldessari, *The backs
of all the trucks passed while
driving from Los Angeles
to Santa Barbara, California,
Sunday 20, January 1963.*

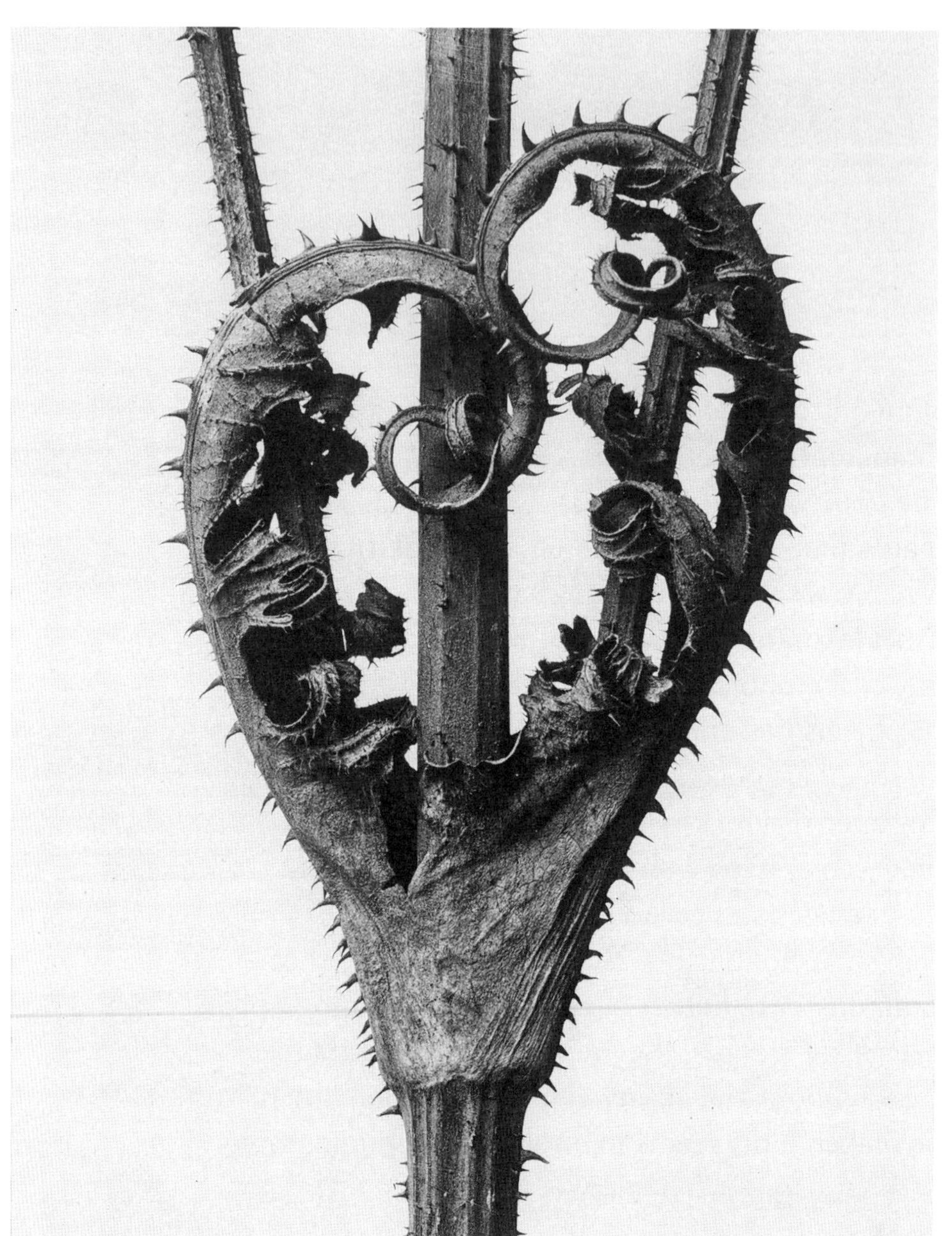

Karl Blossfeldt, *Dipsacus
laciniatus, Cut-leaved reasel,*
1928.

Archival Images

In my introduction, discussing the great diversity of photographic practices presented by Talbot in his *The Pencil of Nature* (1844), I focused on some images that Talbot considered as 'visual inventories'. When photographic images have the function of visual inventories they can be seen as archival; not only of the photographs as such, but as an archive of the objects presented in the image. In light of the dominant approach of photography as discussed by Kracauer, Talbot's visual inventories are quite remarkable. Even a short and superficial look at these images suffices to see how different they are from snapshot images. But according to another common-sense notion of photography, photographic images are records, they represent the world objectively without any expressivity or intentionality of the maker. This seems to imply that all photographs

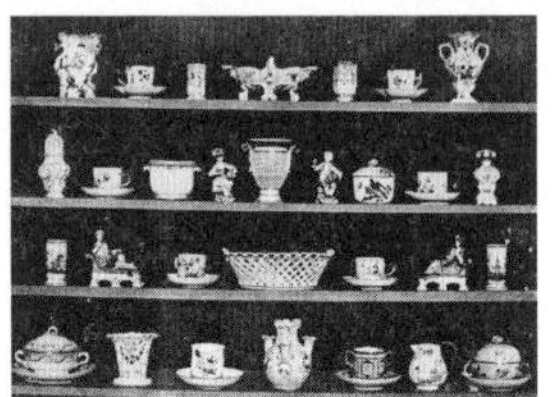

1a   William Henry Fox Talbot, *The Pencil of Nature*, 1844, Plate III: 'Articles of China'.

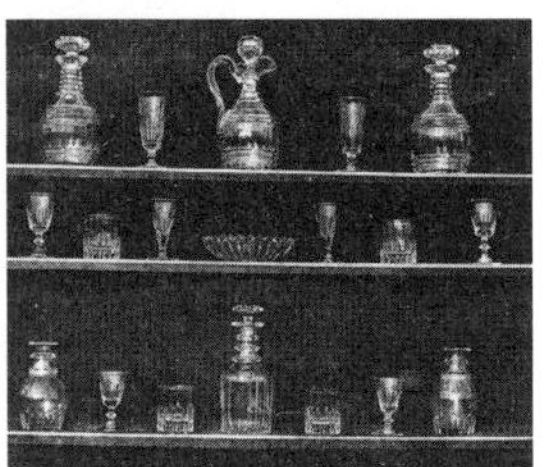

1b   William Henry Fox Talbot, *The Pencil of Nature*, 1844, Plate IV: 'Articles of Glass'.

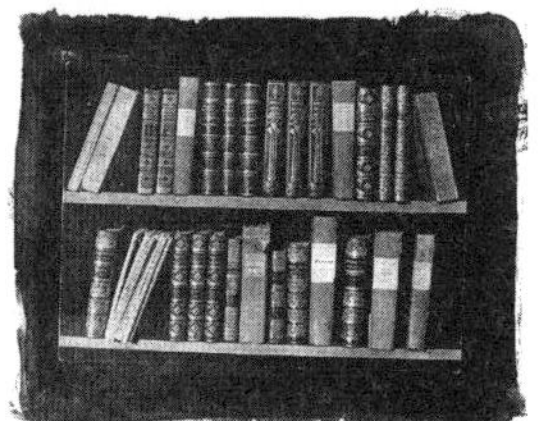

1c   William Henry Fox Talbot, *The Pencil of Nature*, 1844, Plate VIII: 'A Scene in a Library'.

2   Clive Scott, *The Spoken Image: Photography and Language* (London: Reaktion Books, 1999), p. 26.

can be seen as archival and that Talbot's 'visual archives' are exemplary of photography's 'nature'.[1]

In order to show how strange Talbot's visual inventories in fact are, I will examine if the characteristics of the photographic approach as distinguished by Kracauer apply to these images. The first characteristic the German sociologist mentioned was an affinity with un-staged reality. Talbot's images are rather puzzling and paradoxical when evaluated on the basis of this criterion. These collections of china, glass, and books are clearly staged on the shelves on which we see them. A library in which books are shelved is nothing other than a *staging of books*. But it is not obvious that this staging was done for the camera in order to make a staged photograph. These staged collections were probably found in this form by Talbot and are in that sense 'un-staged realities'.

According to the dominant approach to photography, photographs stress the fortuitous. Talbot's inventories clearly don't. They do not show random events, but intentionally chosen and selected objects, even if it remains unclear who did the selecting. The third characteristic is that photographs suggest an infinity beyond the frame, or in terms of Clive Scott, that they have a 'blind field', which is 'the extension of space and time beyond the photographic frame'.[2] That is not the case in these images either. It is not clear if they show the complete collection of china or

222

books or if the shelves continue outside the frame. Still, the spatiality of these inventories is clearly not infinite; but, perhaps, they are a part standing for a whole, a *pars pro toto* or *synecdoche*. The final characteristic is temporal and emphasizes the fact that photographs isolate one temporal moment from a continuity. This does not apply to these images either; if temporality is at all a defining feature here, it is a temporality of duration and not of a singular moment.

If Talbot's visual inventories do not fit into the dominant approach of photography, this implies that we have to rethink the photograph as archival record, and consider how that notion relates to that dominant approach. Although the notion of photography as a record is common sense, at the same time it forms a puzzling problem that cannot easily be integrated into the dominant approach of photography, characterized by the idea of the snapshot. But when exactly can a photograph be understood as archival instead of as a snapshot? And what does an archival photographic practice look like? In the remainder of this chapter I will deal with these questions.

Although the ontological status of the photographic image is complex and variegated, the photographic image seen as archival record is one of the most prevalent notions of the photographic image.

223

From that perspective photographs are considered and dealt with as pictorial testimonies of the existence of a recorded fact. In this respect the camera is a kind of archiving machine: every image it produces is a priori an archival object. Accordingly, over time, the photographic image has become an object of archival ordering and thus has been appropriated for a myriad of scientific, industrial and cultural purposes.

In the history of nineteenth-century photography the archive plays a crucial role, especially in scientific uses. Positivistic science became gradually an archival-photographic endeavour, relying on the photographic image as record. An example of such an endeavour is Alphonse Bertillon's police archives in Paris. Towards the end of the 1870s, this obscure bureaucrat in the police department of Paris developed a method for identifying criminals that was based on anthropometric measurements and mug shots. By means of this photographic archive Bertillon was able to identify criminals by using techniques that had undergone a radical development in the nineteenth century. In the words of Giorgio Agamben:

> Whoever happened to be detained or arrested for whatever reason would immediately be subjected to a series of measurements of the skull,

arms, fingers, toes, ears, and face. Once the suspect had been photographed both in profile and frontally, the two photos would be attached to the 'Bertillon card', which contained all the useful identification data, according to the system that its inventor had christened *portrait parlé*.[3]

These 'speaking portraits' enabled recognition, namely that of the recidivist criminal recognized by the police officer. They were records that were supposed to provide unproblematic access to the referents, in this case, criminal identities. Their status as records means that these images are not separate from their referents.[4]

Evidence for the success of Bertillon's archival classification system is the fact that similar kinds of systems were developed worldwide. In the UK Francis Galton developed a fingerprinting classification system, which enabled the identification of recidivist criminals without possibility of error. He claimed that the statistical survey of fingerprinting was particularly suited to natives from the colonies. Whereas their physical characteristics tended to be confusing and appeared indistinguishable to the European eye, identifying their fingerprints was a solution to this problem.

Another French photographer dealing with images as records was the architectural photographer

3   Giorgio Agamben, 'Identity Without the Person', in *Nudities* (Stanford: Stanford University Press, 2013), p. 48.

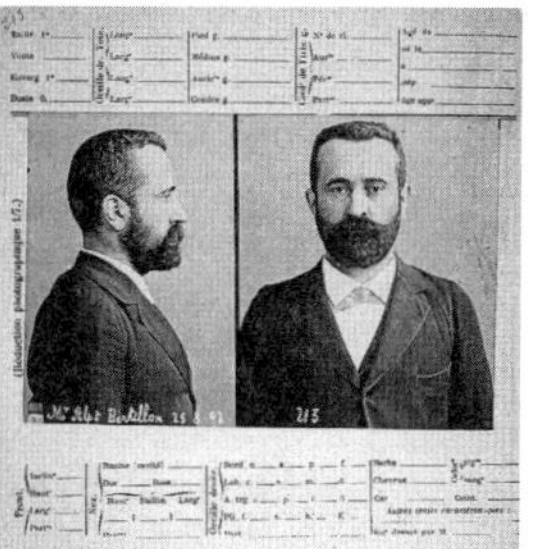

4a   Anthropometry card of Alphonse Bertillon, who originated this criminal identification system of profile and full-face photos and key body measurements, 1892.

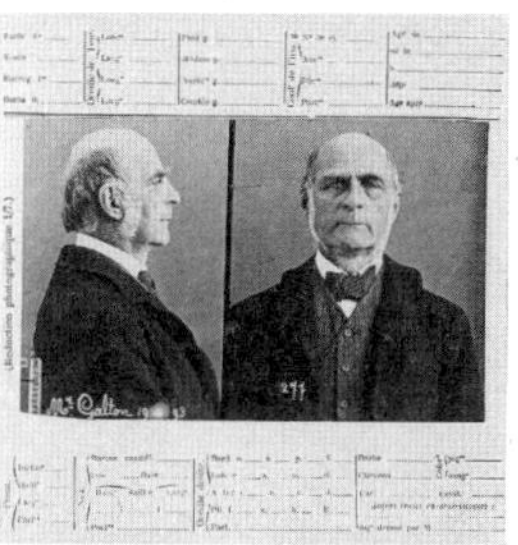

4b   Anthropometry card of Francis Galton, with profile and full-face photos and spaces for key body measurements, taken by Alphonse Bertillon, 1893.

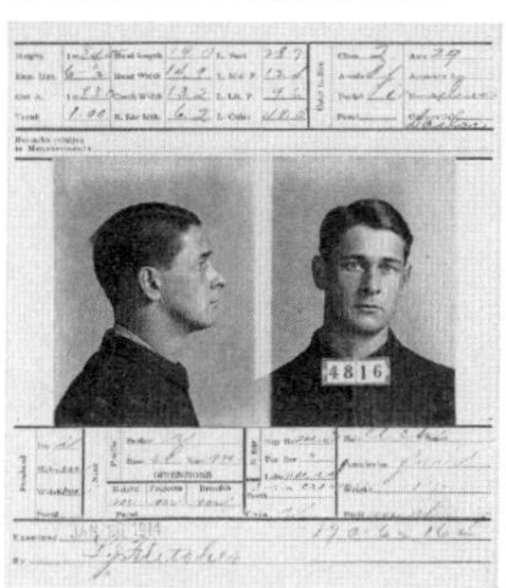

4c   The Bertillon Card for John Welshouse, an inmate of the U.S. Penitentiary in Atlanta, 1914.

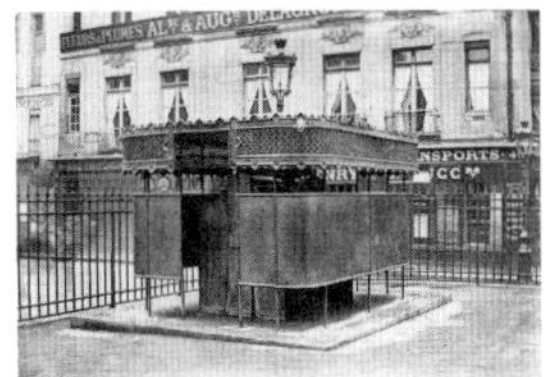

5a   Charles Marville, *Urinoir enveloppe à six stalles*, 1865.

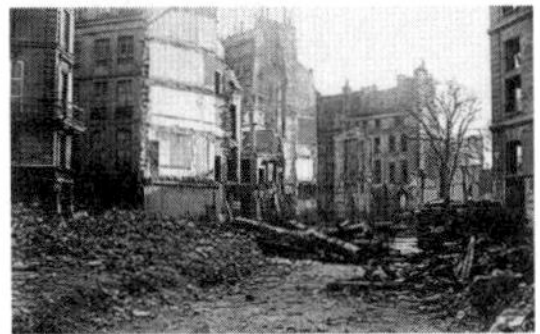

5b   Charles Marville, *Travaux du Baron Haussmann, Avenue de l'Opéra après le carrefour Saint-Augustin*, 1862.

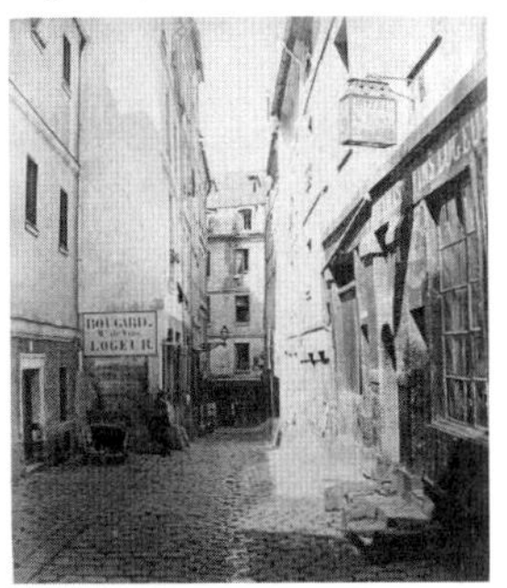

5c   Charles Marville, *Rue d'Écosse vue de la rue du Four Saint-Jacques*, 1865.

6   For a more elaborate account of the role of photography in the modern organization of the archive, see my book *Staging the Archive: Art and Photography in Times of New Media* (London: Reaktion Books, 2016).

Charles Marville (1813–1879). Appointed the photographer of the 'Imperial Museum of the Louvre' he documented and immortalized the great restauration works undertaken in Paris in his days. In his book *Album du vieux Paris* (Album of Old Paris), commissioned in 1864 by the 'department of historical works', he made a testament to what Paris looked like before it was modernized, or destroyed, by Haussmann's reconstruction of the city. All of his images are records or testimonies of how Paris once was.[5]

Within the archive, photographs seem at first to be one kind of document among many. Still, they differ from other, in particular written documents. Documents are older than photographs and therefore command more status; they record acts and transactions and have a legal status. The document's archival status is the performance and record of its act.[6] Photographs, in contrast, do not possess the status of an act in that sense; they are considered more passive; *reservoir* more than record. It is this status of the photograph as passive and as reservoir that posed a problem for the archive, in particular for archival classification and regulation, as the photograph is inherently unstable. It unsettles the grounds of archival classification. In contrast to other kind of documents, photographs are never just established records of the past; once severed from their referents they can always be read differently. This is how the

226

status of the photograph morphs from record to an archive in and of itself.

An archival-photographic practice that demonstrates this morphing of the photographic image from archivable record into an archive in itself is that of the German photographer Karl Blossfeldt. In 1928, this proponent of the so-called New Objectivity in German photography published his book of photographs titled *Urformen der Kunst* (Art Forms in Nature). At first sight, this book can be understood as a kind of scientific publication, as a photographic herbarium, for instance. Reading the book like this means that the photographs it contains have not been severed from their referents: the book is about the plants represented in the images.[7]

But one year later, in 1929, Blossfeldt's images were shown at the famous Stuttgart exhibition 'Film und Foto'; they were hanging in the company of the photographs of the young photographic avant-garde. This artistic context of the exhibition suggests we should not read his images as a herbarium and not focus on the plants as referents of these images. In fact, Blossfeldt's interest in plants from a botanical perspective was very limited. He usually did not take the trouble to identify the plants he photographed. And the kind of images he took, zooming in on small details, dissected most plants beyond recognition.

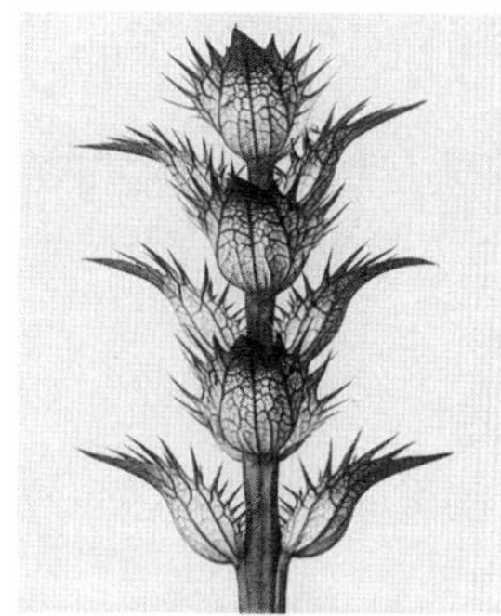

7a   Karl Blossfeldt, *Acanthus mollis, Bear's Breech*, 1928.

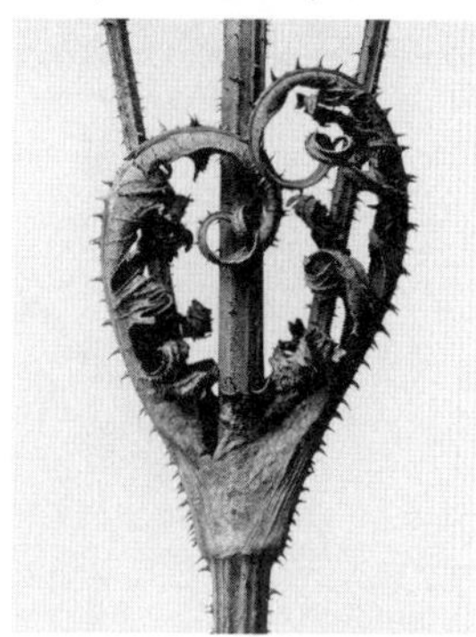

7b   Karl Blossfeldt, *Dipsacus laciniatus, Cut-leaved reasel*, 1928.

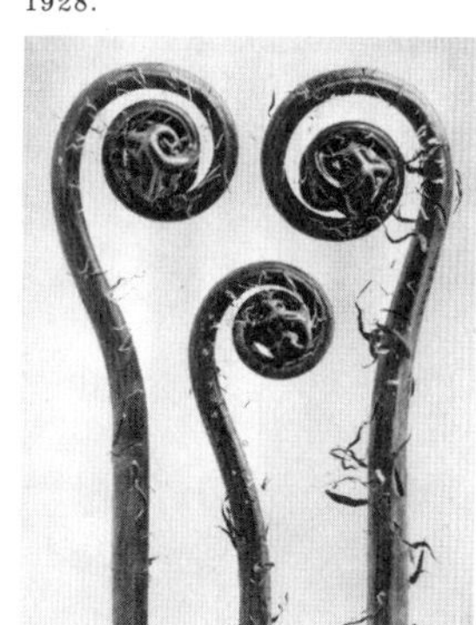

7c   Karl Blossfeldt, *Adiantum Pedatum, Maiden-hair fern*, 1928.

227

8   Ulrike Meyer Stump, 'Karl Blossfeldt's Working Collages: A Photographic Sketchbook', in *Karl Blossfeldt: Working Collages*, ed. Ann and Jürgen Wilde (Cambridge, MA: MIT Press, 2001), p. 15.

All Blossfeldt's images show plant details on a neutral background. They were originally intended for use in classes on plant modelling. Before he became a teacher of the course 'Modelling from Living Plants', he worked as an assistant to the painter and applied artist Moritz Meurer, who had been commissioned to produce a collection of teaching materials for the study of natural forms. The hope was that close study of natural forms and plant anatomy would result in a revival of German craftsmanship to a level that would be competitive with classical antiquity, if only because it would do away with historicism's cluttered ornamentation.

With his images Blossfeldt explores vegetal ornament in its most basic and elementary form; a form that is natural. He used the medium of photography to extract 'the plant's artistic form from its natural form'.[8] He performed this extraction by focusing on details, isolating them from their context, and by magnification. As a result, the plant details achieve an autonomous presence; they do no longer look like details or parts of a plant, but appear as forms, as beings in their own right. This transformation into artistic form implies a severing of the image from the referent. We do not recognize a specific plant or a part of it; we see an image containing a basic form that amazes us. And severed from its referent, it has no longer the status of record; it has become an

archive in and of itself; an archive of details and
forms that only exists in the image. The photograph
no longer has the status of an archival record, as was
emphatically meant to be the case with Bertillon's
images of criminals, but is now an archival image:
a storage of details and forms.

Although this is true for each individual image of
Blossfeldt's oeuvre, the archival status of the image
becomes inescapable in his 'working collages'. While
never meant for exhibition or publication, Blossfeldt
made sixty-one cardboard sheets with arrangements
of contact prints of his negatives. The contact prints
are on a variety of photographic paper—brown gelatin silver bromide and grey gelatin silver chloride
paper as well as cheaper cyanotypes or blueprints—
which were cut out with scissors.[9] This material variety suggests that these 'working collages' are like
sketches or notes, intended solely for Blossfeldt's
own use. This use concerned the grouping together
of similar forms as specific motifs. They each show
the isolation of particular motifs, as if only by grouping the same forms onto one sheet, the motif
becomes recognizable as a basic form instead of
being an arbitrary form. This grouping for recognition is an archival tool in itself. Although each image
is an archive of detailed form, the categorization of
each form becomes much easier when similar forms
are collected into one group. Instead of recognizing

9   Ibid., p. 7.

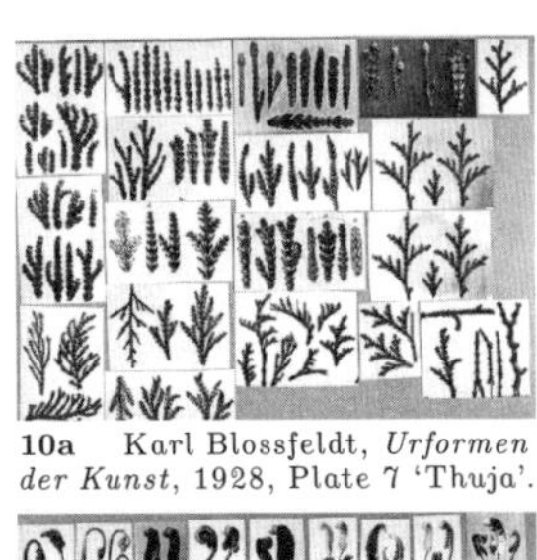

10a   Karl Blossfeldt, *Urformen der Kunst*, 1928, Plate 7 'Thuja'.

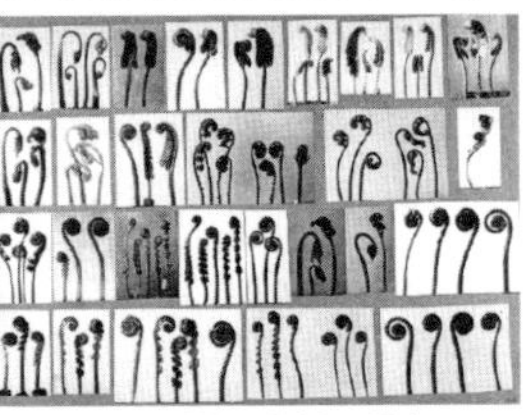

10b   Karl Blossfeldt, *Urformen der Kunst*, 1928, Plate 15 'Ferns II'.

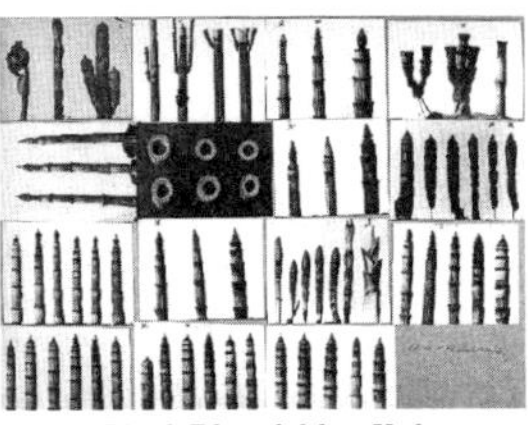

10c   Karl Blossfeldt, *Urformen der Kunst*, 1928, Plate 1 'Rough horsetails I'.

11   The English translation of this essay, 'Photography', is collected in a volume with Kracauer's essays, titled *The Mass Ornament: Weimar Essays*, trans. and ed. by Thomas Y. Levin (Cambridge, MA and London: Cambridge University Press, [1963] 1995), pp. 47–64.

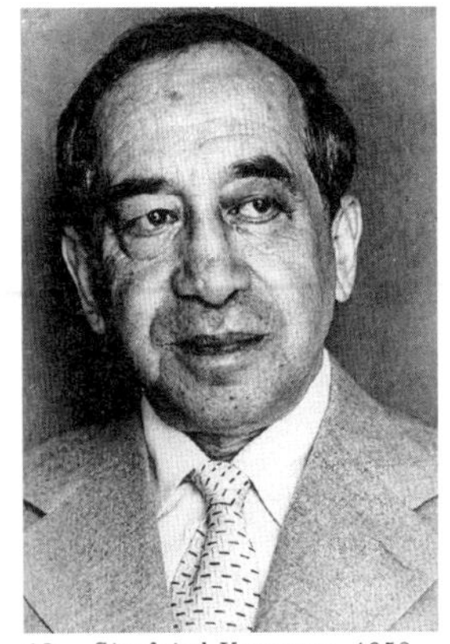

12   Siegfried Kracauer, 1953.

the plant, we now 'see' the form or motif. The seriality of the same form on each sheet confirms that the form is basic. This seriality is a typological arrangement of similar images and forms. The effort of grouping intimates a hesitation concerning the automatically archival nature of photographs.[10]

Photographic Image versus Memory Image

The unstable status of the photographic image, as a record (as an entity within the archive) or as an archive in itself, can also be explained through the ideas of Kracauer, but this time not from the text from 1951 already discussed, but a much earlier one. In 1927 Kracauer published an essay with the short title 'Die Photographie', in which he made a distinction between the photographic image and the memory image.[11] Whereas according to common-sense ideas, the two are more or less the same or in continuity with each other, in the sense that photographic images support memory images, according to Kracauer the two are actually opposed.[12] The main stakes or meanings of these different kinds of images are at odds with each other. Whereas the memory image is highly selective and focuses only on what is significant, the photographic image is not at all selective. The memory image retains only what is

230

significant, whereas the photographic image grasps everything that is present in the spatial continuum of a moment. It includes all spatial elements in front of the camera. As a result, a photograph reveals nothing of a subject: 'a person's history is buried as if under a layer of snow'.[13]

The term 'memory image' used by Kracauer was introduced by the French philosopher Henri Bergson. He argued that when we look at the world our perceptual system conflates the perceptual image as immediate registration of objects with previously registrations stored as memories. They are merged into what he calls a 'memory-image'. Memory-images are partly based on perception, partly on memory, and it is impossible to distinguish the two in such an image:

> If, after having gazed at any object, we turn our eyes abruptly away, we obtain an 'afterimage' of it … but behind these images, which are identical with the object, there are others stored in memory, which merely resemble it, and others, finally, which are only more or less distantly akin to it. All these go out to meet the perception, and, feeding on its substance, acquire sufficient vigor and life to abide with it in space.[14]

Memory-images are interpretations of our actual perception and those interpretations impose

231

13 Kracauer, 'Photography', p. 51.

14 Bergson, *Matter and Memory*, p. 102.

themselves so convincingly on our perceptions that we are no longer able to discern what is perception and what is memory.

To demonstrate that viewers relate not in the same way to old photographs as to new ones, Kracauer describes a sixty-year old photograph of his grandmother when she was still young. The image of the grandmother is pulled from a family album. When Kracauer looks at the photograph of his still-young grandmother she disappears behind details; as a result, she disintegrates into a multitude of particulars. The photograph conveys information but no likeness. He notices, for instance, the particulars of her dress, the fashion of those past days, a hairstyle that now looks dated. But it is the archival context of the family album that enables Kracauer to see the photograph as an image of his grandmother. It must be her; otherwise the image would not have been in the family album. 'All right, so it's grandmother, but in reality it's any young girl in 1864.'[15]

A photograph of a grandmother also plays an important role in Marcel Proust's *A la recherche du temps perdu*. The photograph is evoked when Marcel hears the voice of his grandmother through the telephone, a relatively new medium at the beginning of the twentieth century. Detached from her body and her face the voice generates a sense of alienation in Marcel. This alienation is compared to the alienating effect of a photograph that does not enable the recognition of the portrayed person.

> Of myself—thanks to that privilege which does not last but which gives one, during the brief moment of return, the faculty of being suddenly the spectator of one's own absence—there was present only the witness, the observer, in travelling coat and hat, the stranger who does not belong to the house, the photographer who has called to take a photograph of places which one will never see again. The process that automatically occurred in my eyes when I caught sight of my grandmother was indeed a photograph.[16]

In terms of Kracauer and Bergson one could say that also Proust's notion of photography makes a distinction between photographic image and memory image. Voice and photograph of the grandmother are alienating for him, because they do not merge with his memory-images of her.[17]

Especially old photographs demonstrate that over time the photographic image becomes severed from its referent. It is only in recent images that the referential function of the medium of photography can be assessed. In the words of Kracauer: 'if photography is a function of the flow of time, then its substantive meaning will change depending on whether it belongs to the domain of the present or to

16   Marcel Proust, *Remembrance of Things Past* (London: Penguin Books, 1981), Volume II, p. 141.

17   This reading of Proust is based on Mieke Bal's reading of photography in the work of Proust: *The Mottled Screen: Reading Proust Visually* (Stanford: Stanford University Press, 1997). Also Ann Banfield theorizes the phenomenon of alienating perceptions in the work of Virginia Woolf and Roger Fry as 'the world seen without a self' in her book *The Phantom Table: Woolf, Fry, Russell and the Epistemology of Modernism* (Cambridge, MA: Cambridge University Press, 2000).

18   Kracauer, 'Photography', p. 54.

19   Philip Monk, *Disassembling the Archive: Fiona Tan* (Toronto: Art Gallery of York University, 2006), n.p.

20   Kracauer, 'Photography', p. 62.

some phase of the past'.[18] Philip Monk explains this change over time as follows:

> A photograph, it seems, is only interesting when it ages. When an image is current, we understand it for all the wrong reasons, referred by its mediating role as an 'optical sign' to other functions of identification (i.e. recognition) in which the memory image plays a determining role. … As an image ages, its semiotic value deteriorates, revealing it to be the empty cipher it essentially is.[19]

This deterioration of semiotic value implies more than just that meaning changes over time. It changes the photograph itself in a fundamental way, because now it is based on the severance from the referent. Kracauer formulates this transformation of the photograph as follows:

> The images of the stock of nature disintegrated into its elements are offered up to unconsciousness to deal with as it pleases. Their original order is lost; they no longer cling to the spatial context that linked them with an original out of which the memory image was selected. But if the remnants of nature are not oriented toward the memory image, then the order they assume through the images is necessarily provisional.[20]

234

When there is no longer a referent to direct and channel our look at the photographic image, a great variety of details strike the eye and a great variety of possible meanings proliferate. It is in order to restrict this expansion of possibilities that the classifications of the archive are needed. For the archive provides precisely such a 'provisional order' to the photograph, needed after 'the original order' (of the referent) is lost. This is how a photograph transforms from record to a potential archive.

Earlier I pointed out in which sense the photographic image can be seen as an archive in itself. Photographs are dealt with as recorded facts, as pictorial testimonies to the existence of recorded facts. The camera then has the status of an archiving machine. But the implication of Kracauer's view for this notion of photography is that after its severance from the referent, the photographic image is the messiest archive one can imagine. Because it ultimately utterly lacks any kind of order, it will depend on the classifications of an imposed archival order. Philip Monk explains this dependency as follows:

> … all contingency that we think natural to photography's indexical registrations dissolved as if in a reversal of an image's chemical apparition. All contingency was severed. This, I think, proves an archival problem to classify and house

all these now homeless images, photographs suddenly severed from their referents. Severing contingency instituted the archive.[21]

In the history of early photography, it is the archive that functions as the solution for photography's severance of its indexical contingency and the resulting untidy archive. The archive as institution, then, absorbs the photograph's original status as potentially but incompletely archival itself.

Although the archive is needed as a new home for photographs-without-referent, this solution works only provisionally and partly. It does not imply that within the archive photographs finally find or rediscover their true meaning. A second photograph described by Kracauer demonstrates this. It is an image of a film diva from an illustrated newspaper, which in fact is another kind of archival context. For Kracauer, this photograph of the diva refers not to the woman herself, but to the original referent he watched on the film screen. Without the archival context of the illustrated newspaper in which it has an orderly place, the image of the diva has, however, much in common with the other image, the one of Kracauer's grandmother. For he describes this image of his grandmother ultimately as follows:

> All right, so it's grandmother, but in reality it's any young girl in 1864. ... This mannequin does

236

not belong to our time; it could be standing with others of its kind in a museum, in a glass case labeled 'Traditional Costumes, 1864'.[22]

Pulling it out of the archival context of the family album, Kracauer places his grandmother's image immediately in another archive. It is this other archive which bestows a new identity on her, namely the one of fashion model. Although the diva belongs to Kracauer's own time, represented in her photograph she has probably much in common with the grandmother's image: both look like mannequins, and both could be standing in a glass case in a fashion museum. That Kracauer does not read the diva as mannequin but as diva is due to the fact that in his account she remains embedded in the archival context of the illustrated newspaper, in his days more interested in film stars than in fashion. But that does not mean that in this original archival context the image has a true or authentic meaning. What Kracauer saw happening to the old image of his grandmother repeated itself in the daily archives of contemporary illustrated newspapers, where a 'blizzard of photographs betrays an indifference towards what the things mean'. The problem he first encountered with old photographs repeats itself at the level of the archive. Both were alike in the 'detritus they shored up against meaning'.[23]

22 Kracauer, 'Photography', p. 48.

23 Monk, *Disassembling the Archive*, n.p.

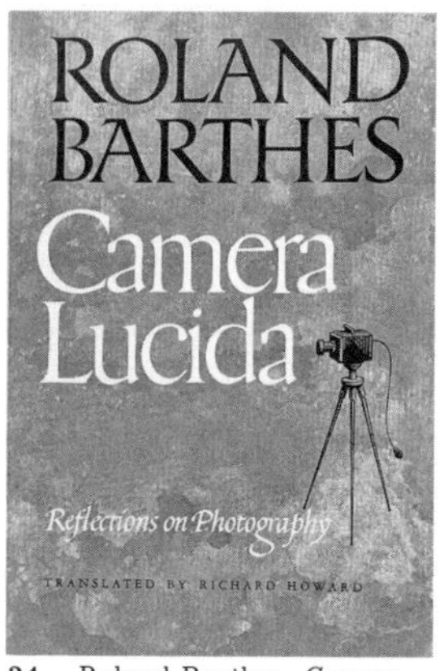

24 Roland Barthes, *Camera Lucida* (New York: Hill and Wang, 1981).

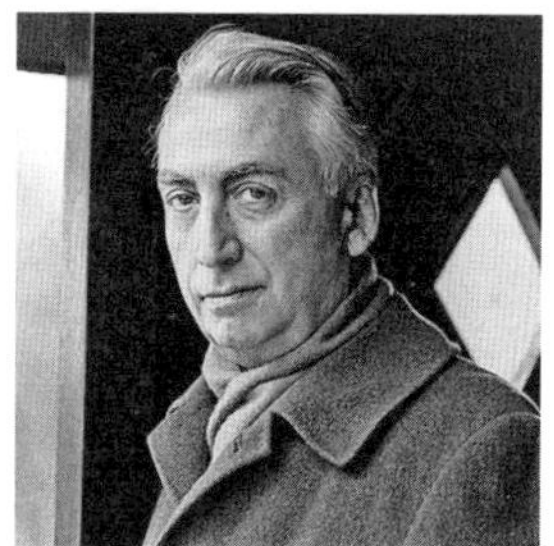

25 Roland Barthes, 1979.

26 Barthes, *Camera Lucida*, p. 64.

27 Ibid.

In his book on photography *Camera Lucida* Roland Barthes notices the same problem concerning the meaning of photography as Kracauer does.[24] In Barthes' case it is images of his mother instead of his grandmother that frustrate him in recognizing her in the image. After his mother had died he went through photographs of her, probably in an album. None of the images seemed right to him, neither as a photographic performance nor as a living resurrection of the beloved face.[25] He concludes: 'With regard to many of these photographs, it was History which separated me from them.'[26]

Here, around 1913, is my mother dressed up—hat with a feather, gloves, delicate linen at wrists and throat, her 'chic' belied by the sweetness and simplicity of her expression. This is the only time I have seen her like this, caught in a History (of tastes, fashions, fabrics): my attention is distracted from her by accessories which have perished; for clothing is perishable, it makes a second grave for the loved being.[27]

Whereas we hope and believe that archives as well as photographs enable us to stay in touch with the past, Barthes experiences the opposite. The archival photographs of his mother separate him from her. Therefore, he feels excluded from the historical dimension in which the mother is portrayed:

'History is hysterical: it is constituted only if we consider it, only if we look at it—and in order to look at it, we must be excluded from it. As a living soul, I am the very contrary of History, I am what belies it, destroys it for the sake of my own history.'[28]

The ambiguous status of the photograph, poignantly articulated by both Kracauer and Barthes, is still a bone of contention for photo archivists today. Photographic archives continue to struggle with it because of the difficulties that photography as an elusive medium presents. Tim Schlak describes the dilemmas of archivists dealing with photographs thoroughly. First quoting Roland Barthes' words 'photography evades us' he then goes on as follows:

> These words get to the crux of the difficulty archivists have writing about (and by extension, working with) photographs. Simply put, photographs are very difficult objects to talk about, let alone classify, describe, and essentially 'own' as archival evidence. Photographs compel us with their capacity to evoke rather than tell, to suggest rather than explain, so that they simultaneously allure and frustrate us with what we naively perceive in their content to be history and fact.[29]

The problem is that, like archival texts and documents, most photographs have the status of nonfictional testimonies to what once was. But as images

28 Ibid., p. 65.

29 Tim Schlak, 'Framing Photographs, Denying Archives: The Difficulty of Focusing on Archival Photographs', *Archival Science* 8 (2008), p. 85.

30   Gabriela Nouzeilles, 'The Archival Paradox', *The Itinerant Languages of Photography*, ed. Edouardo L. Cadava and Gabriela Nouzeilles (Princeton: Princeton University Press, 2013), p. 41.

they do not articulate their content, opening up to a plurality of readings. As witnesses of the past they do not translate easily into words. Gabriela Nouzeilles calls this double status of the photographic image—as archival record and as archive in itself—'the archival paradox':

> The paradoxical condition of the archive—the hesitation between *inscription* and itinerancy—is intrinsic to photography itself. Photography is both Medusan and Protean. It does congeal what it sees, but it also sets itself, and with it its referent, into motion. It both mummifies and sets free.[30]

She explains that photographic images are always subjected to the forces of 'domiciliation' and of 'dispersion'. Although the archive makes them immobile by treating them as records, when they become archives in themselves they become mobile again.

Archival Formats: Series, the Grid and the Book

The provisional order of the archive is not inherent in the photograph, but must be imposed on it. There are several devices to do that. The simplest one we saw Karl Blossfeldt apply when he collected images with similar motifs and presented them on sheets as

240

'working collages'. Each collection of images presents one single archival category. But after Blossfeldt's individual images were shown at Documenta 6 in 1977, they were presented in series or grids. The series and grids are organized on the basis of what the images have in common; they belong to the same family or category. The series and grids are modelled on an archival organization.

Since the 1960s, the grid structure has become the most popular organizing principle for presenting images, especially for conceptual and minimalist artists. A good example is the industrial photography of the German photographers Bernd and Hilla Becher. Individually, their images already have much in common with those of Blossfeldt, but especially when presented as grid or as series. The Bechers make photographs of industrial buildings and constructions such as gas tanks, granaries, coal sheds, water towers, the winding towers that haul coal and iron ore to the surface and the blast furnaces that transform the ore into metal.[31] The Bechers' motifs are always explored in extensive series. To create these works, the artists travelled all over Europe but especially in Germany, visiting large mines and steel mills, and systematically photographed the major structures of those industrial sites. Like Blossfeldt's plant enlargements, the Bechers' motifs in each individual image are centred and detached

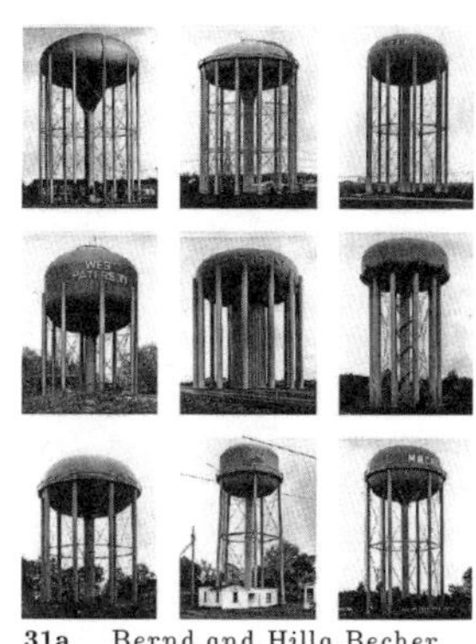

31a Bernd and Hilla Becher, *Water Towers USA*, 1988.

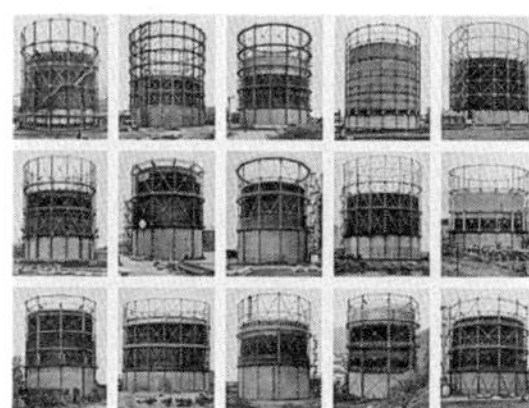

31b Bernd and Hilla Becher, *Gas-holders Germany, Belgium, France, Britain, USA, 1966–1993.*

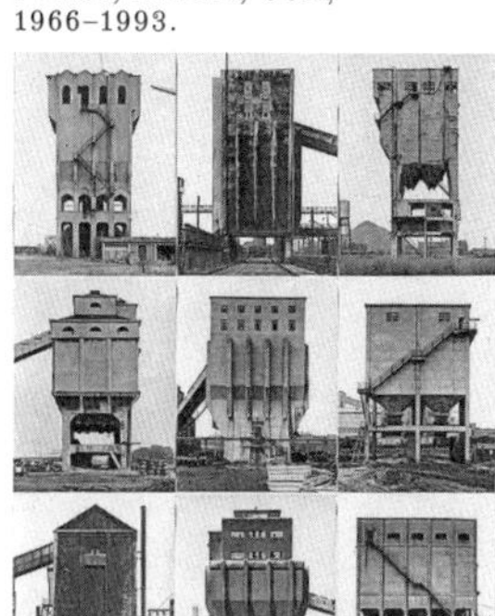

31c Bernd and Hilla Becher, *9 Coal Bunkers*, 1974.

from context.[32] Their rigorous frontality gives them the simplicity of diagrams.

The image collections of the Bechers could be seen as part of a historical project. If seen in that way, they document industrial heritage; historical architecture that has for a long time dominated the German and European landscape, but is now rapidly disappearing. Seen as such, their images are records. But the grid structure that is usually imposed on them when presented in exhibitions, suggests another reading that makes them comparable to those of Blossfeldt's working collages. The grids are typological arrangements. As a result, the referents of these images are no longer the main issue, but the motif or category that enables us to see similar forms in a great number of images. This archival principle provides an order to images that, when seen individually, are too ordinary or arbitrary to understand or appreciate.

Grid arrangement as a formal strategy is part of the conventional vocabulary of the 1960s and after. Many conceptual artists present their images in such a minimalist way. It displaces attention from the image as record, hence, from the referent to the geometrical grid. The individual images presented are integrated within a grid for their formal components; together these images result in a formal, spatial arrangement. This spatial arrangement is a visualiza-

tion of an archival organization. The American artist
John Baldessari formed grids in which to present his
serial images. His *The backs of all the trucks passed
while driving from Los Angeles to Santa Barbara,
California, Sunday 20, January 1963* archives in
the most objective way what the title of this works
says. A similar work is his *Floating: Color, 1972.*
The fact that Baldessari makes the date of the work
part of the title, instead of adding it as a kind of
supplement, emphasizes the archival nature of these
grids, because dates are one of the most important
organizing principles of archives, locating documents and images as historical records.[33]

At the same time that Baldessari made his grids
of photographs, Dutch artist Jan Dibbets also made
grids, but differently, in that he used the grid to
archive time. Two examples are his *Shortest Day at
Konrad Fischer's Gallery* (1970), and his *Shortest
Day at the Guggenheim Museum New York*
(1970).[34]

An artwork that demonstrates the displacement
in the status of the photographic image from visual
record to spatial arrangement in the most radical way
is Sol Lewitt's artist book *PhotoGrids*, of 1977.[35]
Each page in this book presents three rows of
three images. The images show grids as found by
Lewitt on city grates, manhole covers, window
frames, doors, floors, and more. These images are

243

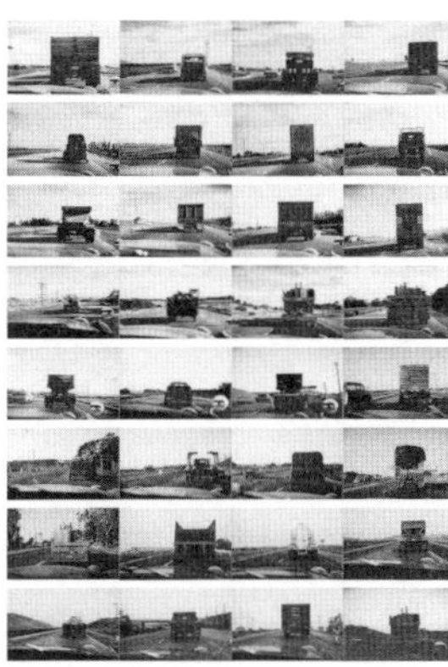

33a John Baldessari, *The
backs of all the trucks passed
while driving from Los Angeles to
Santa Barbara, California, Sunday 20, January 1963.*

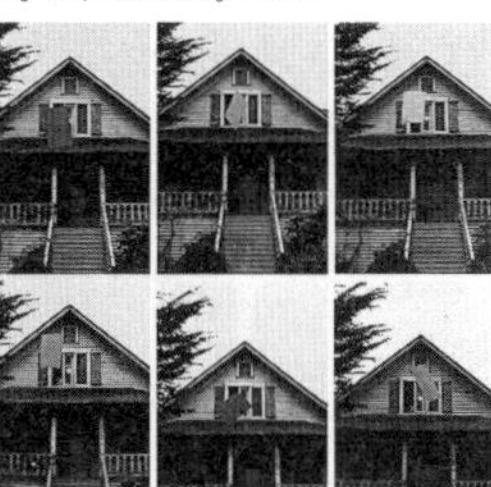

33b John Baldessari,
Floating: Color, 1972.

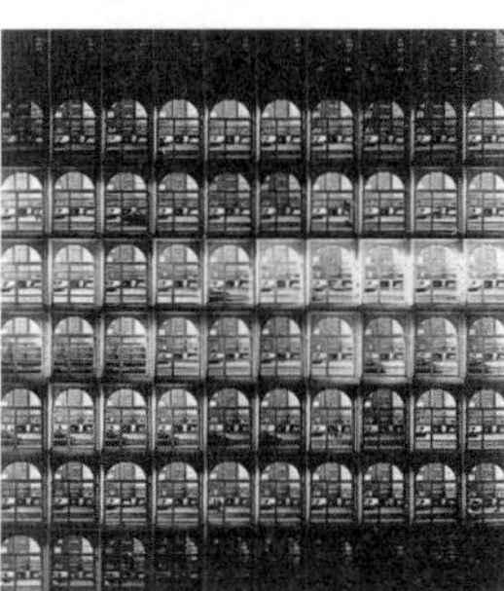

34a Jan Dibbets, *Shortest Day
at Konrad Fischer's Gallery,*
1970.

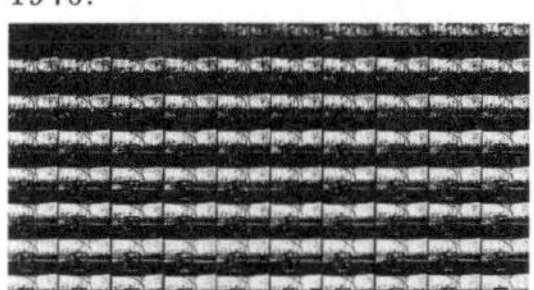

34b Jan Dibbets, *Shortest Day
at the Guggenheim Museum New
York,* 1970.

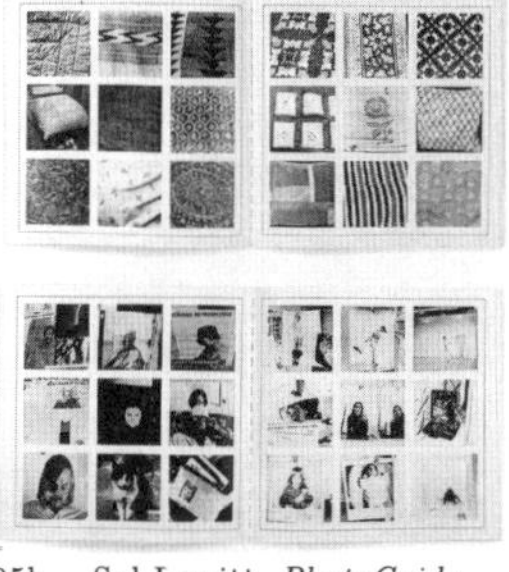

35b Sol Lewitt, *PhotoGrids,*
1977.

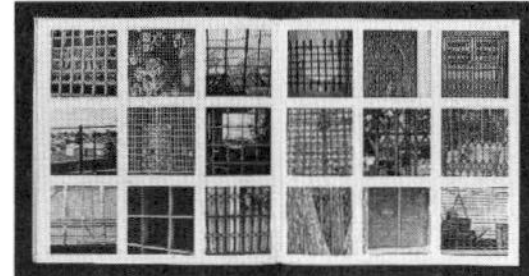

35a Sol Lewitt, *PhotoGrids,*
1977.

36 Sol Lewitt, 'Paragraphs on Conceptual Art', *Artforum* 5, no. 10 (Summer 1967), p. 83.

themselves grouped in grids across the page. The displacement of recorded referent to formal arrangement is no longer implicit or underlying, but happens explicitly before our eyes. The visual arrangement of the book and of each image is what *PhotoGrids* is about. Sol LeWitt describes this focus on the arrangement of form as follows:

> When an artist uses a multiple modular method he usually chooses a simple and readily available form. The form itself is of very limited importance; it becomes the grammar for the total work. In fact it is best that the basic unit be deliberately uninteresting so that it may more easily become an intrinsic part of the entire work. Using a simple form repeatedly … concentrates the intensity on the arrangement of the form.[36]

The artist does not spend a single word on what the basic unit is or refers to. In the case of *PhotoGrids* the images are of the grid structures of, for example, doors, windows or walls. Those basic units are not important as such; all they do is suggest a grammar.

As this example of an artist book suggests, the grid does not only serve the purpose of imposing an archival ordering. Also, the exploration of one single motif, or concept, in the series of images in which that results, is often presented in book format. This has been the case since the very beginning of the history of photography. The first photo book is probably by the botanist and photographer Anna Atkins, who published *Photographs of British Algae: Cyanotype Impressions* in several instalments between 1843 and 1853. Her friend sir John Herschel had invented the cyanotype photographic process in 1842. The very next year, Atkins applied the process to different species of seaweed by making cyanotype photograms that were contact printed. The complete publication contains around 400 images of algae. The name of each seaweed is written on each photogram.[37]

Photographs of British Algae is a photographic archive in book format. In its entirety the book contains only one archival category, namely algae or seaweed. In her introduction to Part 1, Atkins explains that she was attempting 'a systematic arrangement', trying to photographically represent 'The Tribes and Species in their proper order'.[38] In the 1850s Atkins collaborated with her close-friend and fellow photographer Anne Dixon on three other archival publications of cyanotype contact pints of plants. The best-known are *Cyanotypes of British and Foreign Ferns* (1853) and *Cyanotypes of British and Foreign Flowering Plants and Ferns* (1854). The foreign plants included in the last publications came from countries such as Australia and Jamaica, which were British colonies in the nineteenth century, adding an

245

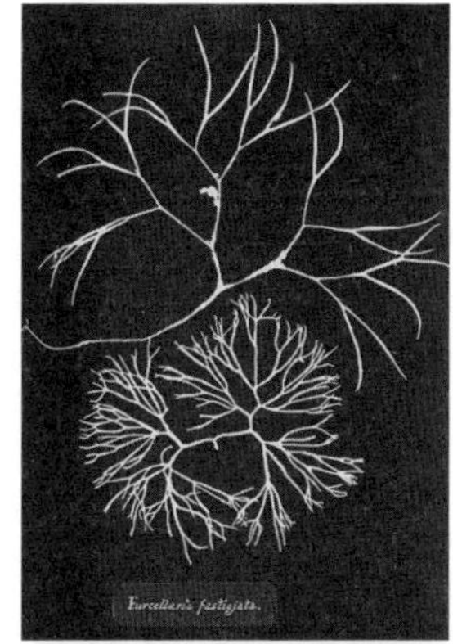
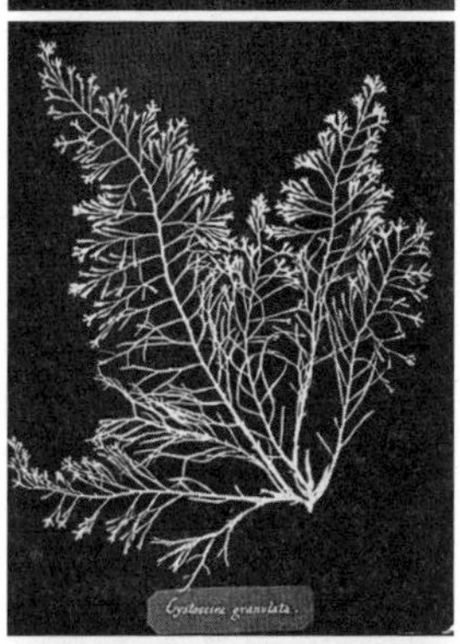
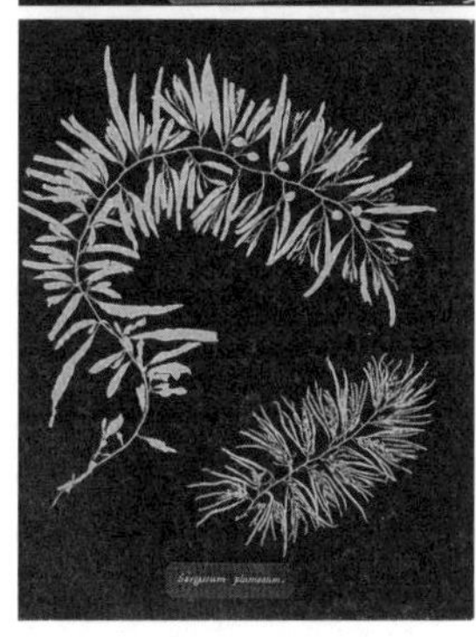

37   Three plates from Anna Atkins, *Photographs of British Algae: Cyanotype Impressions*, 1843–1853.

38   Atkins quoted in Batchen, *Emanations*. Batchen's book provides an excellent, elaborate history of cameraless photography, which changes the conventional history of photography substantially.

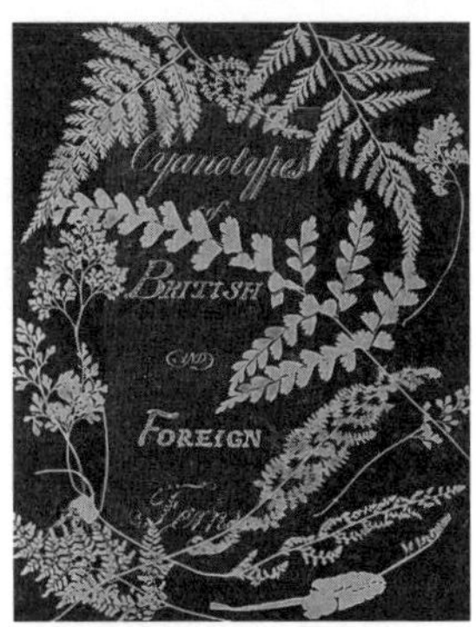

39a Title page of *Cyanotypes of British and Foreign Ferns*, 1853.

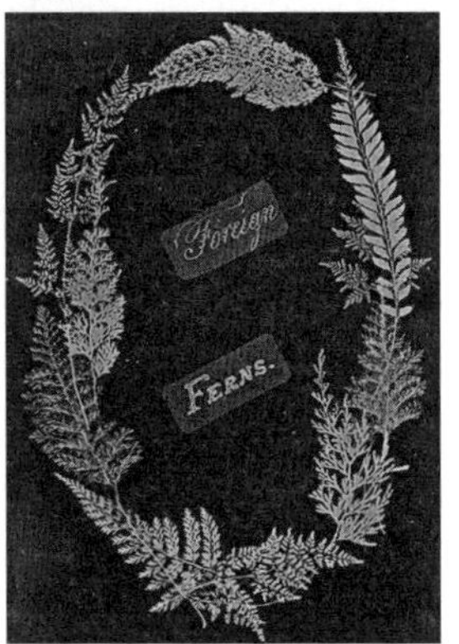

39b First page of the section 'Foreign Ferns' in *Cyanotypes of British and Foreign Ferns*, 1853.

imperial dimension to her earlier project, which had archived exclusively British specimen. Another difference is that the arrangement of the plants is less neutral or objective, as one would expect in a scientific, botanic publication, but much more creative and decorative. It looks as if Atkins and Dixon did not try to reach an exclusively scientific oriented audience for the publication, but also a more artistic one.[39]

More or less at the same time that Atkins published her archival books with cyanotype images, Talbot published his *The Pencil of Nature*. This appeared in six instalments between 1844 and 1846 and competes with Anna Atkins publication for being the first photographically illustrated book to be commercially published. Although Talbot's photo book can also be seen as an archive of images, his archive is not structured on the basis of one single category, but on several. As already discussed in my Introduction, he presented a diversity of photographic practices. That makes his book not less archival, however, because the different images are not arbitrary. His archival book is more diverse in the sense that it encompasses more categories and provides a more complete image of the possibilities of the photographic medium in those days.

The accumulated images of Ed Ruscha's artist book *Twentysix Gasoline Stations* of 1962 are a visual inventory. The book form is used to present a typology or morphology of filling stations between Los Angeles and Oklahoma City. As is the case with LeWitt's *PhotoGrids,* Ruscha's work challenges common assumptions about the materiality of books. The format of the book is conventionally seen as linear: one reads a book from beginning to end. With this kind of visual collection or inventory, however, the book format is more similar to that of a dictionary or encyclopaedia. As with these, one browses the book, leaves through it arbitrarily, because each image exemplifies the same motif. Linearity, conventionally associated with the medium of the book, is made redundant.[40]

The Archive: From Science to Art

In the nineteenth century, the archival paradigm in photography applied to the domain of science, not of art. Pictorialist photographers who wanted to elevate the new medium to the status of art did not make use of archival principles to present their images. Although in some cases their photographs were also published in books, the ordering of those books was not archival, because it was not based on the differentiation of clear categories. In contrast to those artists who had the ambition to produce autonomous

247

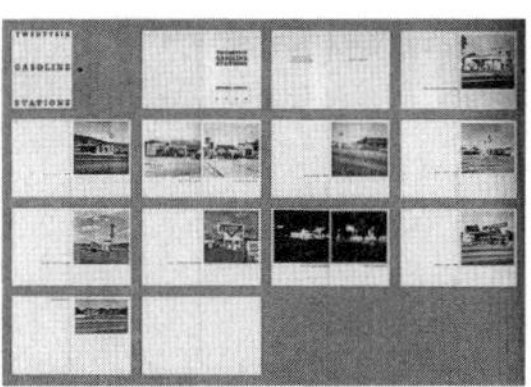

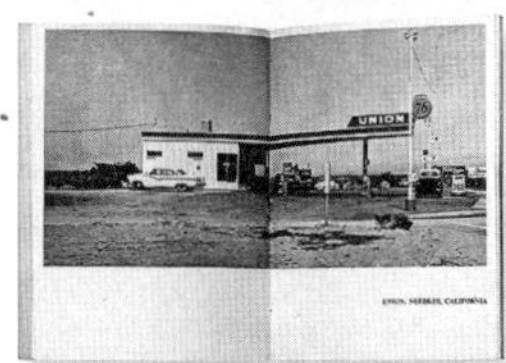

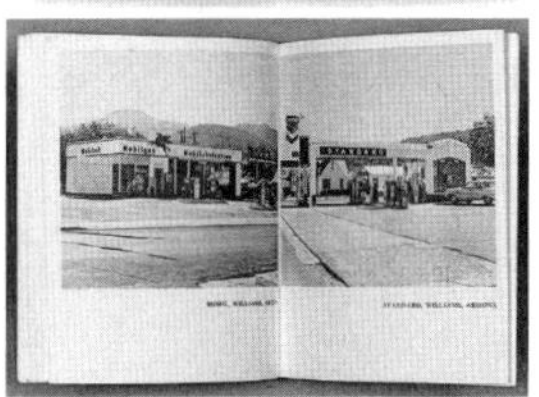

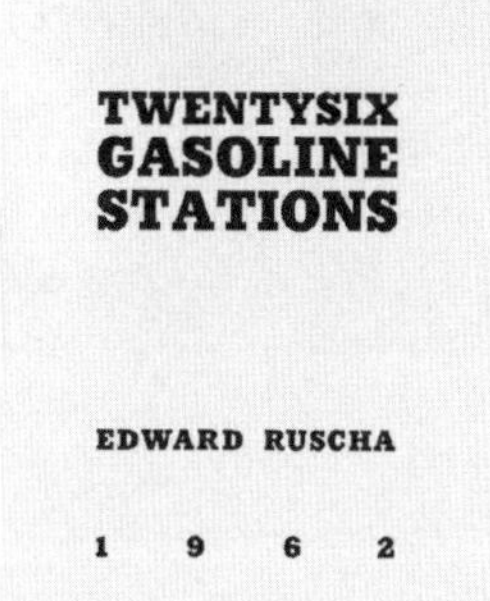

40   Ed Ruscha, *Twentysix Gasoline Stations,* 1962.

art works, for the botanist Anna Atkins the archival format of the book was the obvious framework to represent her images of seaweed. And for police officer Bertillon a filing cabinet with cards for each criminal was the most effective way of presenting his photographs of criminals.

But at the beginning of the twentieth century, some modernist artists and photographers embraced the paradigm of the modern archive as it had been developed in the nineteenth century in the scientific domain. Karl Blossfeldt, already discussed earlier in this chapter, made his archival photographs as teaching material for art students. And when in 1929 he presented his images for the first time at the Stuttgart exhibition 'Film und Foto', the context was clearly artistic, since his images were hanging in the company of the photographs of the young photographic avant-garde. Not long before, German portrait and documentary photographer August Sander applied archival principles to the photographs he made as a photographer who identified as artist. First having had a photo studio in Linz, Austria, later in Cologne, Germany, Sander joint the 'Group of Progressive Artists' in Cologne, in 1920. It is important to notice that as a photographer, he had the ambition to profile himself as 'a progressive artist', and that he was accepted by that group of artists. Although his work includes many different genres, such as architecture, landscape and street photography, he is best known for his portraits. As an artist, he had plans to document contemporary German society in a series of portraits. This resulted in his series titled *People of the 20th Century*. In this series, he intends to show a cross-section of German society during the Weimar Republic. He inventoried his contemporaries by a standard procedure. As in a modern archive he used a classificatory system to order the series. He divided it into seven categories: the Farmer, the Skilled Tradesman, Woman, Classes and Professions, Artists, the City, and The Last People (meaning homeless people, veterans, etc.). In the end, Sander's archive contained over 40,000 images. Most of these show the subjects in full length. They are always facing and acknowledging the camera. The space in which their portrait is taken is usually their own 'natural context': the space in which they live or work. For instance, the pastry cook is portrayed in his kitchen, road workers in the street, a widower with his two children in the living room, circus artists in front of their circus wagon. This supplementary role of the spatial context is crucial, because otherwise the identity of the classified subjects would still be too ambiguous.[41]

In 1929 Sander published sixty images from his *People of the 20th Century* in a book titled *Face of our Time*. Under the Nazi regime his work was seen

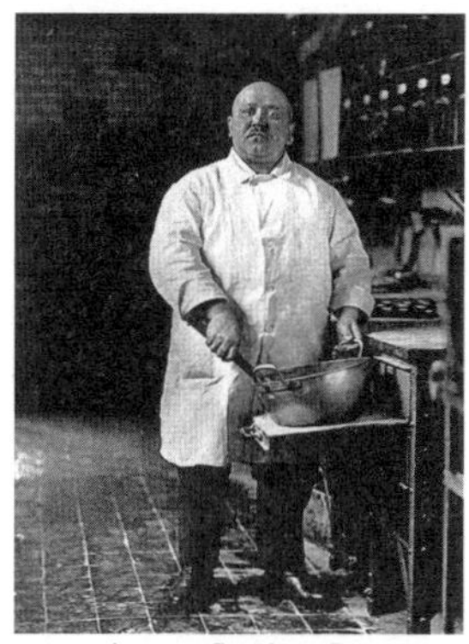

41a   August Sander, *Pastry Cook*, c. 1928.

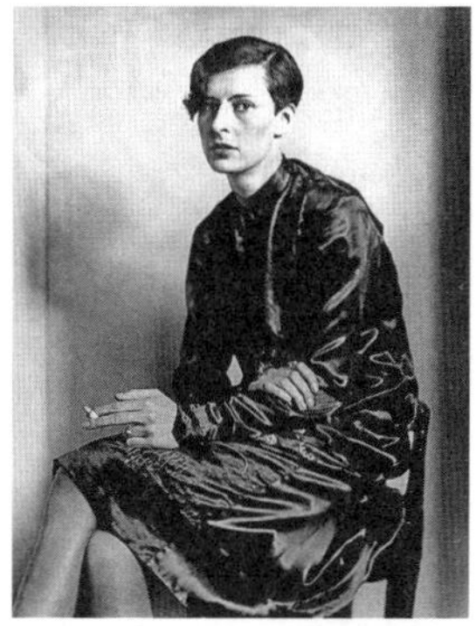

41b   August Sander, *Secretary at a Radio Station*, 1931.

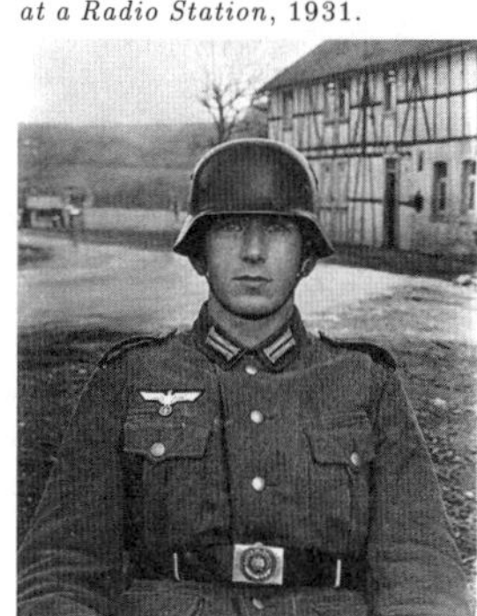

41c   August Sander, *Young Soldier*, c. 1945.

42   Monk, *Disassembling the
Archive*, n.p.

as *entartet,* degenerated, and in 1936 his book *Face
of our Time* was seized and the photographic plates
were destroyed. We can only speculate now which
aspects of Sander's work were the reasons for the
Nazis to condemn it as degenerated and have it
destroyed. But from a certain perspective is it amazing that they did, because the archival art project of
Sander and the political project of Nazism have key
elements in common: they both use a typological
mindset. Whereas Sander's archival project classified
on the basis of occupational categories, the politics of
Nazism used racial categories such as Germanic,
Jewish, Slavic, gipsy. But what they have in common
is an inventorial, encyclopaedic approach to
humanity.

In both cases a specific identity, considered to be
essential, is projected onto human beings on the
basis of a classificatory system. With his classifications Sander, too, pursued the goal to pin down the
identity of human beings, in his case on the basis of
their occupation or profession. The archival structure of his project evacuated, however, any identity
he tried to institute on the basis of these categories,
see,[42] since the identity we are supposed to see in
those images is not the result of who or what these
subjects are, but foremost of the classificatory system
imposed upon them. Within this system, the individual subjects are supposed to express their unique

identity in relation to other similarly unique subjects belonging to the same category. Ultimately, the individual subjects are deemed to be just another expression of the other subjects that surround it. Not from an aesthetic point of view, but from the point of view of his epistemological pursuit of pinning down the identities of the photographed subjects, his project was doomed from the start. In Sander's project the signifying devices of the archive (classifications) and of the still image of photography collaborate. Although the photographs have the status of nonfictional testimonies to what these people are, in other words, what their identity is, they do not articulate their content unambiguously. That is why their problematic status of record, of factual testimony needs to be reinforced by the classifications of an archival system.

The complex role of the photographic medium in this collaboration between photography and archive is exposed in the work of the contemporary artist Fiona Tan. In her video installation *Countenance* of 2002, first shown at Documenta in Kassel in the same year, Tan re-enacts Sander's photographic taxonomies of Germany from the 1920s and 1930s. In this re-enactment of Sander's project photographic portraits are replaced by video portraits. Tan made these video portraits during a stay in Berlin. She explored the city of Berlin through the

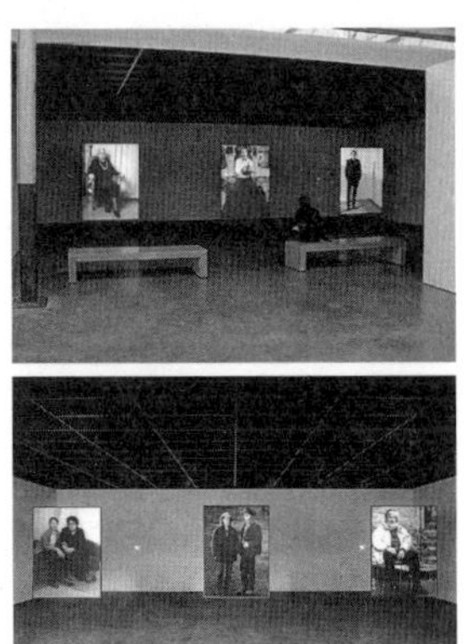

43 Fiona Tan, *Countenance,* 2002, video Installation De Pont Foundation for Contemporary Art, Tilburg, the Netherlands, 2003.

portrayal of its people. Like Sander, she did not approach the people of Germany, or in this case of Berlin, as a homogenous group, but as a collection of people who distinguish themselves through their professions. Again like Sander, the categories Tan employed were from professional and everyday life: a doctor, a carpenter, an architect, a supplier of small supermarkets, a postman, a prostitute, a barkeeper, children in the street, a field labourer, a train driver, a beggar, and so on. As with Sander, Tan's project is clearly archival, but the medium she used for archiving the people of Berlin is different: instead of a photographed portrait, a video portrait. Each person Tan invited for her project was asked to stand motionless in front of the camera for a full minute.[43]

In this difference between the media used it becomes clear to what degree the medium specificity of photography enables the archival classification to do its work. Or, to put it more strongly, to what degree it reinforces it. The status of the photographic still image and of archival organization are very similar. They are supposed to be factual (nonfictional) testaments to what once was, or to what life is. But as I have explained above, in the case of the photographic still image it is hard to sustain this status, because when severed from their referents photographs usually open up to a plurality of readings and therefore they are not very 'factual' in that respect.

The video portraits of Fiona Tan are, however, far from 'still' and thereby they escape any fixed meaning or signification. In the description of Doris van Drathen: 'The people stare at her. One minute is a long time. As each second passes, the mask of their everyday activities slowly begins to slip and fall away, as if an eggshell were gradually metamorphosing back into a soft membrane. In turn, the faces interrogate the one scrutinising them.'[44] The filmed portraits give the portrayed people an uncanny presence, compressing time to the moment of shared duration.[45] Within this shared duration, the look into the camera initiates 'an open, dynamic, sometimes disturbing and discomfiting relay of points of address between maker, subject and viewer, each aware of the other's burden in the exchange yet neither able nor required to share this burden in equal measure.'[46] In the photographed portrait the portrayed person is suggested to be absent, belonging to the past, and only its illusionary shadow is made present in the photographic image. The effect of shared duration of the filmic image results in an almost opposite experience of the portrait. In an interview Fiona Tan herself has described the difference as follows:

> I am more aware of … the artificiality of the
> encounter and simultaneously (in-)voluntary

44 Doris von Drathen, 'Areal Roots', in *Fiona Tan: Disorient*, ed. Marente Bloemheuvel (Amsterdam Mondriaan Foundation, 2009), p. 7.

45 Thomas Elsaesser, 'Fiona Tan: Place after Place', *Fiona Tan: Disorient*, ed. Marente Bloemheuvel (Amsterdam: Mondriaan Foundation, 2009), pp. 20–33.

46 Ibid., p. 23.

47 Fiona Tan, 'Interview with Ana Finel Honigman', *Kultur-flash* 6 April 2005, www.kultur-flash.net/archive/118preview.html (last accessed 16 February 2009).

resistance against it. It is as though as a viewer, I cannot own and cannot pocket the image in the same way I imagine I could if it were only a still photograph hanging on the wall. When looking at a video portrait, I am looking at something which is constantly escaping me.[47]

The collaboration of photography and the archive in Sander's work seems to be successful because the archival classification compensates for the weakness, the instability of photography as objective record. The status of the photographic still image as factual testament, *de facto* problematic, is reinforced, in an attempt to make it unproblematic, by the imposition of archival classification. In the case of Tan's video portraits in *Countenance*, the collaboration between archive and video portrait is untenable; it falls apart. Whereas the archival classification of the portraits promises to produce fixed categories and meanings, the video portraits produce an opposite effect. The portrayed professionals escape us. We don't know what to think of them, and who or what these people are. It is only clear that what they are not is still or stable.

Archiving Time, or Temporal Inventories

A crucial characteristic of the snapshot that has given it its name is a temporal one. The genre's name emphasizes the fact that photographs isolate one temporal moment from a continuity of time. This demonstrates that the snapshot relies on a highly specific notion of time, for time is not necessarily seen as continuity. The Heraclitean conception of the world holds time to be continuous. The counter model also goes back to ancient Greece, namely to Democritus. He describes the world as a rainfall of events of which the drops only accidently touch each other. Every event is random or contingent and remains potentially separate from any other event. Not all photographic practices rely on the Heraclitean model of a continuity of time; Ulrich Baer, who is especially interested in photography visualizing trauma, locates those images in the Democritean model.[48] This specific temporality of the snapshot cannot be recognized either in the archival images that I have so far discussed; a temporality of duration seems to be at stake in those images. This is, however, not the case with the photographic experiments of Étienne-Jules Marey and Eadweard Muybridge. Their sequential images dissect continuous time not by showing one single moment, but by showing a series of moments that

48   Ulrich Baer, *Spectral Evidence: The Photography of Trauma* (Cambridge, MA: MIT Press, 2002), p. 5–6.

49 Quoted in Anita Ventura Mozley, 'Introduction to the Dover Edition', in Eadweard Muybridge, *Muybridge's Complete Human and Animal Locomotion: Volume 1* (New York: Dover Publications, 1979), p. vii.

follow each other by split seconds. When photography was invented in 1839 it was believed to enable the scientific rendering of appearances; the smallest visible details could be reproduced as long as the objects were still objects. However, the camera's inability to record moving figures or objects was lamented. When in 1839 a reporter of the *Foreign Quarterly Review* wrote about one of the first daguerreotype images seen by the public, he immediately noticed the limitation of the new technology developed by L.J.M. Daguerre: 'In foliage he is less successful, the constant motion in the leaves rendering his landscapes confused and unmeaning … the same objection necessarily applies to all moving objects.'[49] It was more than two decades later that technological developments of the photographic process made it possible to make more instantaneous images, albeit that only relatively slow movements such as walking, strolling, or stepping into a carriage could be registered. Any faster movement, like a man or horse running or walking very fast, still resulted in a blurred movement in the image.

A French professor of natural history at the Collège de France in Paris, Étienne-Jules Marey, and a British photographer working in California, Eadweard Muybridge, were the first to register fast motion. They were aware of each other's work but worked independently from each other. Their photographic experiments are often considered as forerunners of the cinema, but in their treatment of time their images relate only superficially to the presence of time in that new medium. Moreover, the conspicuous differences between the images of Marey and Muybridge are not just formal differences; these differences have major implications for the representation of time.

Time and motion are, however, the central issues in the images of both. For motion concerns the correlation of space and time as a body successively changes its position.[50] But their interest in time was merely secondary, 'a by-product of the obsessive concern with the analysis of bodies in motion'.[51] I will first discuss Marey's efforts to represent and store time and then point out the differences between his and those of Muybridge.

Marey had devoted himself, since the mid-1860s, to the scientific analysis of animal locomotion and in 1873 published *La machine animale, locomotion terrestre et aérienne*. Already one year later it was published in English as *Animal Mechanism*. Marey had developed ingenious recording devices to be attached to the animal being studied that enabled the graphic notation of the animal's motion. In that publication he suggested that 'the successive attitudes of the body during walking, running, etc.' could be represented most faithfully by a series of

50 See for a superb reading of the photographic experiments of Marey in relation to cinema: Mary Ann Doane, 'Temporality, Storage, Legibility: Freud, Marey, and the Cinema', *Critical Inquiry* 22, no. 2 (Winter 1996), pp. 324–343.

51 Ibid., p. 325.

52   Marey, quoted in Mozley, 'Introduction to the Dover Edition', p. xiv.

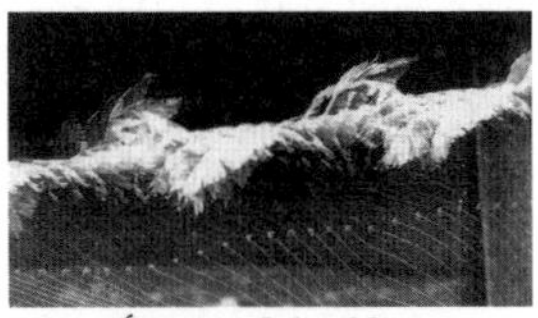

53a   Étienne-Jules Marey, *Flight of seagulls*, 1886.

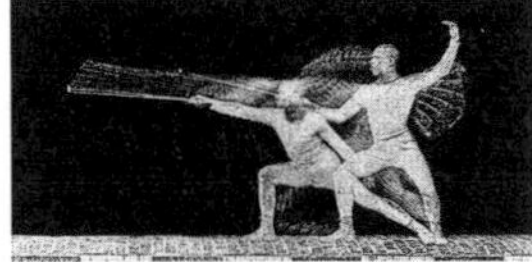

53b   Étienne-Jules Marey, *Sword thrust*, chronophotography, 1895.

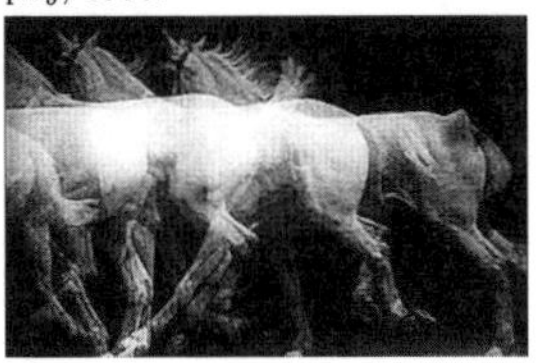

53c   Étienne-Jules Marey, *The movement of a running white horse*, 1886.

54   Doane, 'Temporality, Storage, Legibility', p. 325.

successive images.[52] In the 1880s Marey realized what he had suggested by developing 'animated photography' into a separate field of what he called 'chronophotography', literally the photography of time. His revolutionary pursuit was to record several phases of movement by a single camera and to present them on one photographic plate. These chronophotographs included all of the recorded successive positions of a single body within the same frame. He succeeded in his pursuit and in 1890 he published *Le Vol des oiseaux* (The Flight of Birds), richly illustrated with photographs, drawings, and diagrams.[53]

Although his main concern was the analysis of motion of bodies, Marey was very aware of the tension between spatial and temporal categories in his experimental research. He could only analyse the motion of bodies by privileging temporality and by developing technologies to represent and measure time. The only way to represent time was by 'cutting into time, slicing it in such a way that it could become representable'.[54] Marey's first efforts to represent time were by means of a graphic method. He developed instrumentation for the production of graphic inscriptions capable of translating and representing the movement of horses cantering, trotting, or galloping, and the movement of wings of insects and birds. The graphic inscriptions were indexical traces of these moments. As François

258

Dagognet argues, indexicality is the major semiotic principle in all representational technologies Marey developed.

> Marey's brilliance lay in the discovery of how to make recordings without recourse to the human hand or eye. Nature had to testify to itself, to translate itself through the inflection of curves and subtle trajectories that were truly representative ... The trace was to be considered nature's own expression, without screen, echo or interference: it was faithful, clear and, above all universal.[55]

The qualities of the graphic technology were indexicality, instantaneity, and readability; exactly these qualities also defined the photographic method, which Marey begun to explore after he had experimented with the graphic one. Marey switched to the photographic method after he had read an article by Muybridge in a French Journal in 1878. But Marey's use of photography differed from Muybridge's. Unlike Muybridge he used only one camera and one photographic plate for the registration of all successive positions of the moving body. The resulting chronophotograph differs radically from images of the entire tradition of Western representation, as Marta Braun explains:

55   François Dagognet, *Etienne-Jules Marey: A Passion for the Trace*, ed. Robert Galeta and Jeanine Herman (New York: Zone Books, 1992), pp. 30 and 63.

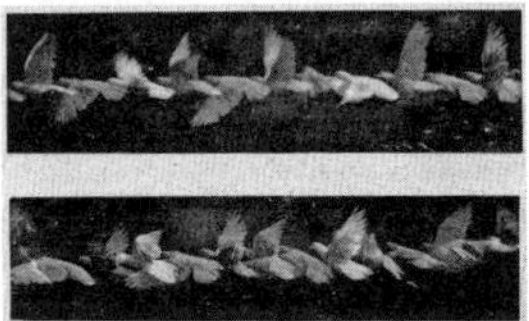

56   Marta Braun, *Picturing Time: The Work of Etienne-Jules Marey* (Chicago: University of Chicago Press, 1992), p. 66.

57a   Étienne-Jules Marey, *Analysis of the flight of a pigeon by the chronophotographic method, 1883–1887.*

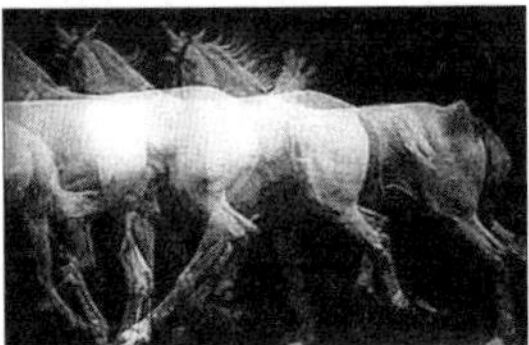

57b   Étienne-Jules Marey, *Cheval blanc monté, 1886.*

Since the advent of linear perspective in the Renaissance, the frame of an image has, with rare exceptions, been understood to enclose a temporal and spatial unity. We read what occurs within the frame as happening at a single instant in time and in a single space. Marey's photographs shattered that unity; viewers now had to unravel the successive parts of the work in order to understand that they were looking not at several men moving in single file, but at a single figure successively occupying a series of positions in space.[56]

Marey gradually decreased the intervals between the successive positions of the subject, because that would result in a more clarifying image of the temporal progression. But as a result, the successive positions were inevitably superimposed and the figures overlapped; outlines became indistinct and blurred. There turned out to be a tension between the progression of time and the representation, in other words, the legibility of time.[57] As Doane has it:

> The legibility of time is seriously impaired since it requires the distinct separation of legible units, and Marey has already stipulated that a pronounced advantage of photography is that it would permit the exact measurement of time intervals. Problems of legibility linked to the

overlapping, blurring, and superimposition of figures were due, in a sense, to the fact that there was *too much* detail in the photographic method.[58]

To solve that problem, Marey excised details by clothing his subject completely in black, using darker backgrounds, and attaching luminous dots to the joints of the subjects and connecting them with luminous striping. The outcome of this solution was a series of almost abstract chronophotographs consisting only of lines and curves in space, which were geometric chronophotographs. 'Marey's trajectory is quite astonishing. He moves from the graphic method to the photographic method only to de-familiarize, de-realize, even de-iconize the photographic image.'[59]

The geometric chronophotographs enhanced the representation of time while limiting that of space.[60] But as a result, the legibility of the photographic image as such is directly affected by the ambition to perfect the representation of time.

The issue of legibility and illegibility of the image can be used for an understanding of Marey's work in how it differs from that of his fellow-explorer and photographer of time, Muybridge. Marey's photography of time presented successive moments in the motion of an animal in one image or frame. The

58 Doane, 'Temporality, Storage, Legibility', p. 328.

59 Ibid., p. 329.

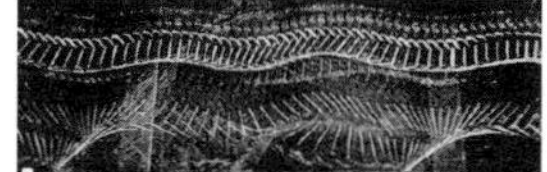

60a Étienne-Jules Marey, *Walking Man*, chronophotography, 1884.

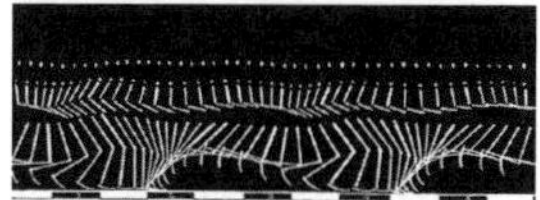

60b Étienne-Jules Marey, *Walking Man*, chronophotography, 1884.

apparatus developed by Eadweard Muybridge presented the successive moments in the motion of animal or human being in a series of frames. The intervals between the successive moments in Muybridge series are longer than Marey's intervals. Each image records one single moment, not different from what a snapshot does.

Muybridge was not a scientist like Marey. He identified himself as an 'artist-photographer'. He started out as a landscape photographer. Having moved to California, in 1872 former Governor Leland Stanford asked him to make a photograph of his horse at full speed because he wanted proof of his theory that a trotting horse at some point in its stride has all four feet off the ground at the same time. This resulted in an image of a trotting horse, which satisfied Stanford but not Muybridge. This was the beginning of a collaboration between Muybridge and Stanford that resulted, in 1878, in an elaborate experimental setup of 24 cameras, set at intervals of twelve inches. He did not use a wheel like Marey did, but a battery of cameras. The results of this photographic investigation were published in 1881 under the title of *The Attitudes of Animals in Motion: A series of Photographs Illustrating the Consecutive Positions Assumed by Animals in Performing Various Movements*. In 1883 the University of Pennsylvania decided to sponsor Muybridge's experiments in the study of animal motion. It was there that he perfected his apparatus of a battery of cameras and made the 781 images for the publication in four volumes that made him famous: *Animal Locomotion*, published in 1887.

Muybridge photographs presented the successive moments in the motion of animal or human beings in a series of images, also called stop-motion photographs. Each image records one single moment by arresting, putting a stop to movement and continuous time.[61]

The successive positions of Muybridge's figures are separated in distinct frames, forming a series. Because the positions do not overlap (within one frame), they do not raise the problem of illegibility of the image, as is the case with Marey's chronophotographs. But Marey was critical of the relatively long intervals between each position of frame in Muybridge's series of images:

> Not only did Muybridge have no way of measuring the time of the movements he recorded, the positions of the figures were too far apart—it was often impossible to determine how the figure moved from one position to the next. Too much time was lost.'[62]

One could argue that Marey's chronophotographs succeed better in representing time than

263

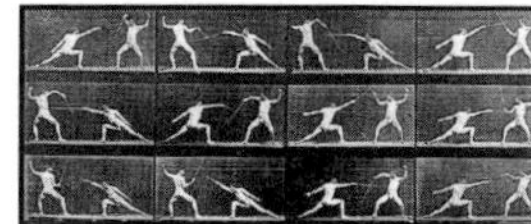

61a Eadweard Muybridge, *Animal Locomotion*, 1883, Plate 349 'Fencing'.

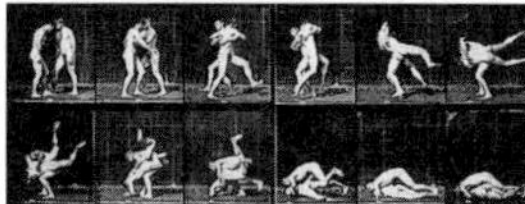

61b Eadweard Muybridge, *Animal Locomotion*, 1883, Plate 347 'Wrestling, Graeco-Roman'.

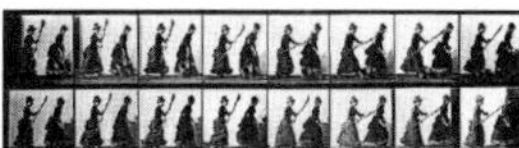

61c Eadweard Muybridge, *Animal Locomotion*, 1883, Plate 464 'Woman chasing another with a broom'.

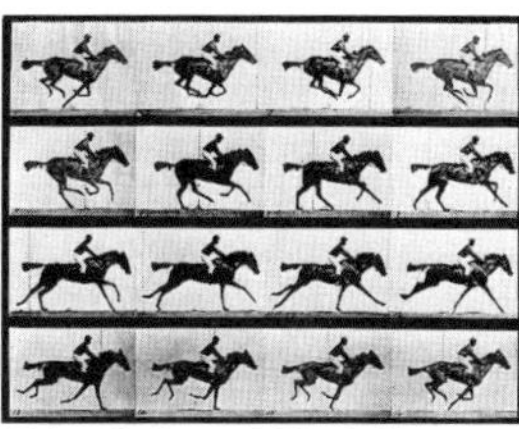

61d Eadweard Muybridge, *Animal Locomotion*, 1883, Plate 626 '"Annie G." galloping'.

62 Doane, 'Temporality, Storage, Legibility', p. 333.

63   Ibid., p. 336.

64   Marey, quoted in Braun, *Picturing Time*, p. 255.

Muybridge's series of images, because the intervals between the successive moments are smaller in his images. But such a conclusion implies that the evidence that Marey's images are more perfect representations of time than Muybridge's consists in the (relative) illegibility of the images. The illegibility of those images suggest that time is ultimately unrepresentable, or is only representable negatively, by means of intervals or discontinuities.

Marey's experiments demonstrate a 'desire for a pure representation of time'.[63] This suggests that he would embrace cinema, but that is not the case; on the contrary, he resisted cinema. Marey claimed that:

> Cinema produces only what the eye can see in any case. It adds nothing to the power of our sight, nor does it remove its illusions, and the real character of a scientific method is to supplant the insufficiency of our senses and correct their errors. To get to this point, chronophotograph should renounce the representation of phenomena as they are seen by the eye.[64]

The perfect continuity of the moving image does not represent or store time; rather, it is time, because it takes time. The discontinuities of both Marey's and Muybridge images—different as these are from each other—are more successful in collecting and storing time, by first cutting time up. Time can only be archived after it has been made discontinuous. Only in the form of distinct entities, lines or images, can time be made legible. In other words, only because the photographic image resists time (unlike cinema), it is able to store or represent it. It does that indexically, using the intervals between successive images as traces of time. Whereas time is usually seen as continuous, it can only be archived in its discontinuity.

Conclusion

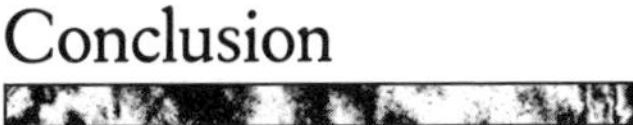

According to common-sense notions of photography, photographic images are records. In that conception, photographs are considered and dealt with as pictorial testimonies of the existence of a recorded fact. And the camera is, then, a kind of archiving machine: every image it produces is a priori an archival object. But as we have seen, the ontology of the photographic image is more complex and diverse than that; a complexity that holds especially in its relation to the archive. Here, time itself acts as an agent of change. The moment a photograph is severed from its referent, and that happens soon when it ages, it is no longer a record but becomes an archive in itself; an archive full of forms and details that can be read and categorized in many different ways.

265

Images, intended as scientific and meant to record referents in the world, transform over time into images that are appreciated not for how, or that they relate to the world, but for their artistic form. As soon as the image is severed from its referent, this transformation takes place, and the possibility of an evaluation and appreciation on the basis of artistic form becomes the new future of the same image. This transformation into artistic form implies a severing of the image from the referent.

When there is no longer a referent to direct and channel our look at the photographic image, a great variety of details strike the eye and a great variety of possible meanings proliferate. This proliferation of meanings, however, becomes a new problem for the image. Paradoxically, in order to restrict this expansion of possibilities, the classifications of the archive are needed. For it is the archive that provides a provisional order to the photograph, needed after 'the original order' (of the referent) is lost. This is how a photograph transforms from record to a potential archive; from detail of an archive to an archive in itself. Photographers, scientists as well as artists have introduced several devices in order to facilitate the imposition of archival order onto the image; primarily those of publication in book form, in the form of series, or in grids. All these different devices bring with them typological arrangements. As a result, the referents of the images are no longer the main issue, but the motif or category that enables us to see similar forms in a great number of images. This archival principle provides an order to images that, when seen individually, are too ordinary or arbitrary to understand or appreciate.

Seriality as a device is also used when not motifs or forms are archived, but when time is archived. The archiving of time is a paradoxical achievement, because photography seems to resist time and its representation. The difficulty of presenting motion in still images demonstrates this problem. But as I have just argued, time can only be archived after it has been made discontinuous. The discontinuity of a series of images, of the intervals between the images in the series, makes them legible negatively, in its absence between the images that constitute the series. In contrast with cinema, it is only because the photographic image resists time that it is able to archive. The continuity of time—for that notion of time is implied by most prevalent photographic practices—can only be made felt and visualized in the form of a series of discontinuous moments. This may well be the greatest paradox of photography.

Agamben, Giorgio. 'Identity Without the Person.' In *Nudities*. Translated by David Kishik and Stefan Pedatella, pp. 46–54. Stanford: Stanford University Press, 2013.

Alphen, Ernst van. 'Skin, Body, Self: The Question of the Abject in the Work of Francis Bacon.' In *Abject Visions: The Power of Horror in Art and Visual Culture*. Edited by Rina Arya and Nick Chare, pp. 119–129. Manchester: Manchester University Press, 2016.

———. 'Visionary Images.' In *Juul Kraijer: Werken 2009–2015*, pp. 82–86. Zwolle: WBOOKS, 2015.

———. *Staging the Archive: Art and Photography in Times of New Media*. London: Reaktion Books, 2016.

Arago, Dominique François. 'Report.' In *Classic Essays on Photography*. Edited by Alan Trachtenberg, pp. 27–36. New Haven: Leete's Island Books, 1980.

Baer, Ulrich. *Spectral Evidence: The Photography of Trauma*. Cambridge, MA: MIT Press, 2002.

Baker, George. 'Photography's Expanded Field.' *October* 114 (Fall 2005), pp. 120–140.

Bal, Mieke. *Narratology: Introduction to the Theory of Narrative*. Toronto: University of Toronto Press, 2009.

———. *The Mottled Screen: Reading Proust Visually*. Translated from the French by *Anna-Louise Milne*. Stanford: Stanford University Press, 1997.

———. 'Timely Remains.' In exh. cat. *Jussi Niva: Timely Remains*, pp. 66–116. Helsinki: Parvs Publishing, 2010.

———. *Thinking in Film: The Politics of Video Installation According to Eija-Liisa Ahtila*. New York: Bloomsbury Academic, 2013.

Banfield, Ann. *The Phantom Table: Woolf, Fry, Russell and the Epistemology of Modernism*. Cambridge, MA: Cambridge University Press, 2000.

Barthes, Roland. 'The Photographic Message.' In *Image, Music, Text*. Translated by Stephan Heath, pp. 15–31. New York: Hill and Wang, 1977.

———. *Camera Lucida: Reflections on Photography*. Translated by Richard Howard. New York: Hill and Wang, 1981.

Batchen, Geoffrey. *Burning With Desire: The Conception of Photography*. Cambridge, MA: MIT Press, 1997.

———. *Emanations: The Art of the Cameraless Photograph*. Munich: Prestel, 2016.

Belting, Hans, 'The Theater of Illusion.' In *Theaters: Hiroshi Sugimoto*, pp. 7–13. New York: Sonnabend Sundell Editions, 2000.

———. *Looking through Duchamp's Door: Art and Perspective in the Work of Duchamp, Sugimoto, Jeff Wall*. Cologne: Walther König, 2009.

Benjamin, Walter. 'On Some Motifs in Baudelaire.' *Illuminations*. Translated by H. Zohn, pp. 155–200. New York: Schocken, 1969.

———. 'Little History of Photography.' In *The Work of Art in the Age of Its Technological Reproducibility and Other Writings on Media*. Edited by Walter D. Jennings, Brigid Doherty and Thomas Y. Levine, pp. 274–298. Cambridge, MA: Harvard University Press, 2008.

Bergson, Henri. *Matter and Memory* (1896). Translated by N.M. Paul and W.S. Palmer. New York: Zone Books, 1991.

Boehm, Gottfried. 'Strom ohne Ufer: Anmerkungen zu Claude Monet's Seerosen.' In *Claude Monet: Nympheas: Impression – Vision*, pp. 117–127. Basel and Zurich 1986.

Bolter, Jay David and Richard Grusin. 'Remediation.' *Configurations* 4, no. 3 (1996), pp. 311–358.

———. *Remediation: Understanding New Media*. Cambridge, MA: MIT Press, 1999.

Braun, Marta. *Picturing Time: The Work of Etienne-Jules Marey (1830–1904)*. Chicago: University of Chicago Press, 1992.

Breton, André. 'Manifesto of Surrealism.' In *Manifestoes of Surrealism*. Translated by Richard Seaver and Helen R. Lane, pp. 1–48. Ann Arbor: University of Michigan Press, 1969.

———. *Surrealism and Painting*. Translated by Simon Watson Taylor. New York: Harper & Row, 1972.

Brougher, Kerry. 'Impossible Photography.' In Kerry Brougher and Pia

Müller-Tamm, *Hiroshi Sugimoto*, pp. 20–29. Ostfildern: Hatje Cantz Verlag, 2010.

Cadava, Eduardo. 'The Itinerant Languages of Photography.' In E. Cadava and E. Nouzeilles (eds.), *The Itinerant Languages of Photography*, pp. 24–36. Princeton: Princeton University Press, 2013.

Cameron, Julia Margaret. 'Annals of My Glass House.' In *Annals of My Glass House: Photographs by Julia Margaret Cameron*. Text by Violet Hamilton, pp. 11–16. Claremont CA: Ruth Chandler Williamson Gallery, 1996.

Cavell, Stanley. *The World Viewed: Reflections on the Ontology of Film*. Harvard: Harvard University Press, 1979.

Chevrier, Jean-François. *L'hallucination artistique de William Blake à Sigmar Polke*. Paris: l'Arachnéen, 2012.

Dagognet, François. *Etienne-Jules Marey: A Passion for the Trace*. Translated by Robert Galeta and Jeanine Herman. New York: Zone Books, 1992.

Daguerre, Louis Jacques Mandé. 'Daguerreotype.' In *Classic Essays on Photography*. Edited by Alan Trachtenberg, pp. 11–14. New Haven: Leete's Island Books, 1980.

Dawdy, Shannon Lee. *Patina: A Profane Archaeology*. Chicago: University of Chicago Press, 2016.

Derrida, Jacques. *Spectres of Marx: The State of Debt, the Work of Mourning, and the New International*. Translated by Peggy Kamuf. New York and London: Routledge, [1994] 2005.

Desnos, Robert. 'The Work of Man Ray.' Translated from the French by Maria Jolas. *Transition* 15 (February 1929), p. 264–266.

Dijck, José van. *Mediated Memories: Personal Cultural Memory in the Digital Age*. Stanford: Stanford University Press, 2007.

Doane, Mary Ann. 'Temporality, Storage, Legibility: Freud, Marey, and the Cinema.' *Critical Inquiry* 22, no. 2 (Winter 1996), pp. 313–343.

———. 'Real Time: Instantaneity and the Photographic Imaginary.' In *Stillness and Time: Photography and the Moving Image*. Edited by David Green and Joanna Lowry, pp. 23–38. Brighton: Photoworks, 2006.

Dubois, Philippe. 'Photography Mise-en Film: Autobiographical (Hi)stories and Psychic Apparatuses.' *Fugitive Images: From Photography to Video*. Edited by Patrice Pedro, Translated by Lynne Kirby, pp. 152–172. Bloomington: Indiana University Press, 1995.

Duve, Thierry de, 'Time Exposure and Snapshot: The Photograph as Paradox.' *October* 5 (Summer 1978), pp. 113–125.

Eastlake, Lady Elizabeth. 'Photography.' *London Quarterly Review* (1857), pp. 442–468; reprinted in *Classic Essays on Photography*. Edited by

Alan Trachtenberg, pp. 39–68. New Haven: Leete's Island Books, 1980.

Elsaesser, Thomas. 'Fiona Tan: Place after Place.' In *Fiona Tan: Disorient*, ed. Marente Bloemheuvel, pp. 20–33. Amsterdam: Mondriaan Foundation, 2009.

Emerson, Peter Henry. 'Hints on Art.' In *Classic Essays on Photography*. Edited by Alan Trachtenberg, pp. 99–105. New Haven: Leete's Island Books, 1980.

Flaubert, Gustave. *Correspondance*. Edited by Bernard Masson. Paris: Gallimard, 1998.

Flusser, Vilèm, 'The Photographs as Post-Industrial Object: An Essay on the Ontological Standing of Photographs', *Leonardo* 19, 4 (October 1986), pp. 329–332.

———. *Towards a Philosophy of Photography*. Translated by A. Mathews. London: Reaktion Books 2000. Originally published in 1983 as *Für eine Philosophie der Fotografie*, Göttingen, 1983.

———. *Into the Universe of Technical Images*. Translated by Nancy Ann Roth; introduction by Mark Poster (Minneapolis: University of Minnesota Press, 2011). Originally published as *Ins Universum der technischen Bilder* (1985).

———. *Writings*. Minneapolis: University of Minnesota Press, 2002.

Foster, Hal. 'Re: Post.' In *Art After Modernism: Rethinking Representation*. Edited by Brian Wallis, pp. 189–202. New York: New Museum of Contemporary Art; Boston: David R. Godine, 1984.

Fried, Michael. *Why Photography Matters as Art as Never Before*. New Haven: Yale University Press, 2008.

Green, David. 'Marking Time: Photography, Film and Temporalities of the Image.' In *Stillness and Time: Photography and the Moving Image*. Edited by David Green and Johanna Lowry, pp. 9–21. Brighton: Photoworks, 2006.

Greenberg, Clement. 'Four Photographers' [review of Atget, Steichen, Feininger and Cartier-Bresson]. *Clement Greenberg: The Collected Essays and Criticism: Volume 4, Modernism with a Vengeance, 1957–1969*. Edited by John O'Brian, pp. 183–187. Chicago: University of Chicago Press, 1993.

Gunning, Tom. 'New Tresholds of Vision: Instantaneous Photography and the Early Cinema of Lumière.' In *Impossible Presence: Surface and Screen in the Photogenic Era*. Edited by Terry Smith, pp. 71–100. Chicago: University of Chicago Press, 2001.

———. 'To Scan a Ghost: The Ontology of Mediated Vision.' *Grey Room* 26 (Winter 2007), pp. 94–127.

Hamilton, Violet, 'Julia Margaret Cameron: The Art of Photography.' In *Annals of My Glass House: Photographs by Julia Margaret Cameron.* Text by Violet Hamilton, pp. 25–30. Claremont, CA: Ruth Chandler Williamson Gallery, 1996.

———. 'Famous Men & Fair Women.' In *Annals of My Glass House: Photographs by Julia Margaret Cameron.* Text by Violet Hamilton, pp. 31–39. Claremont, CA: Ruth Chandler Williamson Gallery, 1996.

Haus, Andreas. 'The Manipulation of Light and the "New Vision".' In *Moholy-Nagy: Photographs and Photograms.* Translated from the German by Frederic Samson, pp. 12–24. New York: Pantheon Books, 1980.

Henry, Karen. 'The Artful Disposition: Theatricality, Cinema, and Social Context in Contemporary Photography.' In *Acting the Part: Photography as Theatre.* Edited by Lori Pauli, pp. 133–160. London: Merrell Publishers, 2006.

Houwen, Janna. *Film and Video Intermediality: The Question of Medium Specificity in Contemporary Moving Images.* New York and London: Bloomsbury, 2017.

Kaplan, Louis. 'Spooked Time: The Temporal Dimensions of Spirit Photography.' In *Time and Photography.* Edited by Jan Baetens, Alexander Streitberger and Hilde Van Gelder, pp. 27–46. Leuven: Leuven University Press, 2010.

Kovacs, Arpad. 'A Painter's Focus.' *Apollo,* December 2012, pp. 74–79.

Kracauer, Siegfried. *The Mass Ornament: Weimar Essays.* Translated and edited by Thomas Y. Levin. Cambridge, MA and London: Cambridge University Press, [1963] 1995.

———. 'The Photographic Approach.' In *The Past's Treshold: Essays on Photography.* Edited by Philippe Despoix and Maria Zinfert, pp. 63–77. Zurich: Diaphanes 2014. Originally published in *Magazine of Art* March 1951, but also as the first chapter in Kracauer's *Theory of Film: The Redemption of Physical Reality.* Oxford: Oxford University Press, 1960.

Krauss, Rosalind. 'Tracing Nadar.' *October* 5 (Summer 1978), pp. 29–47.

———. 'Photography in the Service of Surrealism.' In Rosalind Krauss and Jane Livingston, *L'Amour Fou: Photography and Surrealism.* New York: Abbeville Press, 1985.

———. 'The Photographic Conditions of Surrealism.' In *The Originality of the Avant-Garde and Other Modernist Myths.* Cambridge, MA: MIT Press, 1985.

———. 'Notes on the Index: Part I.' In *The Originality of the Avant-Garde and Other Modernist Myths,* pp. 151–170. Cambridge, MA: MIT Press, 1985.

———. 'Cy Was Here; Cy's Up.' *Artforum* 33, no. 1 (September 1994), p. 70.

———. *'A Voyage on the North Sea': Art in the Age of the Post-Medium Condition*. New York: Thames & Hudson, 1999.

———, and Jane Livingston. *L'Amour Fou: Photography and Surrealism*. New York: Abbeville Press, 1985.

Kristeva, Julia. *Powers of Horror: An Essay on Abjection*. Translated by Leon S. Roudiez. New York: Columbia University Press, 1982.

Leeb, Susanne. 'Suchmaschinen: Ein Interview von Susanne Leeb.' *Texte zur Kunst* 36 (December 1999), p. 71–75.

Lerner, Jillian. 'The Drowned Inventor: Bayard, Daguerre, and the Curious Attractions of Early Photography.' *History of Photography* 38, no. 3 (2014), pp. 218–232.

Lewitt, Sol, 'Paragraphs on Conceptual Art.' *Artforum* 5, no. 10 (Summer 1967), pp. 79–83.

———. Sol. *PhotoGrids*. New York: Paul David Press Rizzoli, 1977.

Lowry, Joanna. 'Modern Time: Revisiting the Tableau, *Time and Photography*. Edited by Jan Baetens, Alexander Streitberger and Hilde Van Gelder, pp. 47–66. Leuven: Leuven UP, 2010.

Lukacher, Brian. 'Powers of Sight: Robinson, Emerson, and the Polemics of Pictorial Photography.' In *Pictorial Effect: Naturalistic Vision: The Photographs and Theories of Henry Peach Robinson and Peter Henry Emerson*. Edited by Ellen Handy, pp. 29–53. Norfolk Virginia: The Chrysler Museum, 1994.

Lyotard, Jean-François. *The Postmodern Condition: A Report on Knowledge*. Translated by Geoff Bennington and Brian Massumi. Minneapolis: University of Minnesota Press, 1984.

Maurer, Bill. 'In the Matter of Marxism.' In *Handbook of Material Culture*. Edited by Tilley et al., pp. 13–28. Thousand Oaks CA: SAGE, 2006.

Metz, Christian. *Film Language: A Semiotics of the Cinema*. Oxford: Oxford University Press, 1974.

Meyer Stump, Ulrike, 'Karl Blossfeldt's Working Collages: A Photographic Sketchbook.' In *Karl Blossfeldt: Working Collages*. Edited by Ann and Jürgen Wilde, pp. 7–22. Cambridge, MA: MIT Press, 2001.

Michaels, Walter Benn. 'Photographs and Fossils.' *Photography Theory*. Edited by James Elkins, pp. 431–450. New York: Routledge, 2007.

Miller, Lee. 'My Man Ray' [interview by Mario Amaya]. *Art in America* May–June 1975, pp. 54–61.

Mitchell, W. J.T., *Picture Theory*. Chicago: University of Chicago Press, 1994.

Moholy-Nagy, Laszlo. 'Photography.' In *Classic Essays on Photography*.

Edited by Alan Trachtenberg, pp. 165–166. New Haven: Leete's Island Books, 1980.

Monk, Philip. *Disassembling the Archive: Fiona Tan*. Toronto: Art Gallery of York University, 2006.

Mortensen, William. *Monsters & Madonnas* (1936). New York: Arno Press, 1973.

———. *The Model: A Book on the Problems of Posing*. San Francisco: Camera Craft, 1948.

Mozley, Anita Ventura. 'Introduction to the Dover Edition.' In Eadweard Muybridge, *Muybridge's Complete Human and Animal Locomotion: Volume 1*. New York: Dover Publications, 1979.

Nadar. 'My Life as a Photographer.' Translated by Thomas Repensek. *October* 5 (Summer 1978), pp. 6–28.

Niépce, Joseph Nicéphore. 'Memoire on the Heliograph.' In *Classic Essays on Photography*. Edited by Alan Trachtenberg, pp. 5–10. New Haven: Leete's Island Books, 1980.

Newhall, Nancy. *P.H. Emerson: The Fight for Photography as a Fine Art*. New York: Aperture, 1975.

Nouzeilles, Gabriela. 'The Archival Paradox.' In *The Itinerant Languages of Photography*. Edited by Edouardo L. Cadava and Gabriela Nouzeilles, pp. 38–53. Princeton: Princeton University Press, 2013.

Owens, Craig, 'The Allegorical Impulse: Toward a Theory of Postmodernism.' In *Beyond Recognition: Representation, Power, and Culture*, pp. 52–69. Berkeley CA: University of California Press, 1992.

Palermo, Charles. 'The World in the Ground Glass: Transformations in P.H. Emerson's Photography.' *The Art Bulletin* 89, no. 1 (March 2007), 130–147.

Pauli, Lori. 'Setting the Scene.' In *Acting the Part: Photography as Theatre*. Edited by Lori Pauli, pp. 13–71. London: Merrell Publishers, 2006.

Peeren, Esther. *The Spectral Metaphor: Living Ghosts and the Agency of Invisibility*. London: Palgrave, 2014.

Pilar Blanco, Maria Del, and Esther Peeren, eds. *The Spectralities Reader: Ghosts and Haunting in Contemporary Cultural Theory*. London: Bloomsbury, 2013.

Poster, Mark. 'An Introduction to Vilém Flusser's *Into the Universe of Technical Images* and *Does Writing Have a Future?*'. In Flusser, *Into the Universe of Technical Images*, ix-xxvii.

Proust, Marcel. *Remembrance of Things Past*. Translated by C.K. Scott-Moncrieff and Terence Kilmartin, London: Penguin Books, 1981.

Ray, Man. 'The Age of Light.' In *Classic Essays on Photography*. Edited by Alan Trachtenberg, 167–168. New Haven: Leete's Island Books, 1980.

Rice, Shelley. 'Parallel Universes.' In *Pictorial Effect: Naturalistic Vision: The Photographs and Theories of Henry Peach Robinson and Peter Henry Emerson*. Edited by Ellen Handy, pp. 59–78. Norfolk Virginia: The Chrysler Museum, 1994.

Robinson, Henry Peach. *Pictorial Effect in Photography*. London: Piper and Carter, 1869; Reprint, Pawlett: Helios, 1971.

———. 'Idealism, Realism, Expressionism.' In *Classic Essays on Photography*. Edited by Alan Trachtenberg, pp. 91–98. New Haven: Leete's Island Books, 1980.

Ruff, Thomas. 'Thomas Ruff' (interview by Marie Luise Syring and Christiane Vielhaber), in *BiNationale: German Art of the Late 80's*. Edited by Jürgen Harten and David Ross, pp. 260–263. Cologne: Walther König, 1988.

———. *Thomas Ruff. 1979 to the Present*. Edited by Ute Eskildsen and Matthias Winzen. Cologne: Walther König, 2001.

———. *Thomas Ruff. Oberflächen, Tiefen/Surfaces Depths*. Vienna: Kunsthalle Wien, 2009.

Scarry, Elaine. *The Body in Pain: The Making and Unmaking of the World*. Oxford: Oxford University Press, 1985.

Schlak, Tim. 'Framing Photographs, Denying Archives: The Difficulty of Focusing on Archival Photographs.' *Archival Science* 8, 2008, pp. 85–101.

Schwarz, Arturo, 'Man Ray: The Wizard of Light.' In exh. cat. *Man Ray: Photographs and Objects,* pp. 1–15. Birmingham Alabama: Birmingham Museum of Art, 1980.

Scott, Clive. *The Spoken Image: Photography and Language*. London: Reaktion Books, 1999.

Silverman, Kaja. 'The Screen.' In *The Threshold of the Visible World*, pp. 195–227. Stanford: Stanford University Press, 1996.

———. *The Miracle of Analogy, or the History of Photography, Part 1*. Stanford: Stanford University Press, 2015.

Snyder, Joel and Walsh Allen, Neil. 'Photography, Vision and Representation.' *Critical Inquiry* 2, 1 (Autumn 1975), pp. 143–169.

Sontag, Susan. *On Photography*. New York: Farrar, Straus and Giroux, [1973] 1978.

Spector, Nancy. 'Reinventing Realism.' In *Sugimoto Portraits*. Edited by Tracey Bashkoff and Nancy Spector, pp. 10–23. New York: Guggenheim Museum, 2000.

Stauffer, John, Zoe Trodd, Celeste-Marie Bernier. *Picturing Frederick Douglass: An Illustrated Biography of the Nineteenth Century's Most Photographed American*. New York: Liveright, 2015.

Stewart, Garrett, *Between Film and Screen: Photosynthesis*. Chicago: University of Chicago Press, 1999.

Stewart, Susan, *On Longing: Narratives of the Miniature, the Gigantic, the Souvenir, the Collection*. Durham: Duke University Press, 1993.

Steyerl, Hito. 'In Defense of the Poor Image' (2009). In *The Wretched of the Screen*. Foreword by Franco 'Bifo' Berardi, pp. 31–45. Berlin: Sternberg Press, 2012.

Stieglitz, Alfred. 'Pictorial Photography.' In *Classic Essays on Photography*. Edited by Alan Trachtenberg, pp. 115–123. New Haven: Leete's Island Books, 1980.

Sugimoto, Hiroshi. 'Conversation between Hiroshi Sugimoto and Philip Larratt-Smith.' In *Sugimoto. Black Box*, pp. 131–175. New York: Aperture, 2016.

Talbot, William Henry Fox. 'A Brief Historical Sketch of the Invention of the Art' (introduction to *The Pencil of Nature*). In *Classic Essays on Photography*. Edited by Alan Trachtenberg, pp. 27–36. New Haven: Leete's Island Books, 1980.

———. *The Pencil of Nature*. Introduction by Colin Harding. Chicago and London: KWS Publishers, 2011.

Tan, Fiona. 'Interview with Ana Finel Honigman.' *Kulturflash* 6 April 2005, www.kulturflash.net/archive/118preview.html.

Thomas, Ann. 'Modernity and the Staged Photograph, 1900–1965.' In *Acting the Part: Photography as Theatre*. Edited by Lori Pauli, pp. 101–131. London: Merrell Publishers, 2006.

Veire, Frank Vande. 'Blind Auto-Reflexivity: Dirk Braeckman's Light on Photography.' *A-Prior* Spring/Summer 2002, pp. 37–53.

Weiss, Marta. 'Staged Photography in the Victorian Album.' In *Acting the Part: Photography as Theatre*. Edited by Lori Pauli, pp. 81–99. London: Merrell Publishers, 2006.

Werneburg, Brigitte. 'Ich dachte, ich würde Prügel beziehen', an interview with Thomas Ruff *taz* (Berlin), 8 June 2000, p. 15.

Winzer, Matthias. 'A Credible Invention of Reality: Thomas Ruff's precise Reproductions of our Fantasies of Reality.' In *Thomas Ruff: 1979 to the Present*. Edited by Ute Eskildsen and Matthias Winzen, pp. 131–159. Cologne: Walther König, 2001.

Zweite, Armin. *Hiroshi Sugimoto: Revolution*. Ostfildern: Hatje Cantz Verlag, 2013.

First of all, I would like to thank the Research and Academic Program at the Clark Art Institute in Williamstown, Massachusetts, for the precious support it granted me in the Fall of 2016. The hospitality and generosity offered by its Director, Michael Ann Holly, and Acting Director, Christopher Heuer, enabled me to write four of five chapters of this book. The special expertise and friendliness of the staff, as well as the research facilities, all contributed to my Indian summer in heaven. My research assistant, Michael Pratt, a student in the Clark and Williams Graduate Program in the History of Art, ably edited the English of these essays.

I also wish to thank a number of friends and colleagues for the discussions we had about photography and for their responses to some of my texts. First of all, Frits Gierstberg of the Nederlands Fotomuseum (Dutch Photography Museum) in Rotterdam who served as sounding board at a time when my ideas for this book had not yet been fully conceptualized. Further, I would like to single out Janna Houwen, Pepita Hesselberth, Peter Verstraten, Maria Boletsi, Ann Banfield, Ali Shobeiri, Marien Schouten, Tingting Hui, Juul Kraijer,

Robert Slifkin, Awoiska van der Molen, Roos Theuws, Cynthia Chase, and last but not least Mieke Bal. Mieke was always there to encourage me, to listen to me, and to respond to what I had written.

It is perhaps a bit unconventional in acknowledgements to explicitly mention those who have *not* contributed to the writing of this book. But in this case I feel pressed to do so, namely my home institution Leiden University and especially the Institute to which I belong, LUCAS. Although this university considers itself a research university, and uses as its nickname 'Harvard on the Rhine', under the influence of the 'neoliberal' culture that is so devastating academic life everywhere at the moment it does everything to prevent people from doing research. First of all by not having an institutionalized sabbatical (and cancelling it when some departments organize it among themselves), but even more importantly by increasing the teaching load, especially of our youngest colleagues, to an irresponsible degree. Instead of stimulating and enabling the academic work and career of the people they employ, they do the opposite: they kill it.

Working in such an academic climate, one can imagine how grateful I was when The Clark Art Institute granted me the Florence Gould Foundation fellowship so that I could spend a semester there and write most of this book.

Ernst van Alphen (1958) is currently professor of Literary Studies at Leiden University. Before that he was Director of Education and Communication at Museum Boijmans van Beuningen, Rotterdam (NL), and Queen Beatrix Professor of Dutch Studies and Professor of Rhetoric at UC Berkeley (US). He has published widely on literature, but also on art and photography. His most important publications on art are *Francis Bacon and the Loss of Self* (Cambridge MA: Harvard UP, 1993), *Armando: Shaping Memory* (Rotterdam: NAi Publishers, 2000), *Caught by History: Holocaust Effects in Contemporary Art, Literature, and Theory* (Stanford: Stanford UP, 1996), *Art In Mind: How Contemporary Images Shape Thought* (Chicago: University of Chicago Press, 2005), and most recently: *Staging The Archive: Art and Photography in the Age of New Media* (London: Reaktion Books, 2016). He also published articles on the Dutch photographers Juul Kraijer and Awoiska van der Molen.

Author: Ernst van Alphen
Proofreading: Leo Reijnen, Els Brinkman
Image editing: Ernst van Alphen
Design: Sam de Groot
Typefaces: Eldorado (William Addison Dwiggins, 1953),
 Computer Modern (Donald Knuth, 1984),
 SKI DATA (Tariq Heijboer, 2014)
Lithography: Mariska Bijl, Wilco Art Books
Printing and binding: Bariet/Ten Brink, Meppel
Publisher: Astrid Vorstermans, Valiz, Amsterdam,
 <www.valiz.nl>

Creative Commons CC−BY−NC−ND

The author and the publisher have made every effort to secure permission to reproduce the listed material – illustrations and photographs. We apologize for any inadvert errors or omissions. Parties who nevertheless believe they can claim specific legal rights are invited to contact the publisher: <info@valiz.nl>.

Distribution
NL/BE/LU: Centraal Boekhuis, ‹www.cb.nl›
GB/IE: Anagram Books, ‹www.anagrambooks.com›
Europe/Asia: Idea Books, ‹www.ideabooks.nl›
USA: DAP, ‹www.artbook.com›
Australia: Perimeter, ‹www.perimeterdistribution.com›
Individual orders: ‹www.valiz.nl›

This publication has been generously supported by
Prins Bernhard Cultuurfonds

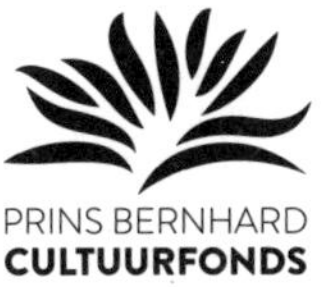

PRINS BERNHARD
CULTUURFONDS

ISBN 978-94-92095-45-9
Printed and bound in the EU

The vis-à-vis series provides a platform to stimulating and relevant subjects in recent and emerging visual arts, photography, architecture and design. The authors relate to history and art history, to other authors, to recent topics and to the reader. Most are academic researchers. What binds them is a visual way of thinking, an undaunted treatment of the subject matter and a skilful, creative style of writing.

Series design by Sam de Groot, ‹www.samdegroot.nl›.

2015

Sophie Berrebi, *The Shape of Evidence: Contemporary Art and the Document*, ISBN 978-90-78088-98-1

Janneke Wesseling, *De volmaakte beschouwer: De ervaring van het kunstwerk en receptie-esthetica*, ISBN 978-94-92095-09-1 (e-book)

2016

Janneke Wesseling, *Of Sponge, Stone and the Intertwinement with the Here and Now: A Methodology of Artistic Research*, ISBN 78-94-92095-21-3

2017

Janneke Wesseling, *The Perfect Spectator: The Experience of the Art Work and Reception Aesthetics*, ISBN 978-90-80818-50-7

Wouter Davidts, *Triple Bond: Essays on Art, Architecture, and Museums*, ISBN 978-90-78088-49-3

Sandra Kisters, *The Lure of the Biographical: On the (Self-)Representation of Artists*, ISBN 978-94-92095-25-1

Christa-Maria Lerm Hayes (ed.), *Brian O'Doherty/Patrick Ireland: Word, Image and Institutional Critique*, ISBN 978-94-92095-24-4

2018

John Macarthur, Susan Holden, Ashley Paine, Wouter Davidts, *Pavilion Propositions: Nine Points on an Architectural Phenomenon*, ISBN 978-94-92095-50-3

Jeroen Lutters, *The Trade of the Teacher: Visual Thinking with Mieke Bal*, ISBN 978-94-92095-56-5

Eva Wittocx, Ann Demeester, Melanie Bühler, *The Transhistorical Museum: Mapping the Field*, ISBN 978-94-92095-52-7

Paul Kempers, '*Het gaat om heel eenvoudige dingen': Jean Leering en de kunst*, ISBN 978-94-92095-07-7